WHEN IN DOUBT, DO BOTH: THE TIMES OF MY LIFE

In this memoir Kay Macpherson, the respected feminist, pacifist, and political activist, takes a delightful look back at a rich and fascinating life, dedicated to the principles of women's rights and social justice, and to an unshakeable conviction that women working together can change the world, and have a marvellous time in the process.

Born in England in 1913, Macpherson immigrated to Canada in 1935. Nine years later she married C.B. Macpherson, then in the early years of his distinguished career as a political philosopher, and together they raised three children. In the late 1940s, a busy mother and academic wife, Macpherson joined the Association of Women Electors. Eventually she served as its national president, an office she held also with the Voice of Women and later with the National Action Committee on the Status of Women. She ran several times as a federal candidate for the NDP. She travelled the world as an advocate of women's rights, and spent most of her time in Canada in the consuming work of social change: organizing, demonstrating, writing letters, giving speeches, and, above all, meeting. From their meetings Macpherson and her colleagues moved into the streets, into Parliament, and, eventually, into history, with one of the most important achievements for Canadian women in the twentieth century: the celebrated equality clause in the Constitution of 1982.

Macpherson's story is the story of second-wave feminism in Canada, which cut across party, class, and language lines, and was characterized by a tremendous sense of unity and of hope. It is also a candid account of family stresses, including strained relations with her children, the death of her husband in 1987, and that of her son two years later.

Kay Macpherson remains unshaken in her commitment to grassroots action. On receiving the Order of Canada in 1982, she was asked by the Governor General what she had been up to lately. 'Revolution,' she replied.

KAY MACPHERSON lives in Toronto.

KAY MACPHERSON

with C.M. DONALD

When in Doubt, Do Both: The Times of My Life

UNIVERSITY OF TORONTO PRESS
Toronto Buffalo London

ISBN 0-8020-0454-7 (cloth)
ISBN 0-8020-7473-1 (paper)

∞

Printed on acid-free paper

Canadian Cataloguing in Publication Data

Macpherson, Kay
   When in doubt, do both

   Includes index.
   ISBN 0-8020-0454-7 (bound)
   ISBN 0-8020-7473-1 (pbk.)

   1. Macpherson, Kay. 2. Feminism – Canada.
   3. Feminists – Canada – Biography. 4. Women in
   politics – Canada – Biography. I. Title.

HQ1455.M33A3 1994   305.42'092   C94-930839-0

The author acknowledges the financial assistance of the Explorations
Program of the Canada Council, and that of the Social Sciences and
Humanities Research Council of Canada.

University of Toronto Press acknowledges the financial assistance to its
publishing program of the Canada Council and the Ontario Arts Council.

This book has been published with the help of a contribution from the Three
Guineas Charitable Foundation.

Contents

Preface

When I started to write this book, my aim was to show how an average, conventional, middle-class woman became involved and active in the peace and women's movements. I would like to tell a story that can show how anyone in circumstances similar (or perhaps not so similar) to mine can make contributions to change which will eventually lead, we hope, to better lives for the people we live and work with and for many others around the world. It would be satisfying if it were possible for some women to say, 'Well for goodness' sake, if she could do it, I don't see why I couldn't.' Or, 'That doesn't seem so difficult; perhaps I could ...' Or even, 'If that's the kind of mess they made, we can certainly do better this time.'

People I've spoken to all have different expectations of this book. Some want a psychological portrait of what prompted me to do things, to join particular organizations, and so on. Others want a minutely detailed history of the women's movement, with analyses of who did what right and who did what wrong at specific times. But I'm not a historian. I've written down my version of things as I remember them, and my memory, like everyone else's, is only semi-perfect.

Most, if not all, of the women I've talked to feel that the part which appeals to them most is how the personal gets involved with the political and how one develops from the other. And how it is possible to lead an ordinary life while at the same time adding some little bit to what is affecting the course of our history. And how individuals have felt about some of the historical events and attitudes of people over those times.

None of us is born determined to head a national organization working for change or knowing Robert's Rules by heart, let alone possessed of a feminist critique showing why consensus-based decision-

making is superior. I wasn't born a radical; it was a step-by-step process. I was given many opportunities for learning, mostly when someone asked me to do something and suggested ways in which it might
be done. The best way to learn is by doing. Almost everything I believe
in and have worked for has been learned from others – by example, by
teaching, or by some kind of osmosis. All I can do is thank my teachers
and hope I can pass on some of the ideals and inspiration they have
given me.

No one takes on the project of changing the world by next week, so
writing about all these years of women's activities is rather like trying
to document the actions of a swarm of bees or a nest of ants. All kinds
of things are going on, and some look aimless or inconsequential, yet
they all have a purpose. When you take them all together, you see the
building and achieving of the aims of a community.

I think much of this coherence is achieved largely by intuition. To
some extent one looks at what others are doing and sees what one
thinks needs adding. Often you do what you feel comfortable doing,
according to a set of principles and feelings you might never make
explicit. Some ways of doing things are instinctively comfortable, such
as the more egalitarian structure of women's groups. And some things,
of course, one knows about. For instance, I always hated and feared
being physically hurt or knowing that others were being hurt. Wanting
to avoid pain and suffering led to the conviction that violence, oppression, and war are unacceptable. I don't think I understood mental dis-
tress and pain as easily, and I've never been very good at recognizing
this in others or even in myself. This is where my education owes much
to my friends and family. Learning never stops.

I hope this story will contain enough material to show that life can
be fun and exciting. Working to change things, to 'save the world,'
doesn't have to be pompous or dull or all those other things that don't
appeal. Certainly one can combine serious work and involvement in
one's community with pleasure and enjoyment.

In many ways, I seem to have been taking things for granted. I've
been elected president of three quite significant women's organizations: AWE, the Association of Women Electors; VOW, the Voice of
Women; and NAC, the National Action Committee on the Status of
Women. I've been fortunate enough to have, or to be able to raise,
enough money to get to all sorts of fantastic meetings and occasions
which were often historic. At one Voice of Women meeting in the 1980s,
I counted eight Persons Award winners who were also VOW members.

I've never missed the annual general meetings of VOW and only one NAC AGM (when I was in hospital). When I add up those meetings alone – thirty years of VOW and eighteen years of NAC – my mind is boggled by the travel, the money, the words, and all the wonderful women I have met, and stayed with, at these gatherings. Everywhere there was something new to learn, about how women do things, how they think, and what makes them tick.

I have NAC and VOW to thank for my love affair with Newfoundland and for my obsession with British Columbia. The Prairies, the Maritimes, and the Territories have given me magnificent friends and exciting experiences, and without VOW and NAC I would not have known such great Quebec women. Women, dozens of them, have stayed with me too, and often I remember what they gave me: a doll, a piece of wood, a button, a jade brooch, a scented geranium, how to peel garlic (hit it), how to finger-weave, political know-how, how to park a car with a trailer, how to light a fire or stop draughts, and recipes, and on and on. I also mourn all the information and history I have forgotten.

I was lucky enough to have a long-suffering family who never prevented or opposed any of my exploits and of whom I am inordinately proud. I bask in the reflected light of my husband's monumental academic achievements, my son's mechanical, mathematical, and musical talents, my daughters' dancing, artistic, teaching, and intellectual abilities – but most of all their love. I got affection and warmth from all of them, more than I deserve, and from all of them an education that goes on whenever we are together.

But I'm not an exceptional person. I can't understand what Kay Macpherson has that most of my friends haven't got too. I don't know what got me the Order of Canada, except for Elsie MacGill's efforts. I'm not indulging in false modesty here. I know I'll have to keep trying to be less lazy, exploitative, unaffectionate, and so on. And thanks to all those who obviously partly disagree with my assessment. I do love you – even if I find it so hard to say so.

WRITING THIS BOOK

The writing of this book probably began in 1941 when I bought a portable Hermes typewriter from a Swiss skiing friend in Montreal. My first piece began, 'In order to practise my typing ...' My first typing lesson was given to me for one penny by a fellow student at St Thomas' Hospital in London, but I never did progress to proper touch-typing.

From then on, I often wrote pieces, at first as a form of diary-keeping, then later also by way of recording events that seemed to me significant or drawing pen portraits of my friends. The pieces I wrote in New Brunswick went into a file and lay dormant for about forty years. Then I wrote mostly reports, letters, and oddments like doggerel, notes for speeches, and a sort of diary (more a date book really).

In the early 1980s, I began creative writing classes and wrote viewpoint pieces, portraits of family events, my friends, and so on. My children wanted to know about their family origins, so that turned into quite a long account. Then people were always asking for short histories of AWE, VOW, NAC, and so on, so I started to think seriously about making my writings into a book.

As my eyesight worsened and it became more difficult for me to read, especially my own writing, I needed to look for help. Thanks to Naomi Black, who applied on my behalf, I received a grant from the Social Sciences and Humanities Research Council (SSHRC) which enabled me to recruit student helpers who came to sort, read, and make suggestions, decipher illegible handwritten notes, type, and retype. They include Marie Hammond, Rachel Gray, Wendy Miller, Les Tager, Linda Potje, Liz Fitting, Michael Mackid, Todd Waring, Loretta Castelaria, and Audrey Hepworth.

I then received a grant from the Explorations Program of the Canada Council, which I'm sure I wouldn't have got without glowing references from Margaret Fulton, Alison Prentice, and Ursula Franklin. This enabled me to employ an editor, Christine Donald, who worked with me for nearly three years in a process she describes as 'very like quilting.' We enjoyed each other's company and worked amicably through changes and rewrites. I had not worked with an editor before and did not realize how much was involved. I cannot sufficiently appreciate the gold-mine of professional expertise Christine provided. I grew to admire her editorial talents more and more, particularly her ability to condense incidents or comments without losing their essential elements. She deserves all my thanks wrapped up in a big bear-hug.

Friends heroically read parts of the manuscript and many helpful comments were provided by Ursula Franklin, Rosemary Brown, Naomi Black, Ann Gertler, Sue Findlay, Vi Thompson and Miriam May, Muriel Duckworth, Anna Lou Paul, Marie Crookston, Mary Louise Gaby, Sheila Macpherson and Bill Smith, Susan Macpherson, Danny Grossman, Stanley Ryerson, Herbert Whittaker, Sarah Henderson, Alice de Wolfe, Dorothy Smieciuch, and, last but not least, June Callwood. They gave all kinds of advice, most of which I tried to follow (my motto being, 'When in doubt, do both'). I owe special thanks to Isobel Warren, who advised on the photographs and their layout.

And all along I would have been lost without the devoted help of Pearl Blazer. In addition to the skills and abilities I knew from her time with NAC, she mastered a computer, made scraps of scribbled writing into usable prose, trimmed my inordinate flights of fancy, plugged the gaps in my memory, argued about my illogical assumptions, and generally set me straight. Her ever-increasing job description includes strange non-secretarial activities such as medical opinions, sewing, finance, cooking and cleaning, and car-driving. She has put up with the fumblings and frustration of one who is losing her sight. I cannot put into spoken words what her support and love have meant to me. I can only write, 'Thanks, Pearl, and bless you!'

Now I have a completed manuscript, the publishing of which has been made possible by a grant from the Three Guineas Charitable Foundation. I owe much to the efforts of my friends and helpers and have not been able to name them all here, but to all the people who helped me get to this point, my thanks.

Toronto
December 1990

WHEN IN DOUBT, DO BOTH: THE TIMES OF MY LIFE

1

Childhood

The world I was born into seemed smaller, simpler in many respects than the technological maze that confronts us today. In 1913, electricity, the telephone, and the internal-combustion engine were marvels enough for us. My family and friends were English, middle-class, conservative, and conventional. They accepted God (generally Anglican), the King, Queen, and all the Royal Family, and a glorious British Empire on which the sun never set and which was proudly pointed out as all those bright red blobs in the family atlas.

My parents were married in 1912. Their names were Frederick Edward Walker and Kathleen Fountain Browne. My father was a doctor, trained at Guy's Hospital in London. Later, he was captain of the Uxbridge volunteer fire brigade. I have a couple of photographs somewhere of my father in his fire-brigade uniform with me sitting on his knee. I also have a photograph of my mother holding my baby brother. She has an ankle-length skirt, a tucked-in blouse, and long hair put up in strange loops and windings that remind me of those old pictures of Lily Langtry and other Beauties of the time.

We lived at The Red House, on the High Street of Uxbridge. Uxbridge was a small place then, and I remember going for country walks to Perivale and hearing the church bells ringing across the valley on Sunday mornings. Going to London for the day on the Metropolitan Railway, which ran from Uxbridge to Baker Street as part of the underground system, was an exciting expedition.

I remember our family being one of the first to own a car, an early-model Buick, which we had because my father needed it for his medical practice. Once, on the way to Nether Wallop, we all had to get out so that the car could ascend a steep hill. In those days, with the combination of unpaved roads and open cars, the women wore motor veils over their hats to keep the dust off and, I suppose, their hats on.

I knew my Walker grandmother as a little old lady in black with a velvet ribbon round her neck. My Grannie Browne moved to our midlands town of Bedford after 1920, so we saw more of her and my 'maiden aunt' Dorothy (Dot) who lived with her. I liked going to visit her and often stayed overnight. One of the treats was to climb into her bed in the morning when she had her tea and I (or we, but I don't remember whether my brother was there much) had a 'buttery crust' to chew on. Grannie had a thin slice of bread and butter, if she had anything.

My mother was the middle child in her family. Her elder brother, Uncle Lex, worked in the family business, a linen-importing firm and outfitter of passenger liners in Liverpool. We all thought his family a pretty dull bunch, and so, later, did my husband Brough, who once misguidedly spent an evening with them during our 1953 sabbatical.

In my father's family, I believe, there were four boys and then my very favourite Aunt May. Uncle Leonard lived in an incredible studio in Hampstead. He was a stained-glass artist whose windows can still be seen at Eton College and the Royal College of Music. He was also a member of the Royal Institute of Painters in Watercolour (I loved the initials: RIPWC – Rest In Peace in the Water Closet). Later, after I was married, we took our three children, Susan, Stephen, and Sheila, to meet Uncle Len, still in the same studio near Swiss Cottage. The children were as impressed as I had always been, and he gave them some small pieces of his stained glass, which I later had assembled into a plaque which now hangs in the kitchen window. He did not paint designs on glass – glass was his design. He mixed the colours into the melted glass so that wonderful swirls and patterns were woven in.

Aunt May was a pianist, an accompanist, and lived in a studio mews flat near Kensington High Street. Her way of introducing herself was always the same: 'My name is May Walker, and I live in the telephone book.' (In the 1930s, of course, it wasn't so difficult to run through the M. Walkers.) May had a grand piano and a cat, a tiny kitchen which overlooked a school playground, and a loft which she later made into an extra bedroom. (Later still, the ceiling of the loft had to be covered with canvas after a bomb fell nearby and blew a hole in it.) Coming from my staid, provincial environment, I was captivated by these two exotic relatives, Leonard and May.

I was four and my brother Richard two when my father died of tuberculosis. He spent some time in a sanatorium, where I once went to visit him. I knew he was dying, but I don't remember much about it. It was wartime. I do remember my mother's sorrow, but not very clearly.

In 1920, after a couple of years on her own, my mother married again. Our stepfather, Maurice John Sarson, was an old friend of my mother's, reported to have been in love with her even before her first marriage. He was at that time first officer on one of the Orient Line ships plying between England and Australia, and they lived a happy if somewhat interrupted life. He was soon promoted to captain, which gave him a little more time at home. Normally the ship was in dock only two weeks out of the three months it took to complete a voyage to Brisbane and back. I suspect my mother was much more of a disciplinarian when Father (no 'Daddy' for him) was at home, which didn't endear him to us. On the other hand, when I was in the Brownies and Guides, I remember him spending hours patiently teaching me reef knots, sheet bends, and bowlines, and even something called a Turk's Head, used to secure the end of a rope and prevent unravelling.

We could all recite the places on the way to Brisbane: the Bay of Biscay, Gibraltar, the Suez Canal, and the Red Sea, calling at Colombo, Fremantle, Adelaide, Melbourne, Sydney, and Brisbane. And often we'd be given exotic fruits, chests of tea, and handicrafts picked up during those trips. The ship's carpenter was co-opted to build a play-pen for my two young half-brothers, Roderic and Barry, born in 1922 and 1924 respectively. It was a very early collapsible playpen, made of teak, which certainly made it unique – and heavy! Dick also had, after we moved from the rented house on Rothsay Gardens to one of our own on Bushmead Avenue, a bunk-bedroom, all beautifully fitted into a small dressing room – probably one of the first bunk-beds made for a house.

My mother was a good housekeeper and very well liked in Bedford where we had moved in 1920. Bedford was only fifty miles from London and was full of 'colonial service' and army wives with families, often minus fathers who were away 'building the Empire.' There were good (and cheap) schools and all kinds of recreation at hand. At first we rented an old house, 7 Rothsay Gardens, which had been used for billeting troops during the war, not long over. It was big, pretty crummy, and very cold. Three stories high, it still had gas-burning lamps, although it did have some electricity too, and a garden with a huge elm at the end of it.

In the 1920s, most middle-class families, however hard up, tried to have some household help. I hate to think what must have been considered adequate wages. 'Help' reflected the household hierarchies of former days, so that one would talk of 'house-parlour maids,' or 'cook-general,' or 'nurse-housemaid,' terms that spelled out the combined functions. Besides a daily or weekly charwoman, there were also 'mother's helps' and 'au pair' girls. I remember that we had some variety of 'cook-general' or 'housemaid' when I was young. They usually lived in and provided built-in babysitting in addition to their many other duties.

My mother ran the house, which meant doing the cooking (when we didn't have someone whose job was cooking), housework (ditto), gardening, keeping chickens, making our clothes, and only sometimes having time left over for bridge with her friends. She kept meticulous accounts (and tried to start me on this methodical road without much success) and sat at her desk, one of those big ones with a roll-top and lots of pigeon holes, writing letters to Maurice and her friends whenever she had the opportunity. I wish I could remember more about the household routine, but I do recall washing days with the 'copper,' boiling clothes with washing soda, the spring cleaning, the putting away for summer or winter of all the appropriate things, and the continual letting down and altering of everything in the way of clothing that could be recycled. I still save string, feel guilty at cooking with butter, and so on. Oranges were a luxury which, when we had them, we ate by cutting a square hole in the top and inserting a lump of sugar through which we sucked the juice, then opening the orange and eating all the rest. Jam-making, preserving, and all such activities went on as a matter of course.

Our next-door neighbour in Rothsay Gardens, who became one of my mother's closest friends, was Miss Baron, known to us as Bardie. A spinster daughter, she lived with her aging parents in a comparatively luxurious house with a parlour maid and a cook, as well as a chauffeur and a Daimler car. There were, of course, many women who had lost their menfolk in the slaughter of the Great War and, for all we knew, Miss Baron may have been one of these. She was a Girl Guide Commissioner, and I learned a lot about guiding from her; knowing her lent me status among my Girl Guide friends. She enlisted me to help with her first-aid groups for Rangers, the older Guides, and I acted as model for bandage practice, artificial respiration, and the like.

Bardie was an opera addict. With a friend whom she had met on a cruise somewhere, a concert singer named Carrie Tubb, she always took in *The Ring* at Covent Garden. Once, Bardie took Carrie Tubb along to Guide camp, which I suppose might be compared with bringing Maureen Forrester along to the Brownie meeting. The singing improved anyway. Bardie's passion for opera was not reflected in my family, whose taste ran more along the lines of Grieg, Gilbert and Sullivan, and 'In a Monastery Garden.' (Until we were hit by the jazz age. Then what we children didn't know about Benny Goodman, Tommy Dorsey, Jack Hylton, the English Ambrose, and others, wasn't worth knowing.)

Until they were old enough to ride a bicycle, middle-class English children were taken for walks. Small children trailed along behind mothers or nursemaids who were often pushing a baby carriage, trudging slowly along pathways, down lanes, beside the river, into parks where perhaps there were swings or seesaws. According to the season, they dawdled beside streams and ponds and fished for tadpoles or hunted other treasures like bluebells or horse chestnuts.

I learned to ride a bicycle when I was about seven and had my first bike when I was nine. Bedford is a flat town, ideal for bicycling, and we lived on our bikes. We could vault on, ride with no hands, stand still on them (slow bike races were very popular), jump them up steps, and of course fall off them. I remember once knocking myself out when I braked by sticking my foot into the spokes of the front wheel and sailing over the handlebars when it caught.

Dr Coombs, our new family doctor, was also a neighbour on Rothsay Gardens. His daughter, Wendy, and I fast became great friends. Our parents became friends too, and Wendy was almost one of our family. In fact, she and I more or less adopted each other's relatives, and aunts and uncles became joint property. Her brother wasn't born until she was ten, making her virtually an only child during our 'Can Wendy come out to play?' days. Although only a year younger than me, she was shy and timid compared with us and was usually cast in the role of slightly scared follower in our boisterous escapades. Her family, however, owned a big house with an orchard and tennis court, which provided grounds and entertainment for the neighbourhood children.

Wendy and I had mutual friends at school who were called Annette and Prudence Scott-Holmes at school and Nan and Prue Pattison at home. Children with a different surname from their parents presented endless confusion to their friends, and I was glad to find others in the same circumstances as me. At school, I was Kathleen Walker; at home, where I was known as Biddy, neighbours called me Biddy Sarson (my mother's name too since she had remarried). This gave me a dual personality that I found quite pleasant.

Nan and Prue's mother, who was very keen on children's theatre, was responsible for providing us with our first theatrical experience. Wendy was usually too shy to be a success in the home-produced plays we put on for admiring parents and friends. I was coerced and rehearsed into performing adequately, though only in male roles – I must have been bigger and louder than the other girls. I only remember two of my parts. One was Sir Francis Drake, the hero of the defeat of the Spanish Armada in 1588. The stage directions called for Sir Francis to 'guffaw.' I had no idea what this meant and, when it was explained, had difficulty squeezing out something between a squeak and a small bark. In the next play, about St George, I was cast as the dragon. This was more to my taste and I strutted about the set declaiming in a gruff voice, through my dragon head-dress, a soliloquy I can still remember:

Lonely, misunderstood, in this desolate wood
I pass an existence profoundly depressing,
Hated, cut, ostracised, feared, detested, despised,
Because of a faint human note in my messing.
Although I enjoy grilled maiden or boy
And greatly prefer curried lady to lentil,
I think, all the same, I fairly may claim
To be in essentials both simple and gentle.
My manners are chaste, I've excellent taste,
I quote by the hour both Shakespeare and Shelley.
For literature light, I read with delight
The Sorrows of Satan by Marie Corelli.

After this, my memory fails. Suffice it to say that St George, played with dramatic flamboyance by Prue, successfully slew the dragon, who had a few appropriate last words to say before expiring.

Wendy and I shared enthusiasms for books, magazines, film stars, and popular songs. She taught me, by showing me the fingering, a beautiful, short Couperin piece which, if I run over the fingering on the piano again and again, I can remember how to play today. And then there was Private Lives. We had the Coward-Lawrence dialogue by heart: 'What are you doing here?' 'I'm on my honeymoon.' 'Very interesting. So am I.' We had a crush on Gertrude Lawrence for years. Wendy's family bought the first recording by 'the best orchestra in the world,' she said. It was the Philadelphia Orchestra, playing Weber's 'Invitation to the Waltz,' and I can still remember where the break came and one had to turn the 78–rpm record over. I first heard Mozart at the Coombs' house.

In the mid-1920s, everyone was experimenting with the newest invention: the wireless. Some had a little crystal set and headphones and twiddled a wire on the crystal until some magic music or a voice was heard. Bigger sets were run by battery or accumulator (like an awkward car battery). We were the first family in the area to have a radio that ran 'off the main,' with a strange circular sounding-board to amplify the sound. Later we had a good automatic record-changing machine for our expanding musical tastes. My portable HMV wind-up player was, however, my constant companion. I could do my home-work with Calloway and the others blaring away, apparently undis-tracted.

Later, I was bosom friends with Beth Hubbard. We were twelve when we first met. The Hubbards were Scottish. Not Scotch. I soon learned that was *not* the word one used for people. I thought Beth had a fascinating accent and used many strange words and phrases. She accused me of saying everything with an extra R in it: grarse, clarss, larf, parth, and so on. Beth used to say 'gerrel' for 'girl,' 'cant' for what I called 'carnt,' 'ruf' for what I called 'roof,' and 'th' for 'though.' Finally, I made up a sentence that included as many of her strange words as I could fit in. It went like this: 'There are miewions of gerrels in Aus-traewia who cant be rud while eating their fud th'.'

And, of course, Beth made quite sure I realized that only true Scots were entitled to wear kilts. She had a beauty, of the correct tartan, nat-urally, and my envy on that score lasted for years. After the war, when the Macpherson family was staying with Beth and her family, I was shocked to hear Beth say, 'Oh, I just buy the prettiest tartan when I get things for the children!' Her old childhood convictions had been for-gotten and, all too late, I was at last free to wear a tartan.

Beth's father was a naval architect, who came to Bedford to work on the designs for the two huge airships, R100 and R101, which were built at Cardington just outside the town. Later, we all followed the fortunes of the airships and their crews, their trial runs, and the beginning of the maiden voyage to India of the R101, which ended in fiery tragedy in the north of France.

I was Beth's opposite in almost every respect, yet we became very close friends, and found we had many interests in common. While I occupied myself with Girl Guides and obsessive games playing, Beth played the violin, rode ponies, drew pictures, and carved wood. She was small, neat, clothes-conscious, artistic, not too keen on games, and later very attractive to the opposite sex. When I grew older, I learned the beginnings of art appreciation from Beth and her family, and it was she who gave me my first political reading material, John Strachey on socialism for beginners.

During my school years in Bedford, beyond the headlines in *The Daily Mail* or the social events and births and deaths recorded in *The Times*, we paid little attention to the political events at home or abroad. The General Strike had few political overtones for us, only the mild excitement when university students were encouraged to drive buses and help to keep the railways running. I think my parents backed the government against the strikers, and we knew nothing about their grievances or demands. People thought the League of Nations was a Good Thing but weakened by lack of international support. The Town Regatta and local football and soccer games provided most of our excitement, unless a member of the Royal Family visited, as when Princess Mary (or was it the Duchess of Bedford?) came to open Bedford High School's new science blocks.

Beth and I were both in the school choir. As well as performing in school concerts and on special occasions, the choir led the hymn- and psalm-singing every day during 'prayers,' which today we would call assembly. There were also piano lessons, which included three deadly necessities: theory, exams, and, above all, practice. Only when I was eleven did I manage to win a medal at the local eisteddfod. After that I fell down on all the requirements and ended up being able to sight read just enough to get me into the Montreal Elgar Choir for a couple of years.

I was mad about games of all kinds, though I managed to get into trouble for not taking them seriously enough and for not being 'responsible' enough. During my four or five years at a private girls' school called St Andrew's (generally pronounced 'Snandrews), I had acquired minimal hockey and a bit of tennis. Bedford High School supplied us with netball, lacrosse, and hockey – my best winter game (I was Left Back). My efforts at sports got me onto most of the teams our school fielded against other high schools, and it was exciting to go on a bus, everyone feeling sick with apprehension, to play another team.

Our school was blessed by having the Bedford Physical Training College nearby, which meant practice coaching from their students in gym and coaching by their staff in all team games. Beth and I both had crushes on the seniors at school and doted on the staff from the Physical Training College who coached us. My two career ambitions were Phys. Ed. (but I didn't much want to teach) or medicine (I assumed that no money was available to learn to be a doctor). In the end, physiotherapy combined for me many of the attractive features of both these occupations.

Schoolwork I found comparatively easy, except of course when I had neglected 'prep.' I was particularly lax about Latin homework and was constantly trying to wake up early on the mornings of Latin classes, either to read a passage or to translate it. I still don't know how I got through my Matric. exams at age seventeen. I later discovered that my high-school grounding in classics and English was at a level Canadians usually achieved only at university, and that facility in essay-writing was far better developed in British children, at least by the high-school level. The rudiments of Latin and even my one year of German have been immensely useful to me in figuring out word derivations and meanings, not to mention being invaluable for such pastimes as crossword puzzles and Scrabble games.

One of the 'extras' I took at school was dancing. English country dancing was, I think, the domain of the gym teacher, but in dancing class we learned all about positions of the arms and legs, port de bras, grands battements, and the like, as well as folk, Scottish, and many other types of dance. It wasn't, however, until my Aunt May took me to see the Ballet Russe in London for my twenty-first birthday present that music and movement first really came together for me. Nothing ever appealed to me so much as this combination of music and dance, not to mention some of the glorious designs of Picasso, Bakst, and others. And I have never forgiven my family for not taking me to see Pavlova dance in the Corn Exchange in Bedford on the grounds that it was too expensive, though I think it was just that their priorities were different from mine.

Guide camps every summer gave me a chance to see parts of England and Wales I might not otherwise have visited. The Guide trips took me to Yorkshire, North Wales, Devon, and Somerset, some of my favourite country. I remember the thick 'doorstep' corned-beef sandwiches we ate for picnic lunches after we had trekked two or three miles to the beach and swum in the chilly ocean; how we watched the farmer's wife making great copper vats full of clotted Devonshire cream; and how a group of us got lost (but not at all worried) roaming the Yorkshire Moors in the misty rain and paddling in the babbling streams without bothering to take off our shoes and socks, which we considered very daring.

Our family could usually afford only a trip to the nearest coast, the east one, where we often shared a house with our Sarson cousins. (Uncle Arthur, a rather jolly clergyman, delighted us all one day by turning up for a swim in his bathing suit, dog collar, and bib.) The first time we ever went I think we hired a car and driver, but on later trips we had our own car, a Morris Oxford four-seater with a top that went down. In order not to be carsick, I would sit with one of the boys' sand-pails on my lap. The sense of security prevented me from throwing up.

On one holiday with Auntie Dot in North Wales, I failed to realize one should never run down a mountainside. I fell on my face and scraped both knees. This was also the expedition in which I took my first and deathless photographs as seen in my first album: Conway Castle doubly exposed over the River Mersey, and so on. I think I was the most conventional, sports-loving, non-intellectual, gawky teenager (the word wasn't invented then) imaginable.

I suspect our living standards and requirements were somewhat lower and simpler than those of today's youngsters, but then the British in general have always had to be a pretty hardy bunch, judging by the way they almost enjoy bad conditions and raw weather, wide-open windows in the middle of winter, chilblains on hands and feet, and children's blue knees between shorts and socks.

When I was twelve, I had pneumonia. It was during a winter when the river and flooded fields froze hard, and the whole community, unused to such freezing weather, scrounged around for every pair of skates to be had. Everyone was out sliding and skating for all they were worth. Whether this cold experience contributed to my getting ill, I don't know. This was a long time before antibiotics, and one just had to wait out the high temperature and shooting pains, using hot plasters of some pasty stuff called antiphlogistine which practically parboiled my skin. I hated it almost as much as it distressed my mother to smear the stuff on.

When I recovered, I was kept out of regular day school and sent to a special small school in Chislehurst, Kent, run by two physiotherapist sisters of my stepfather. The small number of children boarded there combined schoolwork with suitable exercises and treatment. I believe that I was sent to Chislehurst because of a heart murmur following the pneumonia, but nothing ever seemed to come of that, except for a few questions over cardiograms in later life.

My family was not given to many health problems. We children joined our schoolmates in a measles epidemic and indulged with our friends in whooping cough, which seemed to go on forever. I vaguely remember adults suffering in the 1919 'flu epidemic, spelling each other off in crawling from their beds to look after children or do the chores, and my mother suffered one miscarriage before my young brothers were born. Adults were not given to confiding in children, either about illness or mishap. When my grandmother had a fire in her house, no one told me anything. I knew it had happened though, and when we visited her later I could still smell the charring, though no one talked about it. I was afraid of fire, a fear that may have originated in a memorable picture of the Great Fire of London, horse-drawn wagons racing with water to try to staunch the flames.

My mother died in 1933 when I was 19, Richard 17, and Roderic and Barry about 11 and 9. Nowadays women don't often die after a hysterectomy, and even then none of us had really expected it. She had a benign tumour in her uterus and went into a nursing home, and there she died the day after the operation. Middle-class Bedford considered the local hospital infra dig., but I always wondered whether things would have been different had she gone to a larger institution.

It was from one of the big London teaching hospitals that I was summoned. I was in the middle of a lecture at St Thomas' (my first year of physio training) and was called out by Wheeler, one of the staff, who took me aside and told me my mother had taken a turn for the worse and I was needed at home. The bus and tram across London and the hour-long train journey seemed to last forever. When I reached Bedford, I walked the mile or so up to the nursing home where my Aunt Dot met me at the door. She was in tears, saying I was too late, but that perhaps it was just as well, since it wouldn't have helped me to see my mother. I don't know whether it would have made any difference. I went home and found Richard in the garden. We didn't have much to say to each other. Each of us, I think, wanted to be alone, and we didn't know what to do with ourselves. Auntie Dot's emotionalism ('Her strength gave out. Oh, if only I could have been in her place.') turned us both off. She did, however, look after the family until my stepfather could return.

Maurice was on his ship, in Sydney I think. It was not until long afterwards that I heard of his stunned reaction to the news of his wife's death. I learned about it from a woman who had been on the ship, to whom he had turned in his grief. But he very wisely soon remarried, picking a friendly younger woman whom he had met in Australia and who took on the job of looking after my half-brothers Roderic and Barry. Her name was Doris and she couldn't pronounce her Rs, so that the whole family, all of whom (except myself) had Rs in their names, were renamed Morse, Dorse, Wichad, Woderic, and Bawwy.

During the few days before the funeral I got the most comfort from my mother's next-door friend, the Guider Bardie. I avoided my emotional aunt who, poor thing, was doing her best to comfort us all, and found Bardie's matter-of-fact conversation far more comforting than Dorothy's agonized and voluble sympathy. Bardie was the undemonstrative sort, which I suppose I was too, in the good British stiff-upper-lip tradition, and she seemed to understand better how to cope with my bottled-up feelings. She too was reluctant to show her emotions, yet she provided some of the comfort and reassurance I needed, without putting her thoughts into words.

I remember Dick and myself at the funeral, walking behind the coffin, both dry-eyed. To cry in public simply wasn't done. It was years before I learned to show any deep emotion even to one other person, and then seldom in a group. For weeks after my mother's death, I cried only when I got into bed at night. I remember latching on to a make-shift 'she can really see us all and what we are doing' philosophy that provided me with quite a lot of comfort at the time.

I went back to London. I was probably more fortunate than my brothers, who were left at home with all the familiar memories. I could continue my studies in a new setting with many things to occupy my thoughts. It was only when I was in the dark and in bed at night that aching misery gripped me. It seemed a long time before the ache grew less. There was a play on in London at the time. The title, *Grief Goes Over*, struck me as being a rather strange phrase. It showed, however, that grief and despair do get less with time. And of course that is what happened to me, too.

2

London and Selly Oak

When I returned to London, it was May, my beloved aunt, who continued to be my advisor and mainstay and the source of innumerable fun times: expeditions to the theatre, concerts, and the ballet. She took me to the Albert Hall, where I fell in love with Leon Goossens, the bald oboe player whom I worshipped from afar. She took me to Kensington Gardens and Kew, to a polo game at Hurlingham where royalty was sometimes to be seen, to the Trooping of the Colour on the King's birthday, and dozens of other places. She never had much money, but she had all kinds of interesting friends and often fell heir to tickets for things. We'd come back home to cook supper, and I recall how putting the dishes away in May's crammed kitchen was like putting together a jigsaw puzzle.

The postwar recovery led to the excitement of the twenties, and then to strikes, the Depression, and the anxieties of the thirties. By the time the next war came to Britain, I had been living in Canada for four years and my experiences had become very different from those of my family and old school friends. In fact, not many of my schooltime friendships survived the separation caused by the war, though I did keep in touch with Wendy and Beth. Occasionally I would hear news of someone, and my brother kept in touch with many more since he did not come to Canada until later.

But in the 1930s, London was an entertaining place. The Royal Family could be counted on for a wedding or sometimes a coronation, and Londoners and visitors would turn out in their thousands, as of course they still do. In the spring of 1935, King George V celebrated his Silver Jubilee, twenty-five years on the throne. These celebrations, with all the pomp that the British can muster, appealed to almost every Britisher, monarchist or not: the celebration was the thing. A group of us established ourselves at 4:00 a.m. on the Day on the steps of the Victoria Memorial in the middle of the roundabout in front of Buckingham Palace. We must have been there for ten or twelve hours. In those days the crowds were not so enormous, and we had a wonderful view of all the parading guards and carriages and, later, of the Royal Family with the two young princesses on the palace balcony. Everyone was talkative and friendly. After the procession we strolled down the middle of streets with no traffic to mow us down, then watched the fireworks across the river.

I made new friends at St Thomas' and still remember the names of the women in my class: Aiken, Bell, Bickley, Crosbie, Deane, Hamer, Howard-Smith, Lindsay-Scott, Martin, Richardson, Rushworth, Stowell, Walker, Warner, and Wright. We used surnames all the time. Three of us in our 'set' were almost inseparable: Helen Deane, the Canadian from 'far BC'; Martin, a boisterous, deep-voiced Irish woman who was happy to be able to ignore her first names, Lavinia Violet Isabel Brereton; and me, Walker. Even later, for the first year I was in Canada, I continued to be Walker because that had been my name to Rosie Brewin, my Canadian roommate at St Thomas', with whom I again shared in Montreal.

Deane, Martin, and I were boarding in the St Thomas' Hospital nurses' residence in Bloomsbury. Deane and Martin were roommates. Deane and I had first met on the terrace of St Thomas' Hospital overlooking the River Thames and the Houses of Parliament. We were both nineteen, as were most of the other dozen or so would-be physiotherapists who came together on that September afternoon in 1932. Helen had chestnut hair and brown eyes, a beautiful combination. She was very tall and lanky, and her origins in British Columbia seemed romantic to us. We called her 'Queen Helen' as she, a shade more responsible than the rest of us, sometimes acted on our behalf.

Martin had a passion for making up jingles and rhymes, usually to the tune of a hymn or popular song. Helen's twentieth birthday was celebrated with a poem sung as a dirge in our favourite adenoidal accents, to the hymn 'All people that on earth do dwell.' Only our version began:

Happy are we upon this day,
Happier far than we can say.
Today we celebrate with mirth,
The day Miss Deane appeared on earth.

ASIDE
(It don't seem twenty years to me,
Since she appeared in far BC.)

Deaneshaven was the place she chose
Far up amid th'eternal snows
And that is why her knees are queer
Because she had to mountaineer.
etc. etc.

We also made up rhymes to be sung to popular song tunes to help us remember muscles and nerves for our anatomy course. To the tune of 'John Brown's Body':

The circumflex goes backwards through the quadrilateral space,
Anterior, posterior and cutaneous to the base.
Of the deltoid, the anterior supplies the humerus,
    [pronounced 'humerace' to rhyme with 'space']
The posterior supplies the teres minor.

At least that item from my anatomy book, correct or not, remains with me today! And though, with the exception of my famous dragon, I had hated acting and had refused to take part in school plays, as a student at St Thomas' Hospital I began composing skits and pantomimes with the others.

We were so successful in this that we once heard the hospital matron, an almost mythical figure of ultimate decorum and discipline, had said of us, 'Those young women will go far.' But the destination of our journey was not specified since, although Matron attended our house pantomime one Christmas, she had also had us on the carpet for rowdy behaviour. On that occasion, the sister-in-charge had discovered us rehearsing, during study period, a dramatic version of the ballad 'Lord Ullin's Daughter,' for which we rolled around on the floor under a rug to depict how 'the waters wild ... went o'er his child.' 'This is a hospital for the dead and dying,' Sister said sternly, 'not a beer-garden for ádolescents!'

This same sister-in-charge of the massage department (soon to be the physiotherapy department) was quite a personality. Minnie Randell, SRN and Teacher of the Chartered Society of Massage and Remedial Gymnastics, was a remarkable woman who had worked through the First World War and, together with Dr James Mennell, who headed our department, had developed many new treatments for the war-wounded and others. She used to tell us how Herbert Marshall, a current matinee idol who had lost a leg in the war, could perfectly easily, under her tutoring, have walked with no sign of a limp, but he kept a slight limp and hunch of the shoulders because it made him more glamorous for his audiences.

It was due to her that our curriculum included a number of subjects not usually considered regular fare for budding physios. In addition to the regulation anatomy, physiology, pathology, chemistry, and medical electricity, we took painting, relaxation, singing (to exercises – 'Old Man River' was a favourite), and Margaret Morris dancing (a mixture of therapeutic exercise and movements roughly based on classical Greek dance). This was all tied into the pre- and post-natal exercise programs developed by Minnie Randell. All this activity, added to strenuous afternoons of clinical work, made us excellent candidates for lying on the floor for an hour being taught the elements of relaxation. Half the class was fast asleep by the end of those sessions.

Most days, Deane, Martin, and I would ride our bicycles down Southampton Row to the Embankment and over Westminster Bridge to the hospital, dodging traffic and weaving our way between trams and buses to cross an intersection before a traffic light changed. I doubt that could be done so easily nowadays. When it rained heavily or we were going out in the evening, we took the tram running through the Kingsway tunnel. We could never be mistakenly late for classes, since we had Big Ben remorselessly chiming every quarter-hour to remind us of the time.

I remember one day when we were riding our bikes along the Embankment to our hostel, humming any words that came into our heads, we saw and sang the headlines '42 TO 1. LEAGUE VOTES 42 TO 1. JAPANESE DELEGATES WALK OUT.' This headline, which stuck in my memory, is from 1933, when the League of Nations voted to condemn Japan's invasion of Manchuria. (While at St Thomas', I remember getting most of my news from the placards of newspaper boys or occasionally from the BBC.) Meanwhile Hitler's rise in Germany and other significant international crises did not make much impression on us.

For the most part our lives were filled with studying and patients, and of course fun things such as the theatre (with tickets provided free to hospital workers like us) and some brief holidays – to Devon by bicycle or to Jersey, arriving at the boat train twenty-four hours late! Occasionally we tried out different churches; there was one wonderful orator-preacher at a church somewhere in Belgravia. Whenever possible, and usually from the top gallery, we watched Danilova, Markova, Massine, Lichine, and the 'baby ballerinas' of the thirties. To celebrate the completion of our anatomy exams, I saw Fred Astaire in the stage version of *Gay Divorce* (US variation, *The Gay Divorcée*) and I've been an Astaire fan ever since.

At the end of our physiotherapy training, Martin, Deane, and I parted. Martin went to work in the south of England. Helen eventually got married, had children, and returned to Deaneshaven on Kootenay Lake in 'far BC,' where she was head physio at the Kootenay Lake General Hospital for many years. In 1939, I was in Canada too and, on my first trip west with a Montreal physio friend, got off the train at Kootenay Landing and found it just as Helen had described 'my trip home' back at St Thomas'. We saw each other again in the summers of 1940 and 1941, and met next at an international physio convention in Paris in 1959. Each time, we picked up exactly where we had left off.

Helen went from strength to strength. In 1967, she was one of the BC Alpine team attempting to climb new peaks in the Rockies. On another occasion she found the ice axe left by a man called Wright, who in 1915 (I believe) had climbed in the Kokanee area. Helen had an unstable knee joint, as did I, and since we were mad about skiing, this made for a few difficulties. She, however, skied and climbed mountains until her knee and hip finally called a halt. Her friends celebrated her seventy-fifth birthday by having her flown up to the Kokanee Glacier hut in a helicopter for a celebration in the mountains.

Helen made a perfect grandmother, helping the children learn about boating, fishing, and life in the mountains. I loved Helen for fifty years. She was a role model, a brave, independent, peace-loving woman who cared for people and for her beloved natural environment of mountains, trees, birds, and animals.

After St Thomas', my first appointment was to the staff of Selly Oak Hospital, which is just outside Birmingham, near the suburb of Bourneville where Cadbury's chocolate was made. Whenever the wind blew in our direction, it was heavily chocolate-scented. My first pay cheque there was three pounds and ten shillings for one week (the pound was then worth about $5). Even in those Depression days, this did not lend itself to much splurging.

I boarded with two sisters who lived just past the big Austin automobile works at Longbridge, and I took a tram into work every day. The trams were slow, clanking things, but they got you where you were going. Birmingham had good theatres and concerts and I remember seeing some of the London theatre productions either just before or just after their London season, but most evenings I went home to my solitary supper (the sisters preferred to eat separately, and I suspect I agreed) and did a good deal of reading. I read the Webbs' *Soviet Communism*, both volumes, on which I practised speeding up my reading (10 pages, 15 minutes) and by which I was persuaded that communism was a sensible way to try to achieve a good life for everyone. I had been inspired to get this tome from the library by references to the Webbs in the Strachey book given me by Beth Hubbard in her efforts to improve my education.

When I got fed up with reading, I would go on long walks in the Warwickshire countryside, daydreaming, and having romantic fantasies about good-looking interns at the hospital. I suppose this was a delayed adolescent period. The prospect of a long weekend filled me with gloom mingled with what usually turned out to be vain hopes of invitations, phone calls, or exciting happenings. Some friends of my aunt's lived not far away, and I sometimes went for weekends and played tennis with them, feeling that I had returned to the real world.

Not that I wasn't happy. The other four physios were quite a friendly bunch, and I occasionally visited one of them after work, though their Midland accents were strange to my snobbish southern ear. My feeling that everyone who spoke with a Birmingham accent (halfway to Yorkshire after all) was somehow not quite OK was totally inconsistent with my behaviour at St Thomas', where we spoke adenoidal Cockney amongst ourselves nearly all the time.

I had been in Selly Oak for about five months when this rather lonely period was brought to an end by a cable from Rosie Brewin, my former roommate, now back in Montreal. She was setting up a new physiotherapy department there and had more work than she could handle. Would I like a job? I could work part-time at $40 per month and supplement my income by treating patients in their homes. My room and board would cost $40 a month (lunch was free in the hospital) and the tiny income from my parents could make up the difference until I had settled in. I hadn't too many ties in England, but I conferred with my closest counsellor and advisor, Aunt May, and with some of my friends. It didn't take me long to decide to go to Canada 'for a year or two' (!).

So I cabled back to Rosie and began finding out about how one emigrated to Canada. Then as now, no one could enter the country without a job waiting for them that no Canadian could fill. Luckily, there were hardly any Canadian physios and none without jobs, so I was in that category. I remember going to see the Canadian High Commissioner (Georges Vanier, I believe) and having a brief and amiable chat with him – with a predictably favourable outcome.

I was looking forward to an adventure. Sharing a room again with the gregarious Rosie Brewin would put an end to my solitary period. It was to be a few years before I lived on my own again and, the next time round, I had far more resources to fill my time. In fact, there was never enough time then for the solitude I enjoyed.

May came with me to Liverpool to see me safely embarked on the SS *Duchess of Bedford*, and on August 22nd, 1935, I arrived in Montreal.

3

Montreal

When I arrived in Montreal, I was twenty-two, tall, awkward, and very naïve. Rosie Brewin was my opposite: short, vivacious, talkative and, by my standards, very sophisticated. When she met me at the dock, she had just bought and learned to drive a second-hand Ford two-seater with a rumble seat. She immediately drove us out to have lunch at a White Spot drive-in restaurant on Décarie Boulevard on the edge of town, where we had grilled-cheese sandwiches and a milkshake. I was entranced. I'd never tasted these delights and had never driven in what seemed to me to be a huge Canadian car like this.

Rosie had been working at the new physiotherapy department in St Mary's Hospital since she returned from London as a fully qualified physio the year before. Hospitals were opening physio departments, and the fledgling profession was expanding rapidly. I was immediately enrolled as a member of the Canadian Physiotherapy Association. There were only about ten to twenty CPA members in Montreal (most members were in Toronto). However, Rosie announced categorically that it was the done thing and important to build up our profession in Montreal and in Canada as a whole. So I dutifully joined and was immediately made secretary-treasurer, being too dumb to deduce from my friend's generous offer to show me the ropes and help with the bookkeeping that she had had enough of the job herself.

Rosie and I shared a couple of rooms in a house at 4191 Sherbrooke Street West, and she introduced me to all her family and friends. My first Labour Day holiday came around very soon and, after only one week of work, we drove off for the long weekend to Stoney Lake, where Rosie's family had a cottage. Her elder brother Andrew, later an MP, met us in a rowboat for the trip from the landing to the cottage. I met

Rosie's parents (her father was the minister at St Simon's Church in Toronto) and Andrew's wife Peggy, and was completely enchanted by holiday living on a Canadian lake.

Life was very romantic for Rosie, whose amorous adventures I followed with vicarious excitement. I lived somewhat in her shadow and spent much time waiting for her to come in and recount the exploits of the evening with one of her many 'beaux,' as the term was. The long weekend blanks stayed with me when Rosie was away, but sometimes I fell heir to a 'beau' or two, though I was really too tongue-tied and naïve to make the most of the date. I went along, too, on some of her dates. The 'beaux' were delightful young men trying to get themselves established in jobs, though progress was slow since the Depression was not yet over and some had been unemployed since leaving school or college. Brewin would berate me soundly for literally saying nothing during most of an evening when she nobly took me along with her. It's hard for most of my friends now to believe this. But later in September, when Rosie went on her holiday, I did her work and used her car, so I learned my way around Montreal and even went out to a hockey game with Red, the friendly mechanic at our local garage. This quite shocked Rosie, when she was told about it, since I had kissed him goodnight!

My work expanded, as well as my income, when I joined the physio department of the Children's Memorial Hospital, also a part-time job. Soon I was not only working at two hospitals but had sometimes one or two patients in other smaller hospitals (the Homeopathic and the Women's General, now the Herbert Reddy), as well as treating private patients. Many of the patients were French-speaking, which was a challenge, because even with high-school French and a month in Paris I could manage little more than 'pliez le bras.' Rosie and I joined the tennis club, skied in the winter, visited four of Rosie's boyfriends who shared a house out on the lakeshore, and had quite a hectic, not to say hedonistic, life.

I returned to England for summer holidays three times before the war. There were no transatlantic flights in those days, so I dashed across the Atlantic on the SS *Empress of Britain* from Quebec City, five days and nights at sea (other ships were slower). I usually spent the brief weeks of my holiday seeing my brother Richard, Beth, Wendy, some of my physio friends and, of course, my beloved Aunt May, who provided a London base and a warm welcome.

I think it was the 1936 crossing that was made notable by the presence on board of the pipers of the Black Watch, on their way to the ceremonial opening of the Vimy Ridge memorial. The crossing was quite rough, and they lay in their bunks, soulfully practising on the bagpipes. The cabin walls were paper-thin. At the end of that trip, my brother Richard came back with me and rented a motorbike to see the sights of Canada. I rode with him on only one trip, because the bike had no pillion seat, so riding on the back was extremely uncomfortable.

The next year I arranged for Julia Jenkins, a physio friend from England, to fill in for me at the hospital and I went off for seven weeks. As I had the year before, I visited Brother Dick at Cambridge. I arrived there almost straight off the ship and was introduced to Pimm's No. 1, the latest in summer drinks, while listening to Richard's new jazz records in his rooms in Cat's (St Catherine's College).

A friend of Richard's and I attended King's College May Ball, where we had a six-course dinner with different drinks for every course and then proceeded to the ball where there was champagne at every stop around the college. Boating in a punt along the Backs was followed by a mass photograph at 6:00 a.m. on the college lawn (I still have the picture) and a mad drive out to Grantchester for breakfast. Thirty-one years later, when we spent our third sabbatical in Cambridge, my daughter Sheila happily took in as many of these festivities as she could. I think she probably enjoyed it much more than I did, though I wouldn't have missed it for anything.

I went on holiday to Somerset with Wendy, Richard, and other friends. We learned to ride Exmoor ponies. 'Bash their sides in,' said the farmer, meaning we should grip with our knees. We learned, too, about the potency of 'zider' and about the joys (for some) of a rough sea, when we went on a day trip in a small steamer to Lundy Island. Wendy and I were memorably seasick. We then recuperated in the local pub, and luckily the trip back was over sea as smooth as glass.

Later that year, Rosie got married, after a thrilling and romantic engagement to Ralph Crowe, a dashing RMC (Royal Military College) graduate who had recently become an officer in the permanent army. I moved into Miss Rose's boarding house at 1477 Sherbrooke near Guy, and set about finding another physio to help with the expanding work. In 1938, my last holiday in England until 1952, I visited St Thomas' to look for another recruit and talked (mostly about the marvellous skiing in Quebec) to Valerie Ward, who came to join us at the beginning of the next year, followed a short while later by her younger sister, Desirée, understandably known as Kid. The three of us then moved to 1028 Sherbrooke, over the Esse Cookers store, where we stayed until 1941.

I bought a second-hand Ford coupé (or 'coop,' as we pronounced it) complete with rumble seat, and my social life took a leap forward. Anyone with a car was, of course, very popular. My car had once belonged to the traffic policeman to whom we waved at the corner of Côte des Neiges and Cedar every morning on our way to the hospital. At St Mary's Hospital I met other members of the police force who were sent for treatment, and among my first patients was one Sergeant Girard who had an injured knee. A year later, I saw him again. My brother was visiting and hadn't known about the No Left Turn at Guy Street. When I went to the courthouse with the summons, I was so solicitous about the sergeant's past injuries that he arranged to let me off the fine. Another of my early patients was the hospital priest, whom I tried to convince (unsuccessfully, I might add) of the importance of birth control.

At about this time, I also realized that waiting for the phone to ring was not the way to proceed. I had to take the bull by the horns and invite people, men and women, to join me. Thus began the period of counting the days until a long weekend, a far cry from the gloomy anticipation of weekends in Selly Oak. Now weekends were crammed full of trips hither and yon, parties, ski trips, and all the usual activities of anyone in their twenties with a lively circle of friends. A shared beer with a poverty-stricken reviewer from the Montreal *Gazette* after the paper went to bed at 12:30. Long discussions that began at 1:00 a.m. – sleep didn't matter.

The poverty-stricken reviewer was Herbert Whittaker, a lifelong friend, and Sherbrooke and Peel was on his way home from the *Gazette.* He would drop in, or we would meet at the Samovar occasionally, as he was on his way up Peel Street. There are only a few ancient sages who share Herbert Whittaker's friendship over the past fifty years, including Fraser Macorquodale and Valerie Ward (and, later, her husband Leslie Johnston). These friends were brought together by Skene and the 16/30 drama groups. I remember a wonderful mural painted by Herbert, combining scenes from the dramatic triumphs in his and Montreal Repertory shows. I still possess a photo of this masterpiece.

At parties we played games, usually charades. Herbert's Queen Victoria, not amused, was memorable; Fraser's 'Sheep may safely graze' and our joint little cygnets from *Swan Lake* were popular interpretations. The Esse showroom windows offered us a great temptation in the form of clattering venetian blinds on which we performed magnificent versions of Beethoven's 5th and other masterpieces. For years it seemed that Herbert and Fraser vied with each other to see who could attend the greater number of New Year's Eve parties. I remember the three of us sitting in a café on St Catherine Street at about 6:00 a.m., before we trailed off to bed one New Year's Day.

For two years, I sang with the Elgar Choir in Montreal, which I found both remarkable and memorable. Fraser also joined, and he continued his choral efforts for years afterward. Our qualifications for this were minimal, at least mine were. We studied, rehearsed, and finally took part in performances of both Bach's *B Minor Mass* and Edward Elgar's *Dream of Gerontius*. The conductor for this event (it was either 1941 or 1942) was none other than Sir Thomas Beecham, the fiery and unpredictable Englishman who delighted us with his pithy comments and tirades at miscreant musicians during rehearsals. These rehearsals, in a church near the railway, were interrupted by those everlasting shunting bings and bangs made by freight trains (the good old days). Sir T's language was expressive! Since then, I've listened to every performance of the *B Minor Mass* I could. I think the most glorious one was in the summer of 1990, when Helmut Rilling conducted the National Arts Centre Orchestra and Choirs.

In between times, my tennis and skiing improved. I made more friends and led a very full life, punctuated by trips out west and sometimes into the States. I went to New York for the first time, on my own, and spent a whole Easter weekend seeing all the sights, ending with fifteen minutes of the Metropolitan Museum (I got there just before closing time). I also went to the Metropolitan Opera, where there was standing room only. Because it was Easter, they were doing *Parsifal*, so I had to stand through that.

I'd had very few childhood diseases actually during my childhood, so when I began to work at the Children's Memorial Hospital I proceeded to catch most of them. I started with scarlet fever, one of the worst in those days, though now quite rare. Doctors were experimenting with sulphur drugs to deal with strep throat and the like, and were still gauging doses by when the patient turned blue. Patients with acute infectious diseases were sent off to the Isolation Hospital, down near the waterfront and close to the city dump, the smell from which permeated the hospital at all times. I was carted off there in an ambulance on Christmas morning, after a wonderful send-off party for one of my friends, Ruth McCulloch, a librarian at McGill, who was off to some exotic island for the holidays. I had volunteered to clear up all the dishes, plates covered with the remains of spaghetti and sauce, a mess I well remember. I celebrated Christmas in isolation, and when Ruth returned ten days later to find the place exactly as she had left it, her thoughts about me were unprintable.

Then I got mumps. I was so spectacularly swollen on both sides that I was photographed for the medical records, but I do remember having a wonderful few days of spring skiing in the Laurentians by way of recuperation. I then got chicken pox, an itchy nuisance, followed by German measles. The latter I hardly noticed until I saw a rash, which quickly went away. I had, however, infected a polio patient of mine who came out in spots a week or two later. His parents were at a total loss as to how this could have happened, since he was virtually isolated at home and, to my shame, I didn't have the nerve to own up to my crime, other than by eventually speculating in a detached sort of way as to whether I might unknowingly have been infected. What a coward I was. I'm sure they would have been very kind about it.

Of the four of us in Miss Rose's boarding house the next winter, three had come from England. We were all working, two in hospitals, one in teaching, and one in advertising. The snow stayed late that year and, for the three months that it lasted, we spent all our weekends up north. Very few things in town were more attractive than a weekend's skiing.

Several of my friends had taken a cottage at Val Morin, so we would head for the train and make the 1:10 with a few minutes to spare. I always tried to knit on the two-hour steam-train ride, but the white socks just had a couple of darker rows of grey to show for the smoky journey each weekend. Out of Montreal, and soon we would have passed St Jerome. From then on the ground rises and the Laurentians begin, first just a few ridges, then the higher hills. The Big Hill at Shawbridge would be crawling with people. The train would disgorge several dozen more, who took only a minute to buckle on their skis, hitch their packs on their backs, and set off for the village. At Piedmont, Mont Rolland, and St Margaret's it was the same, and the train was getting empty by the time we came out from the hills and woods and the track ran alongside Lac Raymond.

When the train stopped again and we had arrived, we would be out as though we hadn't a minute to waste. I can still remember those clear, crisp, sunny days, the smell of wood-smoke from a cottage chimney, and the sound of the train whistling up the valley, as we walked up to the cottage. After snatching a couple of biscuits to keep us going, we were out making for the nearest hill. This was before the days of ski tows, and we would lose count of the number of times we'd climbed Mont Sauvage. There was never enough time on the downhill run to do all the things one planned to do on the way up, so we always had to have another run. Long after everyone else had gone for supper, we plodded up and down. We slid home along the road with that feeling of exhaustion and utter contentment that comes after physical exertion, combined with the heady exhilaration that a perfect evening in a snowbound countryside gives to skiers.

One night, after we had straggled home from the pub accompanied by our various friends of the evening, we were still far from sleepy and regaled each other with ghost stories. It got colder and colder, so we all dragged our beds into the living room and got as close as we could to the remains of the fire. We put our thick pyjamas on over our long woollen underwear, and sweaters on top of that, and piled all the blankets in the house on top of us, but all to no avail. For hours we lay awake, each afraid of waking the others, and it wasn't until the next morning that we discovered we'd all been doing precisely the same thing. And no wonder. The temperature had dropped to 30 below and there was no heating once the fire had died down. The lack of sleep didn't worry us, however, and after our usual enormous skiers' breakfast, we packed up and decided to go cross-country to St Margaret's.

In 1939, I made my first trip west, by train. I got off the train at Kootenay Landing to visit Helen Deane (now Butling), my physio friend from St Thomas' days. We spent a wonderful few days fishing, swimming, and gazing at the glorious Kokanee Glacier scenery. That trip also gave me my first glimpse of the Okanagan fruit country and Vancouver Island with its huge Douglas firs.

I had become good friends with Ruth McCulloch, and I visited her at home in Penticton. Ruth's father had been the chief engineer building the Kettle Valley railway (now, sadly, closed) and the Field tunnels. He talked about gradients and tunnels and showed us some of the huge trestles built to carry the trains across chasms between mountains. We visited friends on a Kelowna fruit farm, where we ate pounds of ripe purple cherries until our faces and mouths were a rich, dark hue. We then discovered that, if we ate a couple of enormous Okanagan peaches, the peach juice bleached the cherry juice so that we could start again with clean faces. I dreamed about a career as a fruit-picker, but apart from getting a poem printed in the *Penticton Herald* ('On viewing the Okanagan Valley after driving through the Cascade Mountains' or some such) was not suitably qualified – much too slow, for one thing.

A friend and I took the bus down to San Francisco, where we rented a car and toured around. We saw the Boulder Dam (727 feet high, as I knew from Ruth's engineer father), Yosemite, Death Valley, and Las Vegas, which looked like a grade-B-movie run-down cowboy town with mud streets. Then we went back to Vancouver and to Banff, and there we heard the news of the declaration of war on September 3rd. We headed back to Montreal, the joy taken out of our holiday.

During all this time, I doubt whether I knew who the Canadian prime minister was. On one occasion I treated Dr Norman Bethune for a stiff shoulder; I believe I was aware that he had been in the Spanish Civil War, but little more. I learned the story of the Halifax explosion only after I'd met Hugh MacLennan, who wrote a novel about it, *Barometer Rising.* (Hugh taught at Lower Canada College with Avery Shaw, the artist who moved to Saint John, and with Leslie Johnston, eventually Val's husband.) But I certainly never voted and only found out years later that women could not vote in Quebec until 1940. I knew nothing about Canadian politics and had only realized that there were French-speaking Canadians when I met the customs officers at the Montreal harbour.

Although we came home early from our holiday because of the war, nothing much had changed. Work went on, and a year later, in August 1940, two friends and I set off to drive across Canada in a '36 Ford. This was before they started to ration gas. In my account of the trip, written at the time, the only reference to the war occurs when we reached Petawawa where the army was training. 'We arrived in Petawawa without any bother. We were later told that no unattended female is allowed out in Petawawa after 9:00 p.m., so promptly made mental notes to try on the way home, and get a free bed in the gaol. Nothing like experience. It is nice that the morals of the army and/or unattended females are so vigorously protected by the government.'

Food and the scanty washing facilities feature largely in my account, and the heat, the mosquitoes, and the bad roads were, not surprisingly, the major focuses of the trip. Indeed, outside North Bay 'the country became dustier and the road worse, being at intervals surrounded in layers of gravel. As a result of this, we found ourselves charging towards, then embracing and overwhelming a signpost, and eventually landing unscathed in the ditch. The car,' I noted, 'stood up to it well.'

I went on to stay with Helen Deane, before I drove across the US border to meet my brother Richard in Yellowstone Park, a mere 536 miles further on. I arrived too late to cross the border, which closed nightly in wartime, so I slept in my car. Early next morning, I changed a flat tire and set off, arriving in Yellowstone late that evening. The roads were blissful and our celebration, when we met, lustily alcoholic. Driving in my open coupé, I had given myself a slight touch of sunstroke – or maybe it was too much celebrating with my brother.

The next day we toured the park, saw the geyser, Old Faithful, and watched a family of bears raiding the cabins. Dick and I then travelled north, but only as far as the Canadian border since his British passport would not let him into Canada. (He was in the US as a Shell Oil executive during wartime.) We parted in Spokane after a good evening listening to jazz, and I went on to visit Ruth in Penticton. I then drove back to Montreal alone, though a nice young hitchhiker kept me company across Saskatchewan. I dropped him in Winnipeg, where he hopped the freight train, and picked him up again on the road to Port Arthur. I came home to Montreal ignominiously, towed behind a tow-truck for the last thirty miles. The radiator had leaked, so the engine had overheated. I then filled the radiator with cold water, thereby causing the engine to crack. But never mind! I'd driven about 10,000 miles through all varieties of glorious countryside, from mountains to prairies, and met some wonderful people.

I was about twenty-six, often on my own, naïve and inexperienced, incompetent in my knowledge of cars, people, and the world in general, but it was a wonderful experience. There weren't as many travellers then as there are now and the amenities were few and far between, but the countryside felt safe and welcoming.

I repeated part of the trip, with Val and Leslie, as soon as I could. My rehabilitated convertible did yeoman service on that trip, too, and it later served my husband, Brough, and me until the family made it necessary to get a bigger car. We always said he married me for the car and I married him for his record collection! Our good friend Harold King, an artist, took the car, and we have one of his water-colours painted when his horizons had expanded with this new mobility. I don't think driving all over is so pleasant now – too much traffic and too many hazards – but that's partly because I'm getting timid in my old age.

At that time, I wasn't really touched by any of the things happening during the war or with my relatives and friends in England. The war was too far away and news was too slow in coming to realize who had been killed and drowned and blown up and all the other things. It was a pretty sheltered life I had in Canada.

In fact, the war did not touch me closely until the spring of 1941, when the Canadian Armed Forces were recruiting medical personnel to staff Canadian General Hospital Number 1 to go overseas. Many of the bright, young doctors were volunteering and, after what must have been some very high-powered lobbying of government officials, the Canadian Physiotherapy Association was assigned the job of selecting and recommending from amongst its members qualified physiotherapists who would be commissioned as officers in the RCAMC (Royal Canadian Army Medical Corps) and sent overseas with the hospital, which was to be established in England. Being given officer status was considered a great achievement for the still-young profession.

Physios were in short supply since hospitals all over the country were beginning to set up physiotherapy departments, and the association was anxious to be represented by the best-qualified and most-experienced physios they could find. The upper age limit was fifty-five. I'm not sure whether one had to be over twenty-five to be chosen, but I was certainly amongst those who were qualified – unmarried, and with no family responsibilities, therefore a possible candidate. My problem was a moral and philosophical one.

I had been living with two convinced pacifists who later became Quakers, and Richard Gregg's *The Power of Non-Violence* had influenced me a good deal. I was opposed to the use of force, and my conviction was that war was wrong and no way to settle disputes. I had spent my childhood in the warlike surroundings of 1914–18 and, like others of my generation, I had grown up hoping and praying that the aims and promises for which our parents fought might come true. Then when chaos threatened again, war was again proposed as its solution.

Balanced against that were my awareness of the medical profession's responsibility to care for the sick and injured, and the fact that my native country, my relatives and friends as well as the cities and countryside I loved, were being bombed and might quite likely be invaded. Was I also just plain scared of this prospect or of being on a ship that was torpedoed and sunk, as was happening daily? All these conflicting emotions, plus the forceful arguments expressed on both sides of the debate by some of my best friends, contributed to my losing a lot of sleep and about twenty pounds. I decided to sign up, then thought about it all some more, changed my mind, and pulled out. I wrote: 'If people are frightened to hear every opinion, if subversive propaganda is crushed, there is fear of the truth, because if people know they are acting justifiably they do not rule by fear.' And also: 'Suppose England wins the war, is she big enough to treat the German people with methods of love? I am afraid this is doubtful.'

I saw all sides of the conundrum and was totally miserable. Then one day I had a letter from my beloved Aunt May, from right in the midst of everything in her small London flat, pleading with me not to come, to stay, stick to my work in Canada, and help from the other side of the Atlantic. Finally, I decided to stay in Canada.

My Quaker friends, Valerie and Leslie Johnston, were now married, and before Leslie was to start his alternative service as a CO (conscientious objector), we three decided to drive my two-seater Ford out to BC, camping along the way. We pooled our resources, collected sleeping bags and camping gear, and headed west, aiming for Kootenay Lake.

We had to load ourselves and the car onto a ship up Lake Superior, since it was still many years before the Trans-Canada Highway went round the north shore of the lake. We had cabins, showers, and two good meals before we started off on the three hundred miles of unpaved highway to Winnipeg. I think it was that time that I sailed on the SS *Noronic*, the very popular passenger lake boat run by Canada Steamship Lines, which burned while tied up at the Toronto dock a few years later, with shockingly heavy loss of life. Val and I took turns driving, and Leslie took over only once in a while since he was just learning. Both Val and I taught our husbands how to drive. I don't recommend it as a regular practice, but both husbands eventually proved well able to cope. Later, when someone complained to Brough that I was so 'bossy,' he replied mildly, 'Oh, she likes to organize.'

We had a wonderful time with Helen Deane, and the Johnstons still remember it nostalgically after nearly fifty years. I still feel the same way about Nelson, and the Kootenay, and the Okanagan, and have been lucky enough to make more friends there and go back to visit on several occasions.

While I was in Nelson I received a telegram from Marg Finley, who was holding the fort at the Children's Memorial Hospital while department head Esther Asplet was on holiday. It offered me a job organizing physiotherapy services in New Brunswick, where an epidemic of poliomyelitis was causing great anxiety. Before the discovery of the Salk vaccine in 1954, infantile paralysis – anterior poliomyelitis – was one of the dreaded childhood diseases for which there was no known cause or cure. It usually appeared during the summer months, affected hundreds of individuals, mostly children, and left many with some degree of paralysis. If breathing muscles were affected, patients could die unless artificial respiration was administered. Patients could be helped with massage, exercises, splints and, sometimes, surgery. Physios were greatly in demand, since physiotherapy offered remedial measures, greater comfort, and an improved chance of recovering the use of the muscles.

I was still in a state after all my internal turmoil about not joining the Medical Corps, and I expect I had been quite abominable around the department. Marg, bless her, knew all that, and thinking, quite rightly, that I should get away from Montreal, had suggested my name. In 1941, to be asked to head a provincial program for several hundred patients was an exciting challenge. For taking charge and setting up the new provincial organization, the salary was the princely sum of $125 per month, not at all bad for those days. I accepted the offer.

So we set off on our journey back to Montreal. We had a scary skid on the wooden-surfaced bridge coming into Kenora and came almost to the end of our money as we waited for the ferry ship at Port Arthur. The Johnstons were sure that we could cash a cheque the next morning before we sailed, and wanted to spend our last cash on a decent 'city' meal. I was obstinate and not certain we should spend our remaining dollars, and made them dine on whole-wheat bread (I think it was the last of Helen's home-made bread) and store-bought raspberry jam. We survived the ordeal anyway, and cashed the cheque next day.

During the time I was getting packed up and ready to leave for Fredericton, the following appeared in the Montreal Herald:

Fredericton, Sept. 5 –(CP)– Three new cases of infantile paralysis yesterday at Grafton, Carleton County, one at Hibernia, Queen's County and another at Moore's Hills, York County, raising the total number in New Brunswick to 220. The Grafton cases occurred in a house where two others already existed.

A physio-therapist, Miss Kathleen Walker, Montreal, has been engaged by the Department of Health to work with doctors throughout the Province in treating victims of the epidemic.

And on September 4, The Daily Gleaner in Fredericton ran a headline 'Physio-Therapist Is Engaged by N. B. Health Department: Miss Kathleen Walker, Montreal, Will Give Treatment in Severe Cases,' with subheads 'Minimizing Effects Is Great Desire' and 'Four New Cases of Infantile Paralysis Reported To-day – Total 219.'

One of my old friends, Fraser Macorquodale, saw the *Herald* clipping and wrote a poem for the unsuspecting citizens of New Brunswick, warning them of this new arrival.

Friday, September 5th, 1941, A.D.

The public prints would seem to show
That Kay is going down below
To rescue from their sorry plight
Full many a one of N.B.'s white
And coloured folk, and e'en to lend
A helping hand to those who tend
To garner in what salaried wealth
Is offered by the Board of Health.
Oh! Maritimes! I greet thee clear!
But lend me an attentive ear –
This Walker woman who invades
The peaceful quiet of your glades
Brings with her turmoil and unrest,
So hark to this, my sole behest:
Before you welcome, on this mull:
Her motto's 'Ne'er a moment dull.'

Anyway, after a farewell party, Herbert, Val, and Kid finally packed me into the car in Montreal and saw me off from 1028 on the Sunday afternoon.

Never having driven to Quebec City, I had quite an interesting trip. Although it rained intermittently, I tucked myself in, turned on the radio at intervals (they were playing a Beethoven sonata, to my great joy), and sang the rest of the time. By the time I had finished the whole of the *B Minor Mass* and part of *Gerontius*, I was very hoarse and happy and, before it got dark, had time to be very impressed by the beautifully neat old stone houses that one hears so much about and so seldom sees in the welter of untidiness around Montreal. I saw then why the province of Quebec attracted tourists. If only that type of meticulous countryside were a little more general. I took Val's advice and found a cabin outside Quebec City for the night. A soldier boy who wanted a lift told me where to find some good ones. I was quite sorry not to be able to drive him into the city. I was in bed by 9:00 that night, after a wonderful meal provided by Kid, which included even sherry and also hot coffee in a Thermos flask, and I collected a good deal of rather badly needed sleep.

The next morning was cold and sunny, and I drove across Quebec Bridge, through Lévis and Rivière-du-Loup, and turned down towards the New Brunswick border, where the country becomes much wilder and more deserted, and the road does likewise. There was no mistaking the provincial boundary. The road was paved and very good as soon as one entered New Brunswick, and this held good for most of the Maritime roads. I finally reached Fredericton about 6:00, having followed the Saint John River valley almost from the border. The country seemed pleasant: rolling agricultural land, no high hills, farms and small villages scattered everywhere. One had no difficulty in discovering the chief occupation of New Brunswick people. Farming and lumbering, although I don't know the statistics, must have amounted to about 80 per cent of the total.

Reading through some of the pieces I wrote during my two years in New Brunswick, I found a whole period of my experience I had almost completely forgotten. Then I began remembering the open-handed and good-natured welcome I received from the hospital superintendent, Miss George, whom I had met in Nelson the year before. As soon as I arrived, she set about finding me somewhere to stay, and Hattie Harmon became my landlady.

Harriet Harmon had been widowed in the First World War after a few weeks of marriage, and since that time had taught maths in the Fredericton High School. She knew most of the young people in town because she had taught them. They loved her and constantly dropped in to 'visit with Hattie.' On our first contact, she urged me to 'come over right away. No, don't wait until tomorrow; I need some company now for my dinner.' She was a superb cook, like so many New Brunswick women. And so began a lasting friendship with her and her friends and ex-students, and anyone else that she thought I might enjoy meeting.

After I had been in New Brunswick for a few weeks, I went back to Montreal to help close up our flat. Fraser and Ruth and Val and Herbert were there. We dashed about the city, collecting people and objects: a dartboard, my mothball-ridden evening dress, unwanted splints and braces from the hospital for me to take back to Fredericton. Then we got ready for the party. It was a flat-cooling, the opposite of a housewarming: hordes of people, much coffee the next morning, a film (*Major Barbara*), packing cases all over the garage floor. It was a wonderful party, and I wrote an incoherent account of it at the time, called 'Weekend Kaleidoscope, or How We Cooled The Flat – An Appreciation Of My Friends.' My account began: 'Impressions are jumbled, but all as happy as it is possible to be. And by happy I mean that exstatic [sic] peak of pure joy that one so seldom recognizes when it is experienced, but remains as a memory which makes one want to hug oneself with excitement at the thought of it. Badly put, but perhaps you know what I am driving at. We talked and talked. I couldn't stop myself. Everyone seemed so terrifically witty, and it *can't* all have been rum.'

Valerie and Leslie were going up to the Laurentians where he was going to work as a farm labourer, for his 'alternative service' as a conscientious objector. Ruth was moving, and so was Kid. I travelled by train for the trip back to Fredericton, because of the gas rationing, and I made the train with less than five minutes to spare. I kept close ties with Montreal and visited there once a month, until my Montreal friends began to disperse and I discovered the fleshpots (usually lobster pots) of Saint John.

4

New Brunswick

Moving from Montreal to Fredericton in 1941 was more than a change in locale from a bustling, cosmopolitan city of over a million people to the almost rural capital city of New Brunswick with a population of about 7000 and an old university with some seven hundred students. Before I had been in New Brunswick long enough to report on what people discussed and thought, it was impressed on me that this was one of the first-settled parts of the Dominion, that the people I met had been there for generations and were very proud of it, and that for pro-British and almost anti-American sentiments it would be hard to beat.

There were still horse-drawn sleighs on the snowy winter roads, and log booms were towed down the Saint John River by chunky little tugs, after the ice went out. A doctor going out on his rounds often carried a gun in the trunk of his car when the hunting season was open and deer meat available to those who could find it. In the spring came fiddle-heads, Atlantic salmon, and maple syrup, all to be bought on Saturday mornings at the outdoor markets, the stalls clustered around the old red-brick opera house.

After living in Montreal, a city that never went to bed at all, it was rather pleasant to be able to walk along streets that were deserted after 11:00 p.m. Just before I went to bed, usually about 1:00 a.m., I used to stick my head out into the darkness and listen. It was the kind of silence one could listen to. In the winter sometimes, you could hear snow falling from the trees, but you felt the sound rather than hearing it.

A month after my arrival, I wrote (on my new Hermes typewriter):

In order to practise my typing, and so that I won't forget some of my ideas and impressions since I have been in the Maritimes, I'm sitting listening to Beethoven's second symphony, which I don't know well at all and so far like very much, and putting down more or less whatever comes into my head. It is Saturday night, and this is a novel situation for one whose motto is, according to Fraser, 'Ne'er a moment dull.' I'm enjoying it very much. The house is quite silent, as my school teacher has gone to a wedding and, although the town is supposed to be lively, it being market day, there isn't a sound outside. It's a change from Sherbrooke Street.

To set the scene: my room, which I turned completely round as soon as I arrived, boasts a four-poster bed, quite small fortunately, one comfortable chair, a couple of bureaux, a boxy thing to sit or put things on, and a bookcase. It is further enlivened today by some very bright maple leaves which I have duly stuck in glycerine and water in the hope of preserving them, and some yellow gladioli which I bought from the mother of one of my patients, who has a stall in the market every Saturday.

That was the family that almost reduced me to tears after I had visited them on their farm, a small family for those parts, just the parents and six children. The father was in Montreal working for some war firm; the three eldest boys were away in the army (one had already been killed). Joe, aged sixteen or so, was left to help his mother with the farm, although he had applied for the navy. Then Joe got poliomyelitis, and Mrs Clark was left to work the farm and see to the cattle while poor Joe lay in bed and worried himself sick over it all. Not that Mrs Clark wasn't capable. A Londoner, with a distinctive Cockney accent, she would say, 'Well, we get along as best we can. I want the boys to have this place to come back to, whatever happens. All Joe has to do is rest up and get back as much strength as he can.' Then she showed me photographs of the boys in the army, and the flowers she was taking to market the next day, and invited me to drop in whenever I was passing. I left rather hurriedly. On my new typewriter, I wrote:

Never, before I came to this province, has what I call the human interest or sob-sister side of my work been forced on me so inescapably. Luckily for me, but probably most unluckily for my patients, I am not easily moved by what in many cases would bring lumps into people's throats and tears to their eyes. Every now and then, though, an isolated situation hits me, and the thought usually crosses my mind, 'If I were writing this for *The Readers' Digest* or something, what a story it would make.' The trouble is that I will tell the truth, and will not distort it to make the tale a little more harrowing, at least I like to think that. I suppose all reports highlight the most dramatic moments, regardless of their importance in the actual circumstances. What it is to feed the public the stuff it wants.

When I arrived in Fredericton, Miss George had told me enough about the epidemic to get me thoroughly appalled by the gigantic job ahead of me. My work began with planning and discussions with hospital personnel and doctors. One doctor had been assigned to take charge of whatever facilities were set up at the Victoria General Hospital in Fredericton, so he and I worked together, with the assistance of those doctors with polio patients. There were, as I recall, no specialists in neurology and few doctors with any knowledge of physiotherapy. In January 1942, we acquired an exercise pool and an outpatient clinic, so patients received pool treatment and re-education, but antibiotics and other treatments were still in their infancy. We spent hours speculating on how polio was carried and why it struck some people but not others. I wrote:

It all seems such an unnecessary amount of suffering for people to go through, and one feels so helpless. As for the indiscriminate way in which infantile paralysis, or any disease for that matter, picks out often the most needed member of a family, I can't even begin to see any sense in that. I just get back on to my professional horse and look at it objectively and scientifically. It's the best, and by now usually unconscious, protection against emotion on the subject.

By 1942, the new treatments proposed by the Australian Sister Kenny were being examined in North America. I attended her demonstrations in 'Canada' (as New Brunswickers called Quebec/Ontario), and we adopted many of her treatment methods, especially hot packing and the passive/active movement of muscles and joints. Whatever the medical profession said and thought about her theories on poliomyelitis, her treatment was both comforting and generally comfortable for the patients and the end result certainly no worse than those of previous methods. Some patients whom we had considered candidates for double leg-braces progressed to walking with crutches. At later stages of the disease, surgery may well have improved the utility and stability of joints and limbs, but we were dealing with patients dur-

ing and after the acute stage. We all blessed Sister Kenny and her innovative ideas.

There were 427 cases of polio in New Brunswick during 1941. In
1942, there were 41 new cases between January and June, and then in
June another outbreak brought in 99 more. Resources were strained to
the utmost. As the work in the physiotherapy department increased,
the need for more physios became urgent. The first to join me was
Audrey Coleman. I remember that she and I went on expeditions
together to see patients out in the countryside and later worked
together in the expanded department. By the summer of '42, we added
two more workers. Then Audrey went back to her work in Toronto, and
we took on a summer intern. That summer, there were four of us treating the patients who filled the old wooden hospital building.

As I remember, we treated more boys than girls, and in 1942 we
began to have adults who had succumbed to the disease. I have forgotten the names of so many of the patients with whom we lived daily. I
thought I would never forget them. I remember a 12–year-old whose
second name was Leslie, whose devoted parents came to see him daily,
a teenage girl from Grand Manan, Steve somebody from near Moncton. I also remember two young women, each in a respirator (iron
lung), gradually coming out for short periods when they could breathe
by themselves. (One of them died later, the first dead person I had
seen.) And there were patients who improved, then eventually went
home and returned for check-ups from time to time.

In our wing of the hospital, we sometimes had other patients too,
like the woman whose whole back had been terribly burned when her
house caught fire and she shielded her baby from the flames. I saw the
transformation in a small girl with coeliac disease, who looked like a
skeleton when she was first admitted. After she had been fed a diet of
bananas, the only food she could digest, she was transformed into a
lively youngster.

There were moments that I found difficult to get out of my mind.
One boy of twenty, in an iron lung except for the few minutes when he
was taken out to be washed or exercised, was not one of our best
patients. He was in a good deal of pain and was consequently something of a burden on the already overworked nurses. But after exercis-
ing him one day, I offered to prop up on his reading stand some of the
magazines we kept around for boys of his age. 'Look, Miss-Nurse,' he
said, 'You won't laugh at me? What I'd like to read more than anything

else, I'd like the Bible.' I think I felt more like crying than laughing, though I really don't know why.

Here is a touching extract from a letter written to Audrey by the mother of one of our patients:

Dear Friend,

How is Jeans legs coming I am coming down around Xmas to see you people do you want her to stay longer than Xmas I understand that dease is so slow to get better. Is Jean contented or is she a fussy little girl how long do you want her to stay it is lonesome with out her but I want her to get better.

Do you thing Jean will walk some day she is all the little one in the house the other two girls is 17, 15 years old.

Will close with kindness of you to answer tell me about her.

I am willing to leave her as long as you want her.

In fact, it was the children who were not sick enough to be absolutely helpless who suffered in this epidemic; the worst cases had to come to hospital, no matter how great the quibbling over who was going to pay for their hospitalization. For those patients receiving home care, education was the key. The hardest part, and the most important, was convincing the family that the patient must not get up and must not be allowed to walk or to try to stand. It is far more difficult to keep a patient down when he himself feels well and to persuade him not to experiment and see what he can do, than it is to encourage him to try to walk. The children didn't know any better, and the mothers often had too many children at home to give detailed nursing care to the invalid.

There were few social workers or services in those days, so I spent a good deal of time travelling round the province examining and assessing patients and meeting their families. Sometimes, understandably, it was hard to persuade parents that their children would be well cared for and that treatment could help them recover the use of their muscles. Sometimes everyone in the family was terrified of the mere idea of a hospital. Many lived a long distance away, which would make it difficult to visit the patient. On one occasion I wrote: 'It is always difficult to leave a patient's house ... Besides hearing the history of the disease and testing the patient's muscles, there are often unreported cases of suspected polio in the house to be examined, not to mention the family picture gallery, animals and such incidentals.'

Having experienced some rather ungrateful or at least uninspiring patients in my private practice in Montreal, I was unprepared for the way I was welcomed into every house without exception, offered meals, fruit, and anything else to hand. The entire family, friends, relatives, and hangers-on would then, as likely as not, come out to meet me. I realized after a while that I was something quite out of the ordinary to most of the countryfolk, and they might as well get as much gossip and, I dared to hope, information as they could. The patient, young or old, took the audience for granted, and what had I to lose?

Setting off to find an isolated farmhouse in a remote area was often quite an adventure, but I don't remember having any great difficulty in finding my way around the unpaved back roads. Often people knew who I was and they helped me on my way or saved me a trip to some remote farmhouse by pointing out that 'Hoyt Harris' girl is over to MacFarlanes' this afternoon. You'll find her just aways up the straight road.' I do have one lasting memory of trying and trying to unscrew the car wheel to change a flat tire, lying in the snow to get better leverage, and finally unscrewing the nut. Then, after it was all changed, with not a soul on the road, a nice friendly truck driver stopped and asked if he could help.

I ended up driving all over the province, which gave me a good idea of the geography of the place. One day, a doctor from St Stephen asked me to see a patient of his, so I packed myself into the car after breakfast and went off in bright sunshine to do the seventy-odd miles. The people at the hospital there were very cheerful, and I was plied with Chesterfield cigarettes, shampoo (someone had been leaving samples), and invitations to return and see a bit of the town. When I left it was still a heavenly day, so I went on the extra twenty miles to see St Andrews-by-the-Sea. This was where I was disappointed, but solely because I wanted waves and what I got was perfect lake scenery improved by the smell of the sea. There were too many islands off the coast to give the impression of an authentic sea scene. I noted: 'I'll have to wait a little longer before I find my Atlantic rollers. Horrible thought! Perhaps there aren't any on this side of the Atlantic. I must make inquiries.'

Once in a while we would take some patients out to the summer cottage we physios had rented down the river and give them a picnic. Once we took Jack, one of our long-term favourites, home for Sunday tea with his farm family. Here's my account of Jack's expedition.

Jack had been in hospital for nearly a year. He was quite contented and knew that he was improving. One day we were driving out to his father's farm to pick up some deer meat he had promised us, and we said, jokingly, 'How about coming too, Jack?' He knew we didn't mean it, but the longing look in his eyes, and his 'Oh boy, if only I could,' made us suddenly think that perhaps it wouldn't be impossible ...

It was easy enough to get permission from the hospital and the doctor, and the following Saturday we suggested that Jack find out if his family were going to be in on Sunday, 'just in case the physios dropped out,' and this he did without the slightest flicker of a smile or any trace of the excitement he was feeling.

On Sunday morning, Jack woke up at four o'clock, and from then on he studied the weather anxiously. About noon, to his utter disgust, it began to snow. Fortunately, the weather decided to be kind, and the snow stopped. It is quite a job to get a boy of six feet who cannot stand up into a small car, but we managed it quite well with the aid of a wheelchair and Joe, the hospital engineer, who just picked Jack up and dumped him in.

As we got out into the country, he kept marvelling that everything looked exactly the same, nothing had changed. Then he would point out old Phillips' place, or catch a glimpse of someone he knew, usually a relative, walking down the road paying a Sunday afternoon call. We turned into the lane leading up to the McSheffrey's house, and Jack said, 'Boy, I wonder how many hundred times I've walked down this road.' No one stopped to wonder if he would ever walk down it again, because we were getting up to the house.

Mrs McSheffrey came out to welcome 'the girls,' but when I said, 'We've brought a visitor. Come and see,' her face lit up and she clasped and unclasped her hands as she shouted for the others inside. 'Oh my soul, it's Jack. Bill, come and see. Jack's here.' Amid wild excitement and greetings from Jack's father, brother, brother's girlfriend, young sister, and elder sister, Peter, the soldier brother-in-law who was about six inches shorter than Jack, picked him up, walked almost nonchalantly into the kitchen and put him carefully down on a chair by the fire.

We got used to seeing numbers of polio patients together, and their helplessness didn't seem quite so marked when they were with others, but seeing Jack being carried in with his arms around Peter's neck, and sitting in the midst of his family, unable to get up or move around, was apt to make even the most hardened onlooker feel impotent and helpless. Jack was fortunate that his family treated him absolutely normally, taking it for granted that he could not do certain things, and not wasting any sentimental sympathy on him.

We sat down with the men of the family while all the women bustled to and fro preparing the tea. Alec, Jack's six-foot-four brother, put on his denims and lumbered out to the barn. He rode or led out all the horses and the new foal, one by one, while Jack and his father sat at the window and discussed them in monosyllables. There was some difficulty deciding on the foal's name. Then there were the kittens, the cows, and of course Laddie, the big collie dog, who welcomed Jack with a great show of affection. After this, the living room with its new curtains had to be admired.

The other excitements were postponed then, while all ten of us gathered round the dining room table for Sunday tea. This consisted of huge slices of home-made bread, baked beans, spaghetti, all kinds of pickles and cheese, butter straight from the farm, orange bread, raisin bread, stewed plums, and a huge cake covered with whipped cream and known as cream pie. We washed this down with huge cups of tea, and we were just relaxing over our cigarettes – the first Jack had had for a long time – when Father Boyd, the priest, arrived to pay a farewell call as he was moving the next week. An airforce friend of Jack's turned up too, so we redistributed ourselves to allow the newcomers to eat, and Jack lay down for a short rest on the new couch in the living room.

The review of the family's activities continued. Phyllis had been married recently and brought down an armful of wedding presents for approval. She showed us some beautiful blankets, woven at home by one of her aunts, and then asked Peter to bring his tools down for Jack to see. There were metal-working tools, which Peter had learned to use when taking a special course for the Ordinance Corps. He had made Jack a beautiful hunting knife, which he might one day use for skinning a deer. His brother and his father had both already shot a deer this season, and we had benefitted to the extent of two wonderful steaks and a roast. There are few meats which taste better.

Time went quickly, and as it grew dark we realized that we must tear the family apart again and take Jack back to the hospital. Mrs McSheffrey pressed a large bottle of home-made pickles into our hands, and her husband was almost speechless. When someone is almost too full of thanks to speak, and for some little thing which means so much to him and is so easily given by you, you feel that you do not deserve the thanks and it embarrasses you almost literally to tears. That, at least, is how we felt as we drove away.

Back at the hospital everyone welcomed us with shouts of joy. They had all been 'so lonesome for Jack' during the three or four hours that he had been out, and he spent the rest of the evening recounting the afternoon's doings to five other inquisitive youngsters. We went home feeling that we had seldom spent an afternoon which had given us more pleasure, and very thankful that by a very simple action of ours we had made a whole family happier.

(Just after the manuscript of this book was finished, I visited Fredericton and the *Gleaner* published some pictures of me with people I knew in the old days. Then I heard from a Fredericton woman who knew Jack's sister. Jack had managed to walk again, with the aid of crutches. He had gone back to school and had later become a transportation manager. He had a very happy marriage, with four children, and died at the age of 52. His sister said that Jack's cheerful philosophy had had a great impact on the whole family.)

So there were good moments, but I still sometimes got depressed by the limitations of the care we could provide or by the limited impact we seemed to have in the way of educating our patients' families. 'Some of the chief needs of this district,' I wrote in 1942, 'are education in all its branches, especially in public health and the rudiments of preventive medicine. And we need more social service workers, and again education – from grammar to diction and back to reading and writing.' What to do? We worked with the patients and their families as best we could, throwing in hygiene and grammar lessons. At the end of one piece, I wrote: 'Perhaps the depressing effect of a wet weekend enlivened solely by a basketball game and a chocolate sundae is taking its toll of my usually somewhat higher spirits. Whatever the cause, this pessimistic attitude will get us nowhere, and we will end in the depths of gloom. So, let's snap out of it.'

In search of entertainment, I and the other 'polio girls' were willing to brave whatever hazards presented themselves, and a winter trip to Saint John could be particularly hazardous. In February 1942, I wrote:

There are doubtless more pleasant methods of travelling than driving in a convertible coupé through Eastern Canada in mid-February's sub-zero weather, over roads it is often impossible to walk on, let alone drive on, owing to the fact that they are covered by a substantial layer of sheer ice. On this occasion, however, the discomforts and general strain were easily balanced by the events at the other end of the journey. Our Mecca was the frequently maligned city of Saint John, about seventy miles of almost deserted wood and farm land east of Fredericton. One has to live in a small town for some time before being able to appreciate in full the excitement and thrill one gets from once more seeing a blaze of street lights, getting into a traffic jam and, above all, seeing lots and lots of people. It went completely to our heads. The population of Saint John is, I believe, between fifty and sixty thousand, but to us country hicks it seemed like London or New York.

With the ice, we rarely hit more than fifteen miles an hour and, on one occasion, the car turned in a complete circle, blithely ignoring such hazards as the river on one side, the car ahead, and the bus behind. How the buses covered the trip in two hours, I cannot imagine. We ourselves stopped from time to time to dig another car out of a snowdrift. We always finished these trips in extreme high spirits. Then we would go in search of food. Or sometimes it would be the movies. Often I would go to try sketching at Ted Campbell's.

My landlady, Hattie Harmon, had introduced me to Ted. One of the older of our new friends, he taught art at the provincial Normal School (teacher's college) for three days a week and continued his career as an artist for the rest of the time. His warehouse studio in an attic overlooking the harbour was the scene of many wonderful wartime gatherings, and Ted remained a dear friend until he died in the 1980s in Mexico.

The studio was huge, with windows all the way across one end and an open stove at the other. It was comfortably strewn with furniture, pictures, pottery, drawings, books, and gramophone records. A kitchenette and a puppet theatre occupied two chunks of the walls but were barely noticeable as the place was so large. I recognized with tremendous relief the atmosphere in which I had been living in Montreal, a 'do what you like and make yourself at home' atmosphere of general cheerfulness. The group in the studio peacefully absorbed another presence and went on sketching. Later there would be discussion, music, supper, sometimes a puppet show, or a round of tea-cup reading, at which Ted was uncannily accurate. Outside the windows, the harbour lay quietly in the night. In peacetime, the little ferry boats used to be lit up at Christmas like miniature trees. During the war, of course, there were fewer lights and fewer boats.

Going back to Fredericton, whether we faced the hazards of violent snowstorms and glare ice or the beauty of wind, starlight, and the Northern Lights, we were full of memories to mull over and stimulating things to ponder further. With these in mind, there was something particularly pleasant about dozing through the major part of a grey Sunday, with a book to read and a symphony concert on the radio.

In Fredericton, one of the best distractions was food, in which everyone was interested, so that the standard of cooking was, to my mind, very high. I was lucky to be living with Hattie Harmon, one of the best cooks in the city, but all the women and even the men were always to be found swapping recipes. On Saturday, market day, you took your life in your hands walking down Queen Street.

In March of 1942, great entertainment was provided by two big fires happening within two weeks. The first was at the Loyalist Building and happened in the morning when children and working people had to drag themselves reluctantly away. The second occurred in the evening and was much better timed to fit in with the inhabitants' leisure hours. News of the fire jammed the telephone lines, and crowds filled the streets. Only the aged and infirm were left at home. One enthusiastic lady rushed out in her pyjamas covered by a long housecoat. Eventually the firefighters' frantic activity paid off and the flames died down. It was very cold, and we went home in search of hot coffee and hot baths, the latter filled with interesting weeds, presumably from the bottom of the reservoir, which had taken such a beating in the past two weeks.

I welcomed whatever presented itself: amateur plays in the church hall, a few professional concerts, art exhibitions, some rather uninspiring films, and lectures on any subject. 'There are,' I wrote, 'few cities of the size of Fredericton which take such a lively interest in all matters connected with the arts.' This was due in large part to the work done by Madge Smith. Madge (not even the schoolchildren called her Miss Smith) had started a small shop some seven years before, where she sold her beautiful photographs. In 1941, she had moved to a central location, and the shop had become a meeting place, art centre, and general information bureau. When the Maritime artists put on their show, 'Art in Action,' Madge's shop was the general base for activities.

She often provided the inspiration for people to make and sell beautiful things: her scheme for getting the Fredericton farm folk to make hooked mats from scraps of material, for example. Madge was also a friend of Chief Polchis and the Micmacs, and helped them with orders and suggestions. Her shop sold not only their beautiful basketwork, but also woodcarving, picture mats, paintings, and so on. It was in Madge's shop that I first came across the marvellous work of New Brunswick's best-known potters, the Deichmanns, and so began my interest in pottery. Madge always found time to chat with passers-by, and once we had the cottage, she steered a various assortment of lost souls in our direction if they had nowhere to go on a weekend.

For the summer months, the 'polio girls' had rented Sansouci Cottage three miles out of town overlooking the Saint John River. There was a seldom used railway line between us and the riverbank, which provided wonderful wild-strawberry picking as we watched the tugboats hauling log booms down the river. We used bicycles for our transportation as gasoline was rationed. This provided exercise, if we had needed any more than our daily treatments for the patients. We had all kinds of drop-in visitors, including lonely servicemen on leave from army or air-force training camps. Our cabin had a huge studio room, just right for dancing and singing, games of bridge, and long soul-searching conversations. We danced to 'Tuxedo Junction,' 'Moonlight Serenade,' and 'Roll out the Barrel.' Since liquor was rationed too, we usually pooled everyone's contributions, often only an ounce or two in a bottle, and eventually we had 113 empty bottles which made a good photograph at the end of the summer.

I was almost always the first to wake up after our late Saturday night parties, and I would take my typewriter and portable HMV gramophone out onto the grass in the sun or onto the veranda and listen to jazz and write letters and other bits and pieces until the sleepy-heads emerged for some brunch, and the day began. I wrote pieces about New Brunswick as well as general philosophy and pieces expressing my hopes for a better world after the war. I wrote a letter to *Saturday Night*, protesting the idea that the Germans, and particularly the next generation, who were children during the war, should be viciously punished after it. I also wrote 'How To Be a Successful Gooseberry.' Do they exist any more? It began: 'From vast experience extending over a number of years, we have compiled the following hints and tips for those aspiring to be what is known as a successful gooseberry, i.e. the second female, unfortunately for all parties, foisted upon a nice little party à deux. The criterion of success is the attaining of a certain degree of comfort and freedom from embarrassment for all three members of the trio, but especially for the gooseberry herself.'

I dealt with Three In A Space Where Exit Is Possible (including Methods of Unostentatious Exit ranging from taking the dog for a walk to crawling behind the chesterfield and thus out of the door) and proper behaviour for Three In A Confined Space Where Exit Is Impossible (including rumble seats and one-bedroom apartments), as well as Methods of Pseudo-Natural and Unostentatious Intrusion ('only to be undertaken in circumstances of dire necessity when further loitering in street, passages, etc. is no longer desirable, safe or healthy').

For my second winter in Fredericton, we physios shared a wonderfully crummy flat in the Waverley Hotel in the middle of town. It was a haunt of commercial travellers, among others. We had a minute kitchenette and were very happy there. One other apartment tenant worked as an embalmer at the local undertaker's establishment. When Avery Shaw, the Saint John artist, stayed in an extra hotel room one weekend, he was woken early one Sunday morning by a hammering on his door and someone shouting 'Wake up, you're wanted at the undertaker's!' He was a little startled, to say the least, until it transpired that it was the custom of Fredericton men who'd got themselves beaten up in a Saturday night pub brawl to get their black eyes and bruises covered up, or at least toned down, by the local embalmer before returning to their homes.

One of my very good friends, originally introduced by Hattie Harmon or one of 'her boys,' was Frank Park, a Fredericton lawyer who later that year enlisted in the artillery, but ended up in Ottawa editing *Canadian Affairs*, a political commentary for servicemen. When Frank went into the army as a private, he did his basic training in Fredericton. I should say we all did his basic training, since he described his adventures to us in detail and later took us through the rudiments of becoming a private in the artillery. He kept muttering 'bubble, bubble, line, bubble,' which was sheer gibberish to all of us but presumably meant something to him. Then it would be time for him to get on his bike and pedal madly back to camp before curfew, only to return in a great dash for pyjamas, 'mes peejamas' in so-called French. His mother washed his clothes when he was home for weekends, and he invariably left them behind as he visited his friends on his way uptown.

One evening when he came to visit, Frank brought with him a new friend who was boarding in another part of the house where he and his mother lived, on Waterloo Row. This was Brough Macpherson, who had been appointed to the University of New Brunswick for a year to teach political science 'and everything else' (sociology, economics, and so on), since the shortage of professors in small universities was acute. Brough had brought some of his collection of classical records with him, and he invited any of the 'polio girls' who were interested to come and listen. Sitting silently listening to quartets and sonatas was not very much the other physios' idea of fun. However, by dint of taking along my knitting, I managed to fill the time with something constructive, besides increasing my fondness for Mozart and Bach, not to mention the owner of the records.

Luckily, Brough turned out to be capable of enjoying fun and social activities as well as intellectual discussions. I remember one occasion in the fall, when Frank, Mark Neville (the son of a strong CCF mother), Brough, and I went out to look for deer. We probably made enough noise to scare off any sensible deer, so they tried shooting at a tin can stuck on a tree. No one could hit it, although it turned out years later that Brough in fact had won prizes for marksmanship when he belonged to the Walmer Road Church's Tuxedo Boys. Probably the nips of rum, chased down by a bit of apple (we usually mixed rum with apple juice and water) had ruined everyone's aim, though not our enjoyment of the expedition.

That winter, Brough asked me to go as his guest to a reception given by the Lieutenant-Governor, a local dignitary called Clark. We decked ourselves out in evening dress and enjoyed ourselves. The only part that Brough later remembered was that the hairs from my white rab-bit-fur jacket were all over his dinner jacket after our taxi ride home, and it took him hours to brush them off. Our friends thought this a great joke.

Through Frank Park and Brough, I had got to know some of the UNB people. Larry MacKenzie was president of the university then, and Margie MacKenzie and I became good friends. The MacKenzies and Norah and Frank Toole and their families shared the living quarters in the lovely old Arts Building on the hill. The Tooles had a small summer cottage down the river near Saint John, and I have a picture of Brough and me there, chatting with Frank Park and admiring his bathing suit. 'What yer lookin' at, chum?' asked Frank cockily, when we looked at the photos later, so that gave the photo a caption.

I supposedly babysat the MacKenzie children. Larry was often away, and when Margie had to be away at night (she was on the Wartime Prices and Trade Board), she asked me to keep an eye on the three chil-dren, who sometimes were responsible for putting themselves to bed. Since I was living 'down the river' my supervision was somewhat irre-sponsible. This didn't bother Susie (12) and Patrick (10) at all, and the youngest, Sheila, slept at the Tooles' anyway as she was a great friend of their daughter Brigid. Margie reacted in mock horror when she heard I had recommended *For Whom the Bell Tolls* as interesting read-ing for Susie. The hero and heroine slept in the same sleeping bag! This provocative idea had not crossed my mind as being a trifle advanced for twelve-year-olds of the forties. The next year, when Larry was toast-ing the bride at our wedding, he warned Brough about some of the questionable ideas of his chosen wife, which delighted everyone.

I also got to know a number of New Brunswick artists: Jack Hum-phrey, Jack Bishop, Pegi Nicol, as well as Ted Campbell. And I became good friends with the Deichmanns, whose pottery, the Dykelands, was not far from Saint John. Miller Brittain was another particular friend; he went into the air force and, after a time as a rear gunner, became a Canadian War Artist. I believe it was this group, together with Avery

Shaw, that started the magazine *Maritime Art*, which later evolved into *Canadian Art.*

At the end of the academic year, Brough left UNB to go to work in Ottawa. Frank moved to Ottawa soon after, and they both worked for John Grierson at the Wartime Information Board. Brough asked me to pay him a visit if ever I was headed in that direction and, as I remember it, I managed to combine attending Sister Kenny's lectures in Montreal (or was it Toronto?) with a visit to Ottawa that June.

It was, I believe, Arthur Schnabel who played the Schumann piano concerto at Carnegie Hall on the afternoon of June 13th, 1943. Brough and I listened entranced until it was finished. Then he turned off the radio, looked very serious, and asked me if I would marry him. I don't remember whether I said yes right away. I have a feeling I wanted to know if he really was certain he wanted to marry me. He did at some point give me details of his financial state and his prospects for advancement at the University of Toronto, though this aspect of things hadn't entered my mind. Anyway, I certainly thought $4000 a year was a pretty satisfactory salary; mine had been about $1500 for heading the Department of Physiotherapy for the New Brunswick Department of Health.

I was staying overnight with one of Brough's women friends who was working in Ottawa, and I have a feeling she was not too happy to find he had selected me for attention. As for me, I had always determined to marry a man who had good legs. I did a lot of leg-studying of both sexes in those days, and not only from the physio point of view. Luckily for my vow, Brough had stripped to his shorts the evening before while the three of us were dancing and clowning in the hot June weather, and I had noted a pair of shapely and athletic-looking legs as he whizzed around in an inebriated dance. So that was all right. Mind you, he did have a patrician nose, but it didn't seem to get in the way.

To celebrate our engagement, Avery Shaw made a wonderful design for us. It was a marriage bed, and it was unique. A four-poster, it had everything including a crib on top for any eventual baby. It had an alarm-clock-cum-kettle for early morning tea, a gramophone stocked with records, every one a non-favourite like Wagner, and all kinds of plumbing arrangements designed for convenience at all hours.

Brough would be living in Ottawa for the coming year, working as assistant to John Grierson, and we planned to get married in the early fall. Then I would leave Fredericton and move in with him, in whatever space we could find in crowded wartime Ottawa.

5

Marriage

When Brough announced he was getting married, his Toronto friends – mostly women – wanted to inspect this physio he'd met in Fredericton. I wanted to meet them, too, and also Brough's mother (his elder brother Brodie was in North Africa with the RCAF and his sister was living in the States). So, in the week following our decision to get married, when Jocelyn Classey invited me to meet Brough's friends, we set off for Toronto.

Jocelyn was a wonderful friend, who had known Brough since they were in university. Her husband, Joe, was with army intelligence in South East Asia and she was living in a flat with her year-old son Tim. She was a wonderful cook and also an endless fund of trivial and profound information and political advice, and a whiz at the identification of literary quotations and sources (she hadn't got her MA in English for nothing). When she and Joe divorced after the war, Jocelyn supported herself and Tim by editing the 'house organ' at the Bank of Nova Scotia, where the economist was another good friend, Betty Ratz King (now Hearn).

Another two of Brough's best friends were away: Jim (Eugenia, but she naturally preferred Jim) Lawson, a good friend from university days, was in the army; and Jeanne Minhinnick, who worked at Britnell's bookstore and was an expert on children's books before she turned her attention to Ontario's old houses and furniture, was 'down in the county.' Jeanne was disgusted at not meeting me and referred to me as 'that basket-weaver of Brough's,' until we'd at last met 'officially.'

Among those who did come to inspect me were two women, Phyllis Poland and Ann Farwell, who remained amongst our closest friends for

Kay with parents, Frederick and Kathleen Walker (1913)

Sitting on father's knee, Uxbridge (1915)

Team-mate (left) and Kay; school tennis team (1928)

Beth Hubbard (Miller) and Wendy (Coombs) de Mornay in Bedford (1930s)

Brother Richard Walker, Cambridge (1938)

Physio class (Kay 2nd from left, middle row), St Thomas' Hospital (1932–4)

Skiing in Laurentians (early 1940s)

Weekend gramophone music and letter writing, Fredericton (1942)

Physio (Polio) girls: Jean Brereton, Helen Wallis, Audrey Coleman, and Kay,
Victoria Hospital, Fredericton (1942)

Kay and Brough: Wedding photo (1943)

With Susan, Toronto (1946)

Ann Farwell with Stephen Macpherson and Patrick Lawson, South Bay (1947)

With Brough and Susan, Gananoque (1947)

Brough with Stephen, Toronto (1948)

Kay with unidentified friend (left), Ingham Sutcliffe, and Brough at French River (1950s)

Portrait: Susan, Sheila, Stephen (1951)

Stephen, Sheila, Susan: Sabbatical, Oxford (1952)

Association of Women Electors Annual Meeting: Passing on the gavel to June Rowlands (1959)

With Thérèse Casgrain on return from Paris (1965)

Women's International Liaison Committee, Paris: Mirka Hrubesova, Czechoslovakia; Mary Clarke, USA (rear); Kay, Helen Tucker, Canada (1964)

Family photo in Glengowan Road garden: Sheila, Brough, Kay, Stephen, and Susan (1965)

the rest of their lives. Ann was one of Brough's contemporaries at the University of Toronto. A forerunner of the drop-out generation, she helped run a coffee shop for students, then took boring government jobs to fund herself. Finally, with Jeanne Minhinnick, she bought property near Jeanne's birthplace in Prince Edward County, south of Picton, of which more later.

Phyllis Poland worked for the Wartime Prices and Trade Board in Ottawa where she and her husband Fred, a newspaper man then in intelligence work in the air force, were living 'for the duration.' She was down in Toronto on a weekend visit, at the end of which the three of us went back to Ottawa on the train together. We arrived in high spirits to announce the engagement to a disgruntled Fred, who wasn't at all pleased to be woken up with this jolly news.

When I returned to Fredericton to break the glad tidings, I was quite surprised to learn that our university friends had all been expecting we'd get married, something I had not thought of at all. Next, I had to try to find a replacement at the hospital. Although the epidemic was pretty well over, there were still many patients needing treatment. By September, she had been found, and I packed up my worldly goods, managed to fit most of them into the rumble seat of the Ford, said my farewells, and, since gasoline was still rationed, shipped the car and myself up to Montreal by train.

The lock on the rumble seat was broken, but I took the chance and sent it off like that. When I went to claim the car at the freight yard, the Montreal baggage man informed me that he had discovered all this baggage in the back and didn't I know that all cars were supposed to be shipped empty? I didn't, and pleaded all sorts of extenuating circumstances, including getting married. He said I would have to unpack the whole thing and be charged freight on every article, which duly appalled me, and he went off to consult his buddies about this horrible prospect. After a long time he came back and, after muttering some long rigamarole, told me to get lost and waved me and the car in the direction of the exit. I didn't even have a chance to thank him. The only things missing from the car were two full bottles of beer which had been stashed in a sort of side pocket in the rumble seat. So much for bribery!

Wedding plans had been proceeding apace. My friend in Montreal, Fraser Macorquodale, had been acting as wedding agent and had sent us memos on his best legal-firm notepaper, beginning 'I can offer you St A and P with a reception at the Ritz for a bargain rate,' which was invaluable help since neither Brough nor I could be on the spot.

Brough and I spent the evening before our wedding visiting our Montreal friends. Then we discovered that Brough's suitcase, containing his best suit and clothes for getting married, had been stolen from the still-unlocked rumble seat. What a disaster! He spent all the next morning describing the stolen contents for the police and insurance people and getting sewn into a paper suit, as he described it. The resulting blue, pin-striped number, which lasted quite a long time, was always known as his paper suit.

For lack of anyone else, my former flat-mate Val Ward (now Johnston) acted as matron of honour and her husband Leslie 'gave me away.' They were staying with Val's younger sister, Kid, now in her own shared apartment, where we had a party on the day of the wedding. I left the party carrying flowers, thus leading Herbert Whittaker to joke about deflowering the bride. We spent the night in the Windsor Hotel in Montreal, then we drove up to Grey Rocks Inn near Mont Tremblant, with the early autumn leaves blazing with colour all around us, and spent a blissful week being newly-weds.

Our first Ottawa living quarters were in a small house which we shared with the landlord and his wife, on Sunnyside near Bank Street. We had the kitchen and downstairs living-room, and they had the bathroom and a makeshift kitchen upstairs. We used the bathroom, too, and often found a bowl of spinach or other vegetable soaking in the tub. However, we were better off than many other new arrivals to the overflowing city. One woman told us how she waited so long to get into the shared-by-all-the-tenants bathroom to get some water to mix the can of tomato soup heating on her hot plate that in desperation she used Coca Cola to dilute it. Laundries refused to take on new customers, as their facilities and staffs were stretched to the limit. We marked our sheets with the initials of our friends, who added them to their bundles.

In the winter of 1943, the CBC started the series 'Citizen's Forum,' modelled on its successful predecessor, 'Farm Forum.' We joined a group organized by Libbie Rutherford (who later divorced Bill Rutherford and married our friend Frank Park) and met every week to listen to the program. Each program considered a currently important topic, and we discussed the points arising from the broadcast after the show ended. I believe we sent in reports, which were then used in assessing public opinion on the topics discussed. I know we enjoyed the evenings immensely and made some good and lasting friendships in the process.

We moved again that winter, this time to the top floor of friends of friends who lived in Rockcliffe. This was a much more comfortable set-up than our previous one, where we'd become unpopular with our landlord because of having Val and Leslie and their small boy to stay overnight. (On thinking about that, I can't really blame him). Anyway, we had the top floor of the Adams' house to ourselves, with a bathroom of our own and a lovely cupboard which we made into a kitchenette. The Adams, Eric and Jo, had two small girls and a large red setter called Flynn, and they have remained dear friends ever since. It was the time of national friendship with the Russians, and Shostokovitch was becoming very popular in North America. Eric used to play their new record of the Soviet national anthem to wake us up in the morning.

When spring came, we arranged to share a rented summer cottage up the Gatineau River with the Polands, the Rutherfords, and Frank Park, who were all working at wartime jobs. Somehow we all fitted ourselves into the cabin at Burnet, and we had some wonderful weekends during what turned out to be one of Ottawa's hottest summers.

During that year, I had kept up my physiotherapy practice, working first at the Ottawa Civic Hospital and later at the Rideau Rehabilitation Centre. We were due to return to Brough's teaching job at the University of Toronto that fall, and were just starting to lay our plans in the spring when I realized I must be pregnant. We had been dutifully using contraceptives, or so we thought.

Not only was I pregnant, but we also had to find somewhere to live in Toronto, a city that had even less 'moderate-income' housing available then than it does today. Luckily, we had the chance to join Jim Lawson's friends, for whom she was converting a big house on Deer Park Crescent into flats to provide accommodation for three families, the stipulation being that they must have children. Jim was still away in the army, but she commissioned Jocelyn Classey and her widowed mother, Mrs Moore, to find and obtain a house and to do all the arranging with contractors and dealing with the wartime difficulties over building permits and supplies. It all worked out very well. Jocelyn and her small boy Tim were on the ground floor, we were in the middle, and our friends the Johnstons moved into the top floor. Mrs Moore had the basement flat. Life was full of activity when we lived in Deer Park Crescent. Although our flats were separate, we often combined over meals, babysitting, and various household projects. We swore that Jocelyn and Jim used to be able to talk to each other simultaneously and to listen and answer the other as they went along. They used to do this up and down the stairways, and usually everyone around would join in. We moved in in October, a month or two after we arrived in Toronto, and Susan was born in November, thereby fulfilling the landlord's requirements.

During a recent wakeful night, I picked up Margaret Laurence's *Dance on the Earth*. Given the frequency with which war is considered the greatest experience in the lives of men, she suggests that motherhood could be thought a similarly tremendous experience in a woman's life, yet it is, by comparison, seldom written about. So I thought for a while. How often do women's biographical notes record, 'After marrying and having a family, she began (or continued) her life's work, research, law practice, stage career, and so on'? And I may be about to do the same thing. So let me try to redress that omission.

When we were still at St Thomas', one of the physio students had caused us great hilarity by asking during a class, 'Sister, what does "pregnant" mean?' We told this story as evidence of the incredible naïveté of our younger fellow students, though we were all about nineteen or twenty at the time. Yet, on thinking a little more, I realize that, although I may have known the meaning of those words when dealing with the process and mechanics of reproduction, I was just about as ignorant and naïve as my younger colleague. My own mother had not been skilled in discussing sexual facts with either sons or daughter. Menstruation, I knew, meant a girl was growing up and could eventually become a mother, but how this occurred was never spelled out to me.

I contrast my secretive acceptance of the facts of life, as far as I knew them, with my daughter Susan's delighted announcement that she had started to menstruate (though perhaps this is due less to me and more to the help and advice of Jim Lawson and other friends). I remember the exact moment, after I had written most of my exams, when I realized that a man's penis was actually inserted into a women's vagina to transfer sperm to the ovum. But I had had no actual sexual experience until my social life improved at the time when I was working as a substitute physio for Rosie Brewin when she was on holiday. It can be seen from this that I lagged considerably behind my own daughters, who knew all this in their early teens.

I started my sex education gradually, after I arrived in Canada at the age of twenty-two, and it proceeded along conventional lines with no great emotional moments or great decisions to be made. Eight years of light-hearted fun and games until faced with my one and only proposal of marriage, which, after deliberating briefly, I accepted (only to be plagued by bouts of uncertainty for the next few months). This had been preceded by a good many discussions with women friends, married and single, about how one decided on a mate. At that time, there was little talk of living together or not marrying, amongst my friends at any rate. But could one be sure? Did one have to be 'in love'? And so on. I don't believe I was 'in love' with Brough until several years after we were married. We were lucky.

In the six months after our wedding, Brough and I (at about the same pace) had begun to consider that it might be an interesting and gratifying experience to have a family, so our 'accident' was well timed. Margie MacKenzie, our good Fredericton friend, said firmly that the best obstetrician in Toronto was Marion Hilliard at Women's College Hospital. And so the Macpherson children, like the MacKenzies' and hosts of others, were all Hilliard babies, and Marion Hilliard, that cheerful and inspiring woman, was an early role model for many of us. On my regular visits to Marion Hilliard, her office was packed with cheerful and friendly women waiting to hear her quick footsteps coming down the corridor, usually late from a delivery.

Although at St Thomas' we physios had had extensive training in pre- and post-natal exercises, posture, rest, and giving attention to the physical well-being of mothers, the actual delivery process was not stressed or even considered very much. Anaesthetics and episiotomies were almost routinely given. Young women today, if they want, know much more about labour than I did. When I came to the point of delivering the first baby of mine, I was almost unprepared for the physical sensations and the exquisitely painful labour pains which inevitably grew as my apprehension grew. Of course, no one thought of letting husbands into the delivery room, and most of them would, in any case, have been ill equipped for this. I remember asking the nurse whether there was anything I could do to help, or to make things go smoothly, or *anything*. I was getting desperate. Her reply was, 'There's nothing you can do. Just wait it out.' I was so thankful when the doctor finally gave me chloroform or whatever it was they stuck over my nose and mouth.

In contrast to this and to the experiences of most of the mothers I knew, I have never known anyone enjoy pregnancy as much as my daughter Sheila later did on Hornby Island, with her partner's participation. In fact, I think they both slept in the big hospital bed the night Darian was delivered.

When I came round, thankfully free from any more labour pains, I had never in my life felt so exhausted. It was bliss just to do nothing and then to see and fondle this small bundle of living humanity which Brough and I had produced. Breast-feeding is a wonderful sensation, as is knowing one can so pleasurably and so easily fill the hungry needs of the baby. And the resulting stuffed, quietly burping, satisfied baby is wonderful too – until hunger strikes again!

So Susan/Nicholas, as the unknown had been called, became Susan and arrived just in time for one of Toronto's biggest snowstorms and, later, a communal Christmas dinner where the turkey weighed more than Susan did. Jocelyn refused to consider a Christmas pudding and made a torte which rose so high that it stuck to the top of the oven. Susan joined Tim Classey and David Johnston, both two years old, as the three small fry in our friendly house. When babies are somewhere between four and five months old, they change from babies to people. I have a lovely picture of Susan at about five months obviously cele-brating 'personhood.'

Marion Hilliard had been known to say one should start over and deal properly with the second baby. I don't think she said to throw out the first! She did say, I believe, that parents should disappear when children reached the age of sixteen. Certainly Susan, when she reached sixteen, announced that she was now old enough to look after herself and proceeded, in general, to do so.

In 1946, Stephen arrived. Stephen had a delightful habit of lying with his head draped over the back of my shoulder and his bottom almost sitting on my arm; it was rather like going around with a warm hot-water bottle or heating pad, which occasionally wiggled or grunted. It's a lovely feeling, having a small body clinging to one. The other adults who babysat, later, when Brough and I went out together, swore that as soon as we left the house Stephen would wake up and keep the sitter busy trying to get him to sleep again, which, they said, usually hap-pened two minutes before we returned to a peacefully sleeping baby.

After the first one, subsequent labours were quicker and uneventful, except for the disaster of stillborn twins – the umbilical cord had torn from the placenta and this starved the babies in utero. I think that was when Susan and Stephen were nearly four and two, so it must have been 1948. We were in the county down by Milford, and I used to drive up regularly to see Marion Hilliard. (I remember going up one time, as I neared eight months, and being stopped by a policeman. He'd been driving along at fifty miles an hour, and I had been meekly following him, until I got fed up with it and passed him, whereupon he promptly nabbed me. I told him I was on my way to the hospital, and maybe that scared him. I don't think I got a ticket.)

Anyway, I had a haemorrhage, which turned out to be the torn placenta. So Brough and I drove in, leaving the kids with Ann Farwell, and eventually I had a pair of stillborn twin boys. Marion Hilliard was away at the time and came in after it was all over. I remember Brough and I commiserated with each other, but accepted it as a sad waste and so on. We didn't spend too much time talking or analysing our feelings, and I had never been demonstrably emotional. I remember Libbie Park coming in and sympathizing, but in a positive way, that, you know, we might get another chance, and not to worry, and so forth. So it wasn't, from what I recall, a great traumatic experience.

But it was a sad occasion, and Marion Hilliard told me, 'No more babies for six months, then try again if you want to.' And so we did and the result was Sheila. There was almost a repeat of the tearing, so she was induced at eight months. Satisfactorily, she weighed over five pounds, the cut-off weight for leaving the hospital on time. She was remarkable for her big, blue eyes, which reminded one of our friends of a painting, in the British National Gallery, of a small angel peering round a church door.

Occasionally afterwards I would imagine how old those two would have been, a couple of years younger than Stephen, and how it would have altered the shape of the family. But, although four is a neater number than three, I certainly had enough to do with the three we had not to want any further excursion into family life.

Allan Burnett, who was married to one of my physio friends, became our family doctor and friend. He had a nice sense of humour and a flexible attitude to conventional treatment. When confronted with an active two-year-old with a temperature, he would say, 'Well, you should keep him quiet in bed, but' (as the patient was doing his best to climb over the crib sides) 'just do what you can to stop him jumping around too much.' When I once went to him, very indignant because the blood-donor clinic had turned me down because of a low red-blood-cell count, Dr Burnett said 'Well, you need some iron. You could eat some nails, or shoot yourself, but I guess you'd better get some iron pills.' On one occasion, when Brough took him a visitor with a blistered foot, Dr Burnett seriously worried the young man by remarking, 'Well, Brough, we'd probably better amputate, but in the meantime, let him soak his foot.'

In 1945, when the war ended, the service people came back for jobs and education and Brough got used to teaching classes of two or three hundred students. One of the large halls pressed into service had in its basement some of the Banting Institute's experimental poultry, whose crowing and squeaking made a nice accompaniment for political-science lectures. One of the returning veterans was Jim Lawson's husband Lon, who was said to have been one of the most brilliant sociology students at the U of T at that time. But he preferred working with children and chose to go on to social work. In any event, he was a wonderful teacher of anything he wanted to teach you.

When the Gouzenko affair hit the headlines in 1946, we discovered that many of our close Ottawa friends were involved. Brough and Frank Park were immediately involved in the Emergency Committee for Civil Rights, since the way the so-called suspects had been picked up by the RCMP, often in the middle of the night, and held incommunicado for weeks, was totally contrary to all their legal rights. After their release, there were long-drawn-out legal wrangles and trials to be faced, with devastating and lasting damage to the health, careers, and families of many completely innocent people. I had by then developed a sufficient mistrust of the ways of the RCMP and of the anti-Soviet bias that clearly increased as the war ended and our noble Russian allies became dastardly communist subversives.

Because we would regularly put up visiting Ottawa suspects and their families and friends, our old day-bed in the living-room became known as the Spy Bed. Not for one moment did I believe that our friends could ever be guilty of the spying activities which sounded to me like the plot of a cheap thriller by an indifferent author. In the end I was right. None of our friends had done anything reprehensible. Still, they had their careers ruined and their futures jeopardized by a government-sponsored witch hunt. Canada was the first trial run for the Churchill-devised Cold War.

After the whole sordid business had run its course, Fred and Phyllis Poland moved back to Montreal. Fred, denied the work in External Affairs for which he had hoped, went back to the *Montreal Star* and became their expert writer on scientific and medical subjects. Phyllis went back to McGill and completed her social-work degree. She then became chief psychiatric social worker at the Royal Victoria's Allan Memorial Hospital and, with Dr Alistair McLeod, was responsible for setting up the innovative well-being clinics run for years for the women employees of Bell Canada.

Some of the university's board members apparently asked questions about Brough's activities, but the story goes that Harold Innis, the department's most influential and highly regarded scholar, put his own job on the line in defence of his young colleague. After all this was over, the Adams, the Polands, and the Parks remained our dearest friends for over forty years.

Our friends continued to involve us in both politics and entertainment. After 1947, when Herbert Whittaker took over as drama critic of *The Globe and Mail,* he and I went to almost every ballet performance in town. There were all kinds of shows, and Herbert was never short of companions. He and I have only to mention Riverdale Collegiate to conjure up a marathon dramatic endurance test ending at one in the morning, and we still remember with pleasure the glories of the Bolshoi in – of all places – Maple Leaf Gardens. Whittaker's phenomenal memory for films and dance is like having a friendly human encyclopedia available on demand. 'Who played David Copperfield, and in which version?' 'When did you first, or last, see Danilova dance, and in what?' And he can name and date every painting in the Grant McDonald collections.

I have a Whittaker column from the 1960s, written from New York and beginning, 'I dropped into the lobby of the Algonquin, and who should I run into but ...' There followed a beautiful name-dropping mixture in the best Zena Cherry society-column style. And Herbert and I have a mutual experience we love to recall. Gielgud. Supper at the Savoy with Sir John! What a nostalgic theatrical delight that was, with Lord and Lady St Just joining the party. The names sounded straight out of Coward or Wilde, but they were for real!

And, with the younger generation knocking at the door, Herbert Whittaker became the perfect godfather to myriads of little nippers, many of whom became first aspiring and then real actors, dancers, and various other kinds of stars.

6

Children

Soon the apartment on Deer Park became too small for our growing family, and we bought our first house, on Wilberton Road. We had to pool all our resources, including my mother's pearl necklace and some rings, to make the down payment, and took married students on our top floor for several years until we were better off and needed the extra rooms ourselves.

Mary Rous, sister-in-law of my friend Ruth Davidson, introduced herself by pulling apart the fence-posts where our two back gardens met, between Gormley and Wilberton. Mary's son Christopher became bosom friends with Sheila in junior kindergarten, and her daughter Tony (Antoinette, to be formal) was a year younger than Susan. Altering the fence was a good idea, since there was no sidewalk along Lascelles Boulevard, which joined the two streets, and riding tricycles and wagons was a risky business for visiting five- and six-year-olds.

Neither Mary nor I had paid jobs, though Ruth occasionally did some teaching. Later, Mary and her husband separated and she was suddenly faced with supporting herself and her children; she became Brough's assistant when he was asked to chair the university's investigation into undergraduate instruction in the arts and sciences. Although we never had the intense and controversial political discussions that Ruth and I enjoyed, Mary has always been a stalwart and cheerful friend. We've probably disposed of gallons of sherry during the years we've known each other and enjoyed each other's company.

In the November of 1947, my brother Richard arrived from England, along with his wife and two small daughters (ages: five and three), and we found them a tiny, cramped apartment on Lauder Avenue (housing was still at a premium). They spent their first Canadian Christmas with us.

A couple of years later, the Adams came for Christmas. Excitement was at a high pitch. The children had finally calmed down enough to go to bed, and Eric had started to wire the tiny electric lights into the doll's house we had been furnishing for Susan. When this exacting job had been finished, and we were all getting ready for a few hours' sleep before the stocking-openers woke up, small thumps were heard coming down the stairs. Stephen, refreshed from his first sleep, came bumping down the stairs in his pale blue sleepers, demanding his favourite pastime: 'Daddy, let's fix the furnace.' (This was in the days of coal furnaces when the embers had to be raked out and new coal added to the furnace once or twice a day.) Stephen was used to going down with Brough for this enchanting entertainment and couldn't understand the groans of his exhausted parents. He was placated somehow, probably by Brough doing a short trip to the basement, and finally we all retired to bed. It seemed no time at all before the Adams girls, soon joined by Susan, were noisily opening their stockings and demanding that the day begin.

When the children were little, Brough was often away at conferences or other universities, and weekends were sometimes dull, though never empty. But when the children were bigger, we all went off on weekend trips. For summer holidays, we would make a short visit to Macpherson Island in the St Lawrence at Gananoque, which Brough's family had bought around 1920, and which was used and cared for by a local family. Then we spent five or six summers (at any rate, until the children could swim well enough to spend the summer in boats and deep water) near Milford, on South Bay in Prince Edward County.

We used to rent a farm-labourer's cottage, or stay in Ann Farwell's farmhouse, and we had wonderful times with the Lawsons, who had built a waterfront cabin nearby. We carried our water from the well to Ann's house or dipped pails in the lake when we stayed in 'the rural slum,' as we called the old cottage. We cooked on an old oil stove and used oil lamps. (We still have oil lamps at Gananoque.) We picked wild strawberries and raspberries as we explored the county, including the cheese, pea, and canning factories. Eric Adams introduced us to cheese curds, which we could buy straight out of the big vats where they were prepared. Our friends visited often, and we always had Jeanne Minhinnick and Ann Farwell and their friends nearby.

Jeanne and Ann had moved a beautiful old clapboard farmhouse to a point overlooking South Bay, where they restored and finished the house and planted a garden. They were both connoisseurs of books and furniture, and they furnished the house with old pine and other furniture of the early days in the county. Jeanne was so good at this that she became an authority on Ontario houses, gardens, and furniture. At first, they had almost no money, and Jeanne continued working in the city for several winters, at Britnell's bookstore. She went on to write her book on old Ontario houses and furniture and to tackle the jobs of planning and procuring the furnishings and interior decoration of Upper Canada Village, the Grange in Toronto, and some of the fort at Louisburg, Nova Scotia.

Ann became a sheep farmer, school trustee, carpenter, plumber, plasterer, and painter. There was something about Ann that set up immediate connections with people of all ages. The kids loved her. She was leader of the local younger scouts for several years. Their activities were perhaps unorthodox. I remember one summer the local army unit had carelessly left cartridges around some fields. Ann's response was a small-arms-management course for her cub pack, with additional pupils from the visiting holiday-makers. As one might expect, Ann was not interested in dressing in anything but comfortable clothes. She owned one skirt for her infrequent trips to the big city, otherwise farm boots and a khaki shirt and pants were her usual outfit. She smoked all the time and enjoyed good food and drink whenever it was available.

Ann was an astute political analyst. We had many discussions of 'the situation' and her assessment was always worth hearing. When she turned her hand to politics, she was an able organizer and could argue well and convincingly. She read voraciously and in later years took to rereading the classics, as well as keeping up to date with current writing. Her friends were artists, farmers, politicians, teachers and, above all, young people. Her consuming and compassionate interest in everyone came through in everything she did. This endeared her to us all.

Our children, even when they were grown up, never tired of hearing Ann describe the days when they were small: Stephen emptying peas into the flour barrel, tipping out groceries, and so on; Tim Classey and Susan painting each other instead of the out-house; the four-year-olds Bridget Lawson and Sheila greeting each other after a year apart with the exchange, 'How was it at England?' 'I learned to skip on the Isle of Wight. The stairs had a black bannister,' before they returned to splashing in the lake. One summer, when Ann was left babysitting Susan and Stephen, aged approximately four and two, and they disclaimed all interest in eating their dinner, she put their plates on the floor and told them they must get on their hands and knees and eat like puppies. The supper disappeared in short order.

It was her sense of humour that appealed most to us. This was part of her whole outlook on life: people and incidents were fun. For the last ten years or so, when she lived by herself, she always greeted us with some new anecdote from her daily life and told it in a way that was irresistibly amusing. Ann's stories improved with repetition. A favourite story was about the uproarious sex life of her elderly tabby, Edward the Cat. We had dropped in on Ann in her farm kitchen one day in the late spring to see how the winter had treated her and to hear some of her tales of snow drifts and winter nights in the barn, spent helping the arrival of the newborn lambs. 'Let me tell you about Edward's sex life,' said Ann, and we settled down for a tale:

He always picks the iciest, blizzardy, and most freezing day to start mooning about. He wanders around, sniffs at his food, spurns my friendly overtures, and finally paces back and forth between my chair and the door. He's very apologetic. He really doesn't want to bother me, and he knows it's lousy weather, but 'This is bigger than both of us,' he tells me. 'I just can't resist it.'

Finally, I'm forced by his pitiful story to let him out of the house. The wind hurls itself through the door. In a flash, Edward is out and battling the elements in search of his destiny. That night there is no Edward. Nor the next. After three days, just as I'm beginning to give up, this THING comes dragging its way down the garden path. Edward is a scrawny, bedraggled, bloody, and battered shadow of his former self. He totters in without so much as a nod, makes straight for his food and drink, and gobbles everything up. Then there's a long pause. He's obviously very uncomfortable. Suddenly he brings all his dinner up – at my feet – pays no more attention to it or to me and immediately falls fast asleep in his spot by the stove. For two days he hardly moves. Then he gradually comes to life – eats, drinks, and begins to tidy up. He licks and polishes until he begins to look more like a well-groomed gentleman cat. He lolls about for a few days, living like a king, as is his wont. Then, you won't believe it ... the whole routine starts again. Don Juan is off on another of his thousand conquests.

Ann's lambs, one of which was always called Pet, her neighbours, and the CBC were all magnificent sources for anecdotes. 'Nothing could be further from the contrary,' said a football player interviewed on the radio, and Ann noted this gem. She took a local housewife to see the film *Dr Strangelove.* 'It makes you think, doesn't it? I must brush up on my thinking,' said the woman. The stories became part of our family's language.

Stephen and Sheila particularly loved Ann. One of my saddest memories, when Ann was very ill with cancer and had moved into a friend's house, is of Stephen driving all over the county, trying unsuccessfully to find her to say goodbye. But when we knew she was soon to die, we all had a wonderful pancake and maple-syrup outdoor breakfast with farmer friends of hers, and Stephen took a beautiful picture of her. It was always fun to be with Ann; she made things better for all of us. When Ann Farwell died, in Picton in 1976, it touched the lives of three generations of country and city folk.

Wherever we made our summer base, at some point we packed everyone into the car to go camping and visiting our friends. This was the postwar period, when many middle-class Toronto families wanted to move outside the city – to live, to commute, or just to have a year-round retreat. So we had lots of generous friends whose hospitality we exploited ruthlessly. Fortunately many of them had children themselves or were those incredible adults who really like children. Brough would often find a nice corner to read or write or talk with our hosts. I loved bird-watching, as it gave me an excuse to wander off and be by myself when I needed solitude.

I think our most favourite place of all was French River, where we visited the Sutcliffes, whose blueberry-laden property was a delight. I could almost feel the tensions of the city winter rolling off as Erma and I picked blueberries and talked, with the kids swimming and canoeing and doing all those things with fishing and water that kept them busy. Erma's husband Ingham, a chartered account, would be pottering around mending things – he was an accomplished engineer in his spare time. Allan Sangster was a good friend of the Sutcliffes, and he had a generator, so the sound of his big record player came to us across the water, and we visited him and his wife Peggy to listen to music and watch the little field mice climbing around the rafters of the roof.

Back in Toronto, none of our children was particularly interested in competitive sports, or any sports at all really, except swimming and sociable games like ping-pong or badminton. I remember being severely shocked, a few years later, at a high-school parent-teacher meeting when the issue of competitive sports came up. One mother reported that her child had been told there would be no room or time for kids in his class to play basketball unless they had been picked for the team. I was expecting an accommodating answer and was astonished to hear the teacher reply, in effect, that the mother had better realize that, in this world, competition is what it's all about. Either you win or you take the consequences. Nothing about enjoying, cooperating, improving skills, playing together. I was disgusted. I don't think I went to another of those meetings.

Time that other parents spent picking up hockey players and skaters, I spent on dancers, but then I liked watching dancing anyway, particularly Susan. Perhaps it wasn't all parental bias, in view of her future success as a dancer. After her three years at the U of T, where the only physical-education class she could contemplate was modern dance, she spent several years learning dance at the Graham School in New York and later became a founding member of the Toronto Dance Theatre. I was always an enraptured audience any time Susan was dancing.

The children were certainly all exposed to professional ballet, since I was a complete addict and took them to everything that came to town from year one. How dull it must be to listen to that first-act music from *Giselle* without being able to imagine the drama of the mad dying and stabbing scene. I remember Stephen, aged four or five, angrily wiping the tears from his face as the intermission started. I was chided severely by all three Ss – Susan, Stephen, and Sheila – when I waved across from the balcony at the Royal Alexandra Theatre at some friends. 'Mother, DO behave,' they would say.

Both Stephen and Sheila played an instrument during their high-school careers, and I think music was the only thing that Stephen really enjoyed during his extended stay at North Toronto Collegiate. As he struggled through high school, I think his trumpet and music saved him from despair. He hated his one year at Waterloo, and it was improved for him only by the fact that our friends Len and Anita Gertler lived there. He came home on his motor bike most weekends and took back bagels (which were unobtainable in Waterloo) for the Gertlers. When we left for the Cambridge sabbatical, he built his own career in computers, and then put himself through Sheridan College as a woodworker and builder of furniture and, later, of harpsichords.

High spots of the high-school careers of the three Ss for me were Susan's choreography for *Night Train*, Stephen's playing first trumpet in the *Water Music* and *Pictures at an Exhibition*, and Sheila singing the telephone song in *Bye Bye Birdie*. Which leads me to the Beatles and taking Sheila and friends to the drive-in at Kingston for their first viewing of *A Hard Day's Night*. I swore I'd drive straight home if they screamed, and they managed to contain themselves until the very end, which was remarkable given the times. Betty Nickerson of the Voice of Women once spent the night in Sheila's room at Glengowan and said it gave her quite a turn to wake up staring into the close-up face of Paul McCartney on the wall beside her nose.

There was some political awareness, too. When Stephen was spending his reluctant year at Waterloo, he wrote a very good letter to the university paper about Vietnam, which surprised and delighted me since he hadn't shown much, if any, interest in any 'socially significant' affairs. I also remember Sheila spending all night in front of the American consulate at the time of the bus boycott in Selma, Alabama. She got to sleep out on University Avenue in February, with everyone providing groundsheets, coffee, doughnuts, and all. We have photos of this, which are on a card on the basement stairs. I also have a picture of Susan marching around Parliament Hill carrying a banner for some 'just cause,' as the Vietnamese say. And Brough once went on a professors' march to the US consulate to protest the bombing of Vietnam, apart from all his letter- and petition-signings, money-giving, and so on.

Brough's growing academic eminence, on the other hand, was not paid much attention by Brough's family, including his wife! His mother, until she died, was his most proud and loving admirer. The rest of us accepted as a matter of course his continual reading and writing, which he usually returned to after dinner unless we went out or people came in. He would leave the table in the middle of a meal saying, 'I just had a thought ...,' or get up in the night for an hour or two at his desk because some theory needed to be caught and recorded.

During the fifties, sixties, and seventies, Brough's career was marked by prodigious intellectual activity: the writing of books and numerous papers; a growing reputation; increasing numbers of graduate students anxious to work with him; lectures and academic visits in Canada, the US, and overseas. He served on numerous university committees and the senate. He spent one summer working on the committee that produced the Hall-Dennis report for the Toronto Board of Education, and he also headed the University of Toronto president's committee that wrote the 'Macpherson Report' on undergraduate instruction in the arts and sciences. Brough's last undergraduate lecture before he retired was given to a packed house, and he said, when he came home that evening, in a mildly surprised voice, 'and they gave me a standing ovation!' We were proud when he gave the Massey Lectures, 'The Real World of Democracy,' when his major work, *Possessive Individualism*, was acclaimed academically all over the world, and when he was made an officer of the Order of Canada, a fellow of royal societies, and the recipient of honorary degrees.

In spite of all this academic eminence, it was mostly Brough whom the Ss consulted when they had problems. They would also ask our other friends for advice, particularly Jocelyn Classey, and Phyllis Poland, Jim Lawson, Ann Farwell, and Herbert Whittaker, who were among their godless parents, as we called them. Later the children were able to draw on my VOW and NAC friends, who, in turn, picked Brough's brains on many occasions. Many were the long discussions, and I remember Brough and Rosie Abella laying the groundwork for human-rights lectures together at our kitchen table.

It must have been difficult for the kids to cope with their parents' activities. I remember we went to a Liz Keenan harpsichord recital at the U of T's Edward Johnson Building one evening, where Matthew Redsell (Stephen's boss at the time) gave Stephen a nice tribute as the one who had built the harpsichord and the virginal. When we went down in the intermission to say hello, Brough introduced himself as Stephen's father. Later Stephen said that, after years of being Brough's or Kay's son, he'd waited thirty-five years for that introduction!

When she was home, Sheila was the solid rock on whom I depended for years to give me the point of view and an update on what 'youth' was thinking, as well as the latest 'heard it in grade 8' information or jokes. When I'd got myself into a bind, her advice was always excellent. It still is. She went on to Scarborough College for her BA, sampled various jobs, and settled into Coach House Press before she made the big move to the west coast. She took one summer to become a bicycle expert and conducted high-school bike tours with Jay Richardson. They biked down the west coast to Mexico one winter and back the following spring, crossing the flooding Mississippi on their way home. Jay later married Sheila's best friend, which was somewhat traumatic at the time, but later their two little boys had a good time together when Jay visited Sheila and Darian on Hornby Island.

Susan and John Faichney settled in what was originally John's house on Sullivan Street near the Art Gallery of Ontario for over ten years. They came with us to Guelph once when Brough was receiving an honorary degree there and were greeted by the president as our son and daughter. (John is tall and looks surprisingly like a mixture of Brough and Susan.) Later, when John and Stephen both took to motor bikes, they looked like two huge monsters in their biking gear as they parked outside our front door when they both came to dinner. And finally Stephen met and then married another North Toronto Susan.

7

The Oxford Sabbatical

In 1952, Brough was due to take his first sabbatical. In those days, it was six months at full salary or a year at half-salary, so it was good if one could get a fellowship or grant to make up the other half to allow for a full year of study or whatever was planned. It was a Nuffield Fellowship which allowed us to spend a full academic year in Oxford. We duly rented an almost unheated North Oxford house, ordered a new Austin car for us to pick up when we got there, shipped ourselves over the Atlantic in a Cunarder from Quebec, and proceeded to find schools for the children and to look up relatives and make new friends.

Susan and Stephen were enrolled at Cranescourt School, a small private school, within walking distance of home, run by a Miss Crane. The children wore purple blazers with grey shorts or skirts, according to sex, with purple caps for the boys and purple bands round their grey felt hats for the girls. Sheila was at the Squirrel Nursery School, run by a motherly youngish woman and a couple of her friends, where the atmosphere was informal and comfortable. We were greeted by a large dog and a couple of cats when we arrived, and Sheila settled down quite happily amongst her new friends. One of these was Johnny Visozo, from Spain. He was four, a little older than Sheila, and a non-stop talker. We knew it was schooltime when we heard Johnny's voice as he came along the street with his mother every morning.

We were thrilled to be in the centre of this wonderful old city and the Cotswolds countryside with its thatched cottages and old stone villages. There was a playground with swings and seesaws at the end of St Margaret's Road, and we would trundle off over the railway bridge and along beside the allotments, with the river meadows stretching away over towards the Perch, a well-known waterside pub, watching sundry rowing crews practising far off on the river. We took the children blackberry-picking and picnicking at weekends, and we dashed up to London whenever we had a chance or could park the children on friends.

I remember one occasion when I was sitting on the top of a number-two bus going down Finchley Road on a cool autumn day after all the tourists had left. What was so great about being on top of a bus in grimy old London? It's hard to tell, but it had all my roots in the past and my happiness in the present bound up in a package almost too precious to grasp. I have a feeling of holding on to these moments, marking them in my mind as one of life's highlights.

Brough had a wonderful time pursuing Hobbes and Locke, exploring the Bodleian Library, and dining with his colleagues in their various colleges. We met and became friends with Christopher Hill, who was master of Balliol. On one occasion, we had Sunday lunch with Janet Vaughan, the principal of Somerville – we arrived an hour early, since we had forgotten about daylight-saving time, and had to wait one whole hour before we were served any sherry. (We didn't discover our gaffe until the BBC news that evening.)

Brough's cryptic date books for this period make interesting reading and are sometimes useful for setting me straight chronologically, though it is difficult to decide, when the note says 'Lecture LSE,' whether he listened to or gave the lecture, and, when it says 'Dinner Robson,' whether I was included or not. Often we both went to London but usually, when a college meal is noted ('Lunch Balliol'), he was on his own. Oxford was very exclusive of wives in those days, although apparently not as bad as Cambridge. Once in a while there would be a Ladies Night at a college to which wives were invited.

That winter was a cold one, and we even had snow. Our house was icy cold. One coal-oil radiator in the bathroom provided the only heat upstairs, and the whole family got dressed in that one small room. Brough would wrap himself up in an old academic gown when trying to read in the evening, and everyone watched for his congealed breath to form a drip on the end of his nose while he fumbled in the robes for a handkerchief. We felt sorry for all those poor little boys in the many Oxford prep schools with their blue knees poking out below their grey flannel shorts and their bedroom windows wide open to the freezing wind. We did have an anthracite stove in our basement dining-room, which was quite warm until the chimney caught on fire and we had to wait two weeks before it was swept. I wrote the following.

We English are a Spartan race;
Heat centrally, and we lose face.
Contempt could not be well-concealed
For other folk from far afield
Who shiver in a weak-kneed way
At 'slight ground frost' or 'showers today'
If stately homes were warm inside
And windows never open wide.
Fresh air, y'know, is what we need
And exercise – this is our creed.
'Of course,' we say, 'heat's so expensive,'
If once we're put on the defensive,
Forgetting that the cost of tweeds
And extra blankets far exceeds
That item in those sissy lands
Where no one needs to warm their hands.
For chilblain cures, hot bottles, gin
Are where *our* heating costs begin.

However, when the winter ended, we all delighted in the English spring. We went to Lyme Regis for Easter and were enchanted by the hedgerows with bluebells, cowslips, primroses, and violets, just as I remembered them from my childhood.

We went to see my stepfather and his wife, in the New Forest, and visited my stepbrothers and their young families: Barry, chartered-accounting in Oxford, and Roderic, apple-farming in Kent. We had fun visiting Wendy Coombs, her RAF husband Patrick, and son Simon in Goodeaster, their remote Essex village. We also visited the Johnstons: Leslie had recently been made vice-principal of the first London County Council boys' boarding school, in the grounds of Wolverstone Hall in Suffolk. The school had one main building, and Nissen huts provided dormitories for the boys. We stayed several times with the Johnstons during our sabbaticals, and the children enjoyed each other's company.

We visited 'the stately homes of England' whenever they were open to the public, and steeped ourselves in manor houses, castles, churches, and a good deal of British history. We watched rowing, May Day singing, and Morris dancing in the streets of Oxford, and went to concerts and plays. The children managed to enjoy themselves on these expeditions, especially since many of our friends had kids around their ages for them to get to know. I took photos wherever we went.

Eighteen years after George V's silver jubilee, I again joined the London throngs for the sheer joy of those friendly crowds during Queen Elizabeth's coronation ceremonies. The children had German measles, and I deserted them and Brough. The late train back from Paddington was full of people deep in exhausted sleep, having been up since well before dawn. I remember wondering how many of them would wake up in Birmingham or Liverpool by mistake.

At the other extreme (or is it?), I remember attending a full day of lectures and discussion on how to convert sewage into fertilizer, and how to clean up polluted river water and clear up smog. This was the beginning of the program which cleaned up London's air considerably and made the Thames habitable again for fish and swimmers.

Sometime in the early summer we all went to St Hilda's College for an outdoor riverside performance of *The Wind in the Willows*. The setting was perfect, but sometimes the wind in the willows made it hard to hear the dialogue. Later on, Brough and I had dinner in the college, after sipping sherry with the principal, whose dress, Brough insisted, was made of purple plush. I remember another academic dinner where I sat for most of the time amongst these brilliant scholars, several of them women. After a long period of high-level academic shop-talk, one of the women turned to me and said, 'And what do you do?' At the time, I was acting as a parent helper at Sheila's nursery school. Such lowly employment was more than I could own up to in that august gathering. I can't even remember what I actually answered.

On another occasion, as part of the program for making visiting 'colonials' feel at home, I was invited to have tea with one of Oxford's institutions, Mrs Haldane. She was, I believe, the widow of one of the university's great professors, and she herself was a pillar of Oxford's academic society. She lived in a big North Oxford house that looked more like a museum than a home. I was thoroughly intimidated and sat uncomfortably making small talk for the allotted period of time (I have no recollection of whether anyone else was present). I made my way thankfully home to the chaos of children's homework and supper and to relieve Brough of holding the fort.

During this period, Brough was on the executive of the International Political Science Association, which was given to having its annual meetings in exotic places like Florence, Prague, or Geneva. It became known as the Gravy Train, and Brough was much envied for his chances to go to these cities so long unseen because of the war. John Goormaghtigh, the secretary, became a good friend of ours, and we later visited him and his family in their home outside Geneva. John was a Belgian, had grown up trilingual, and was completely at home in most countries where his work and travels took him. We collected his matter-of-fact statements, which to us were the height of sophisticated European living: 'We didn't take a villa in the south of France this year'; 'Salzburg is acceptable' (as a place to live if they were to leave Geneva); 'It's cheaper in Vienna'; or best of all, 'We didn't stop in Florence this time. Couldn't find a place to park.' He was quite unconscious of our delight.

To Brough's disappointment, the year we were in Oxford, the association met in Oxford, thus depriving him of another continental trip. When they were eventually able to meet in the United States (some of the East European delegates had previously not been able to obtain US visas), they met in Pittsburgh, not the most romantic site. The university there was called 'the cathedral of learning' and was a skyscraper of some sort, which did not appeal to those used to the gleaming spires and ancient domes of Europe. However, no sympathy was expended on those poor deprived gravy-trainers.

8

Into AWE

On our return to Toronto, life was not appreciably less full than before. Our friends and neighbours in the fifties and sixties tended to be grouped according to their association with us. We saw Brough's colleagues and their wives at university functions; many of them were invited to our house and we to theirs. Sometimes we got to know their children, but they were not always around the same ages as ours. We saw a good deal of neighbours who had children at school with ours but did not always share social visits with them.

Some friends, of course, fell into more than one category, and others stayed good friends regardless. Our community then was more white, Anglo-Saxon, and Protestant than nowadays. Many of the neighbourhood children were from church-going families, and Susan went through one or two harassing sessions with friends because her parents were non-churchgoers. It's the only time I remember Brough and Susan shouting at each other; they were both so upset by the situation.

We made some good friends among the Brown School parents and some of the staff but fewer at North Toronto, as the area covered by the school was much bigger and we no longer met while waiting for and picking up children. The Brown School Garden Fête was one event that brought many of the parents together, although the Home and School Association did have regular good discussions at their meetings. My main contribution came with the Garden Fête, when I was one of the parents responsible for the white elephant (jumble) stall, and we enjoyed ourselves sorting and pricing all the contributions and then hauling in the money. Any parent who happened to have an available car would offer to pick up children in bad weather (I'm sure I counted eighteen children in the station-wagon one time, though I may have been seeing double), and we spelled each other off and fed each other's families when one parent was busy or some crisis occurred.

Because we were almost at the border of the school district, the children had nearly a mile to walk four times a day when they were at Brown School. I remember one time when Sheila got knocked down at the traffic crossing. I was phoned from the hospital, so I rushed down, to find that Sheila was just fine, but Susan, who was about ten, was absolutely devastated with shock and remorse because she had been in charge. On another occasion, Stephen got knocked off his bike at Lonsdale and Oriole Parkway. He too was all right but terrified that I would find out, since they had been told not to bike around the short cut on that corner. His friend Pat Lawson, although sworn to secrecy, told his mother Jim, and so I found out. I can only hope, since I don't remember, that I wasn't the ogre that Stephen expected.

One of our more notable neighbourhood institutions was the Ladies' Liquid Lunches. Mary Rous, Ruth Davidson, and I were all enthusiastic Ladies' Liquid Lunchers together with other neighbours from Gormley and Duggan and a few from farther afield. It was confined to mothers of children attending Brown School and fitted in perfectly with the school routine. Babies would be put to bed after their noon meal and older children packed off to afternoon school. Occasionally we must have brought an infant or toddler along to sleep in the hostess' house, but it was strictly an adult gathering. We did not discuss our children, and we generally banned religion and sometimes politics, although this was usually more entertaining. The one acknowledged CCFer amongst us was considered the most conservative in her attitudes and opinions.

The sherry bottle was produced and glasses filled. Conversation became animated, and the noise level rose significantly. The hostess then provided the soup, sometimes extravagantly adding sandwiches or crackers, and the meal ended with strong, sobering coffee, just in time to fetch or meet the returning schoolchildren. As the children grew older and mothers decided to go to work or occupy themselves in other ways, the LLLs became less frequent, but for a number of years they brought cheerful companionship and fun into the daily routine, at least once every month or so.

One of the households of whom we saw a good deal was the Hall family – Brian, Elspeth, and the three boys – who lived on the next street. Their Stephen and Nick matched our Stephen and Susan in ages. The children all went to Brown School. Brian worked in a job he

hated at Goodyear Company. He was an outdoors man, a paleontolo-
gist, very good at handling machines and constructing buildings and
furniture. Elspeth was a sculptor and loved pictures and beautiful
things. She was a city person, yet she learned all about the lake country, where they eventually built a cottage. We had many happy camping and boating visits with them there, and learned a lot about wildlife
and flowers. In town, we parents spent many evenings having a beer or
coffee before bedtime. Elspeth and I worked together for the Home
and School Association, were both Women Electors, and later worked
together in Voice of Women.

These were the days when most university professors were male,
mostly with wives and families. There were women's auxiliaries who
met either for improving or just entertaining activities or for fundraising, usually for the University Settlement. The Settlement had a swimming pool and gym and a very good music school, and was in constant
use with neighbourhood mothers' meetings, classes of all kinds, and a
summer camp for the kids. Later, I was asked to sit on the board of the
Settlement, which was made up of professors and some wives. It
proved to be a rather frustrating job, since there was always too little
money and fundraising was always on the agenda.

Although I had given up practising physiotherapy by about 1950, I
kept in touch through various committees of the Canadian Physiotherapy Association and I attended meetings of the local branch. The profession was expanding rapidly and schools of physiotherapy had been
established at universities across the country. There was much discussion of how to incorporate those already qualified and practising, and
how to set the standard for newcomers to Canada who wished to practise their profession. Eventually, the government of Ontario, where the
majority of physios were working, decided to set up a Board of Directors of Physiotherapy under the Drugless Practitioners Act to decide on
procedures for accreditation, determine standards, establish regulations, and register all physios under the Act. The board was to consist
of two men from the Ontario society and three women from the CPA
and, after long negotiations with the old society of physiotherapists
and the government, I was asked to chair the board, which I did for ten
years with some leave (for a sabbatical) in the middle. Eventually a new
Physiotherapy Act was passed, a procedure that had earlier been followed for chiropractors and other groups.

While we lived on Wilberton Road, the Deer Park Residents' Association was formed under the energetic leadership of a busy Association

of Women Electors member called, at her own request, Mrs Albert Nordheimer. The residents' association played an active role in neigh-bourhood and municipal affairs and became a strong member of the Coordinating Committee of Toronto Ratepayers. This and similar groups gradually took over many of the local candidates' meetings at election time.

Politically, we and our friends considered ourselves to be to the left of the CCF. Some of them had been members of the Communist Party before the war or were still members. Others, like us, belonged to no political party, although Brough was known as teaching from a Marxist viewpoint. I didn't join a party until the 1970s, and Brough never did, although he and Frank Park once drew up the constitution for the fledgling CCF Party in Fredericton.

So when Jocelyn Classey had persuaded me, one evening in the late forties, to go to our neighbours across the street for a local ward meet-ing of the Association of Women Electors, I remember thinking that, in my books, they were quite a conservative (large and small C) organiza-tion, and that, if I did anything, I would try to radicalize some of their ideas by 'boring from within.' I soon discovered that even though some AWE members might well have voted Conservative, they were com-pletely dedicated to making Toronto a better city to live in, particularly for the poor and underprivileged citizens and their families.

A good friend of Brough's mother and very active in the Women's Musical Club in Toronto, Betti Sandiford, was president of the Women Electors at the time. In fact, I think she was the first president of an all-women organization I had ever met, and when I first watched her chairing a meeting, I knew I had seen an expert at work. She was charming and efficient, and wasted no time, yet one felt that all essen-tials had been dealt with and no one cut off. She and Theresa Falkner, a past AWE president, served as wonderful role models of public-spirited women. Theresa was AWE's official observer to Toronto City Council for twenty years, a job she filled with extraordinary ability and flair. Later, she wrote a history of AWE, and she also went on to chair the Toronto Housing Authority.

AWE had been formed in 1937 by a small group of civic-minded women in North Toronto and had an active influence on Toronto municipal affairs until it ended its formal existence in 1986. The associ-ation was non-partisan, non-sectarian, and non-profit by its constitu-tion, and it was kept going by membership fees, donations in kind, and many hours of volunteered time. Most AWE members were housewives, some retired, some with children, but there were a few 'working women' and women with young families. Remember, the postwar baby boom was only just beginning, and Betty Friedan's *The Feminine Mystique* was still unheard of. After the war, there were many middle-class women not in the paid workforce who could take time to observe the growing numbers of committees where much of the policy discussion took place.

There were many reasons for women to take action. There were crying needs in welfare, housing, education, and child-care services, but no one in the city appeared to be concerned about what went on at City Hall. Few outsiders were present at City Council meetings. The press took little interest and rarely reported City news, unless of a sensational nature. To have one or two sharp-eyed 'ladies' watching and recording every move and decision was a new and chastening experience for councillors and committee members, some of whom learned to appreciate and to cooperate with these well-informed and well-intentioned women.

A special corner was set aside at City Council and Board of Education meetings for the official observers. Members of AWE scrutinized every move made there, and out of these observations AWE built its policy and program for action. Women Electors formed groups in each of the city's nine wards to read and discuss their observers' reports from City Council and the Board of Education. The City provided the use of the Council Chamber at old City Hall for the monthly meetings of the presidents and vice-presidents of the ward groups to exchange information and plan action.

Conversion of wartime housing and establishing day-care centres, health classes in the schools, and parks and recreation facilities were high priorities. AWE also campaigned for extension of the franchise, an end to multiple votes, the phasing out of high-school cadets, and the establishment of junior kindergartens. They made public requests for women as caretakers and as TTC commissioners, showing a concern for women's status some twenty years before the Royal Commission on the Status of Women. Women Electors campaigned for women to be appointed as election officials during municipal elections, and eventually this came about, together with a change in the date of election day (from New Year's Day) and the two-year term for aldermen and trustees.

At municipal election time, the Women Electors organized public all-candidates' meetings, conducted along strictly non-partisan lines, with equal opportunities for each candidate to be heard and questioned. They also helped during elections, and at one time drew up and established a school course in municipal government, including the election process. School classes were encouraged to observe Council and the schoolboards in action.

Before undertaking any action to achieve change, it was an unbreakable rule in AWE to study all aspects of the situation. Some AWE members became experts to the extent that eventually they were appointed or elected to civic positions. Women Electors helped plan and organize the first of a whole series of neighbourhood planning meetings with full citizen participation – these eventually led to the Toronto City Plan. Women Electors were among the originators of the Regent's Park project, which provided the City's first public housing. A number of AWE members were appointed to the Housing Authority, the Library Board, the Board of Health, the Planning Board, the Police Commission, and the citizens' advisory committees. Others ran for office and became trustees, as well as Council and Board of Control members.

AWE tended to concentrate on certain subjects when their presidents were specialists in one area or another. When Elizabeth Vickers was president, it was the era of parks and planning. The Annex was used as a pilot project, and other areas followed. Audrey Burger made herself an expert in all aspects of child care and homes for the aged. Margaret Walker, as observer for the Metro School Board, developed extensive knowledge on education financing, and Pat Murphy followed Theresa Falkner as an expert on City Hall policies and practices.

For several years, I did not attend the AWE daytime reporting meetings, partly because I had to be home to meet children coming in for lunch, but also, to tell the truth, because I was scared of having to read out my report in front of the twenty or so women who attended the meetings in the Council Chamber. Soon after my first few neighbourhood meetings, I had been persuaded to take on the reporting of the meetings of the Toronto Board of Education. The Board met in the evening and this was actually convenient for me, as Brough could babysit and happily get on with his writing – although the era of long evening meetings was just beginning and there were times when they finished around 1:00 a.m. In addition to making reports of each meeting (every two weeks or so), the job entailed giving a comprehensive annual report of the activities and trends in Board business. This was like making a convocation address or a major speech and took hours of procrastination and work time. (Incidentally, we still have some of the old Board of Education committee reports. For years I used them as rough paper, and on that very same paper Herbert Whittaker did some wonderful set designs and drawings for the children when visiting Gananoque. Recycling started in our household during the early fifties.)

I had no idea, when coerced into taking on the reporting job, that I would continue it for ten years or so and also end up president of the Association (for some years having to write both the observer's and the president's reports). There is a Mozart piano and violin sonata played by Yehudi and Hepzibah Menuhin, which I must have played a hundred times to calm or inspire me, or both, during one of the years while I was trying to write my AWE reports. I found myself doing everything except report-writing for days, and finally, as zero hour approached, putting pen to paper with a sort of light-headed fatalism. Nobody was going to bite off my head, after all, and everyone was on my side, and it would soon be all over (I hoped).

Thus one prepares over the years for the making of speeches, the chairing of meetings, the lobbying and political negotiating that is part of being in the women's movement, the peace movement, and all those other busybody actions that one feels must be undertaken. There were nerve-racking moments in learning how to be a committee woman. I remember standing with shaking paper in my hand, reading a report, or trying to remember Robert's Rules of Order in speaking at meetings or in running them. But it was an excellent education in many aspects of committee work. I also learned some discretion in introducing what might appear to some as radical or revolutionary ideas or procedures. Remember, when I joined AWE, we were all Mrs C.B. Macphersons or the equivalent, and we addressed our elected representatives very formally.

Eventually, I learned to be at home with both ends, as well as the middle, of the women's movement, but, of course, in the fifties there was no movement as such, and it took about twenty-five years, just before AWE folded, for its members to realize that they were perhaps among the pioneers of the movement. I have some lovely 1950s photos of Women Electors in hats, and sometimes gloves as well, at meetings and deputations. There's one of Madge Hermant handing me the president's gavel, and another, ditto, of me to June Rowlands. June came to AWE with two neighbours of hers in the suburbs who had been befriending families and working in housing developments. She continued in her career as a City and Metro councillor, became head of the Metro Police Commission, and was later elected mayor of Toronto.

A wonderful woman joined us in the late 1950s, Nellie Hall-Humpherson. Her mother had been a suffragette and friend of the Pankhursts. A little old lady, perhaps in her early seventies, she held us spellbound as she told us of some of her exploits in Britain during the Votes For Women days. Fortunately, she has told much of her history to the CBC or NFB, so it's on the record. 'I was on the roof of the town hall in Birmingham, with a brick in my hand, ready to break the glass when Mr Chamberlain arrived,' began one story. 'When the police were on the lookout for us,' she added, 'we took our ammunition (bricks or propaganda) in our market baskets with cabbages and so on as camouflage.'

Nellie told us of one of the times she went with her mother and Mrs Pankhurst to visit Lloyd George (or was it H.G. Wells?), and George Bernard Shaw was there trying out his new play *Press Cuttings*, which is the one in which feminists invade the prime minister's office and take over. They read through the play, moving the furniture round to fit the stage directions and everyone taking a part. (When I recounted this, Herbert Whittaker told me that, to fulfil copyright laws at that time, and thus to escape copying or plagiarism, a play had to be given a 'public performance,' and this might have been Shaw's way of complying with the law.)

Life with the Women Electors was full of humour. Elected officials provided us, sometimes unintentionally, with many entertaining speeches, and AWE reports have been given in deathless verse. As the aldermen's actions became 'curiouser and curiouser,' Theresa Falkner developed a whole fantasy, 'Alice in Metroland,' about the goings-on at City Hall. One of my better efforts, a take-off of Tennyson's 'The Brook,' was trotted out on many occasions. It was Tennyson who suffered, I'm afraid.

> We come from sinks and stoves afar
> To form a deputation
> And, by reporting, make or mar
> Somebody's reputation.
>
> By car or bus we hurry down
> From all around the city;
> We will not miss the fun downtown
> At council, board, committee.

We chatter on, in voices low,
Though when observing, never!
For Councils come and Councils go
But we go on forever.

Each month we meet to sift the facts,
Discussing all with passion.
We wonder why the Council acts
In such a curious fashion!

We hear reports, express concern:
'This really calls for study.
A subcommittee soon will learn
About this fuddy-duddy.'

We poke about and in and out
With paper, file, and letter,
Till finally we raise a shout
That something CAN be better.

We move, we vote, we write, we speak
To every politician
Until, convinced at last, they seek
Permissive legislation.

We murmur here, officials muse,
Then comes *their* inspiration;
Skullduggery's the word we use
For ladylike persuasion.

We draw them all along with us
To join a delegation,
Then after years of talk and fuss
We reach our destination.

At once we find there's more in store
Requiring our attention;
The problems so prolific are
Too numerous to mention.

We may be few, we may be slow.
To see we will endeavour
Though Councils come and Councils go,
That we go on forever!

ADDENDUM
But times have changed, observers gone
To other nooks and crannies
Which need efficient women's work –
There are those active grannies.

For monit'ring the city now
More groups are growing clever,
And though the Councils come and go
The task goes on forever.

Let's raise our voices, hail the days
We toiled and slaved together;
Though Councils come and Councils go
Our history's here forever.

The Association of Women Electors formally closed its activities in 1986; all the regular reports of the Association are on file in the Toronto Municipal Library at the City Hall. It is interesting to note that, within a short while, a new women's group, Women Plan Toronto, had come into existence. Although this organization is more directly concerned with women's issues as such, it followed AWE's methods of studying questions, observing municipal bodies at work, and lobbying for better housing, transportation, health, and education for the city's inhabitants.

Against all my expectations, I had become very involved with the Women Electors, not to mention the Settlement, the Home and School, and the physio board. I looked forward to Brough's upcoming sabbatical (1959/60), which we planned to spend in England, this time in London. I wanted to make a break from all the meetings and organizing.

Before we left Canada, Brough had spent a considerable amount of time doing meticulous (as usual) research to prove that we could afford to buy a Jaguar in England. You bought a car as a visitor in

England and brought it back here as a used car, thereby saving all kinds of money. (Two years later, we had 'done' Jaguars, and Brough sold it to a friend who happily drove it back and forth on the highway behind Kingston until he too found it too expensive to run. We then acquired a utilitarian Studebaker station-wagon, which took us safely camping across the continent in 1962 and was replaced by a Volvo station-wagon in 1967 when we again went to England.)

Everything worked out according to plan. We settled in Hampstead in a rented house with a sedan chair and an Epstein bronze bust of Einstein in the hall and a spinet in the attic. And we took possession of a brand new white Mark X Jaguar saloon car, with walnut let-down tables for the backseat riders, and two of everything, tail pipes and mufflers in particular, *and* a red sheepskin rug. This was the cad's car par excellence! And the first thing that happened was that some American cad in a Thunderbird careened down Platt's Lane one evening and bashed our fender, just when the Jag was peacefully parked doing no one any harm.

Soon after we arrived in London, I was booked to attend the International Congress of Physiotherapy in Paris. I had a date with my old St Thomas' friend Helen Deane. I found her, as I had often done before, in a hot bath soaking out the fatigue after her transatlantic flight. We gossiped and talked our heads off, as usual.

Meanwhile, Phyllis Poland came to London for a while. She was welcomed by all of us and designated Mother's Help. She and the children laughed their heads off over the strange school uniforms required by the British schools and had a great time seeing the sights and 'doing' Hampstead and London. Then the three Ss started at their three schools. Susan soon made a long-lasting friend, Louise Medawar, and we all got to know the Medawar family. She had a good year at Camden School, and Sheila enjoyed her local prep school, but Stephen, stuck in a comprehensive, was only saved by learning to play the trumpet.

Brough visited old academic colleagues and gave guest lectures, wallowing in memories of his two years at the London School of Economics during the 1930s. I went off to keep-fit classes and made friends and, for the first time, at a 1960 rally in Trafalgar Square, I heard Bertrand Russell speaking on banning the bomb. At that time, Europe was ahead of Canada in the numbers at, and the frequency of, demonstrations. We went on family expeditions when we had a chance and visited friends all over England and Scotland. Plays, the ballet, dinner parties, music, and sightseeing filled the rest of our time. The Jag could find its own way from Hampstead to the Festival Hall and got to know all the pubs on Hampstead Heath.

When Carole Chadwick, the girls' dance teacher, now a long-time power in the National Ballet School, came to visit, we rushed her straight off the boat (I don't think it was a plane in 1960) up to the gods in Covent Garden to see the last act of the Royal Ballet's *La Fille Mal Gardée*. Still in London, the girls' ballet class was thrilled to be visited by Svetlana Beriosova of the Royal Ballet and later to see her dancing the Lilac Fairy in *Sleeping Beauty*.

We were also able to see old friends like Beth Hubbard (now Miller). After we left school, Beth had taught domestic science until the war, when she joined the RAF as a driver. She then married a Bedford boy, another Scot, who had been considered charming but dumb at school. His army career showed he had a great flair for working with men, and he became a successful prison governor, first on the Isle of Wight (where Beth had a chance to indulge her passion for sailing) and now with Winchester prison. We took the children to see King Arthur's round table in Winchester and heard Barbirolli conduct in the Cathedral. Beth had also worked with the prisoners, and she became, if anything, more successful than her husband in running things. Later, when they finally separated, she embarked on the career she had always been cut out for, that of a lay analyst. After long years of training, she came into her own with a private practice, a lovely apartment near Harley Street in London, and two hearing aids which don't seem to bother her at all.

In the summer, while Susan was in Switzerland with a group of high-school friends improving their French in a convent and eating lots of the students' favourite local pastry, Sainte-Vierge, the rest of us set off to spend the summer in France. En route, the Jag had what was called a fuite d'huile, its only other mishap of the year. On that occasion some wonderful, casual acquaintances of schoolfriends of Sheila's took pity on us, foreigners in a strange French city, and put four of us up for the night.

We camped our way across France, buying local wine in Chablis and feeling guilty when we still had some on hand by the time we reached Mâcon and wanted to switch to the local wines there. We wandered through lanes of vineyards and found the villages of Pouilly (en haut) and Fuissé (en bas). We sat in the courtyard of the local tavern drinking tumblers full of that delectable wine, while Stephen tried his hand at shooting at a target for which the prize was a case of cognac. Too bad

Brough didn't try too; with his youthful prizes for marksmanship he might have won it! The only words of French that Stephen could bring himself to attempt emerged when the local baker called at the campsite in the morning and S2 was dispatched to buy 'deux baguettes s'il vous plaît.' Meantime the French campers, with beautiful fancy blue tents, were busily grinding their fresh morning coffee. A wonderful camp life.

I still have a vivid memory of watching my ten-year-old daughter Sheila on the top of the Pont du Gard (built by the Romans, picture featured prominently on the wine-bottles of the region), three hundred feet or more above the river, as she bent over the edge of the bridge to pick a flower growing in the cracks of the stone slabs. I couldn't stand the suspense and rapidly returned to ground level, leaving Brough to cope.

In Verona, we were tempted to stay for the performance of *Aïda*, with elephants yet, in the old Roman forum, but we couldn't quite cope with the prospect of trying to find a campsite after midnight.

In August 1960, the Macpherson family arrived back in Toronto with the Jag, many badges and emblems from all over Europe, some interesting variations on Cockney and glottal-stop accents, and a new dog called Duff. We also had the first of the CND peace buttons, those black-and-white anti-nuclear symbols. After our travels, we helped Sheila make a wall-map with our route, photos, and souvenirs attached, and it won a special prize at the next year's Brown School hobby show. And, as we settled back into the school and university routine of North Toronto, one of my friends said, 'There's a new women's group that got started while you were away. You'd better look into it. It's called the Voice of Women.' I expressed mild interest, thinking how nice for all those ladies in hats and gloves to have a good cause to work for.

A new women's group wasn't exactly what I was looking for right then. In fact, I'd blessed that sabbatical year, as it had released me from the Women Electors and the University Settlement and all that. I was looking forward to taking up a few other things, improving my French, and keeping fit after all the tennis I'd been playing in England. So I put the idea out of my mind.

9

VOW, Part One

For over thirty years, Voice of Women has been a major part of my life. The amount of the involvement has ranged from attending the odd meeting and reading newsletters and reports to full-time work (as much as any housewife can do, as well as running a house and looking after family needs). This work often extended late into the night and took me to meetings all over Canada and into other countries. Through the Voice of Women I have met many of my closest friends.

Back in the sixties, the Voice of Women seemed to operate by the 'do you know anyone who' method of recruiting volunteers. If one woman knew another woman who could keep books, organize a sale, speak in public or, even more important, who didn't mind 'having a go,' then she was persuaded to come and help and usually stayed in, absorbing, as I did, the policies, objectives, and philosophy of the group.

Thus it was that one day in the winter of 1960/1, my friend and neighbour, Elspeth Hall, said to me, 'If you have a little spare time, the Voice of Women president has asked me to collect a committee to organize a conference. They know the Women Electors are good organizers. Can you help?' I should have known better. Of course I supported the aims and purposes of VOW, more or less, but I certainly didn't join because of a deep-rooted conviction that women could change the world. Now I'm convinced that they'd better do just that.

Actually, it was journalist Lotta Dempsey who set off the spark that fired the Voice of Women. It was at the time of one of those far-off summit conferences between the US and the USSR. The summit meeting had failed; Krushchev banged his shoe on the desk at the UN; an American U2 spy plane was shot down over the USSR; the Cold War was rapidly getting hotter, and we all believed we were on the brink of nuclear war. In the spring of 1960, Lotta wrote a column in *The Toronto Star* which said, 'The men surely have made a mess of things ... if only the women could get together, perhaps they could do better.'

The response was overwhelming. She was swamped with letters from women all over the country. 'It's time women did something to stop war,' was the theme, and 'I want to be part of it.' At a packed peace meeting in Toronto that June (which featured Rabbi Abraham Feinberg, UK Nobel Prize winner Philip Noel-Baker, and other notables), a peace activist called Helen Tucker suggested calling the women together. After several planning meetings, a founding meeting was held on July 28 and the Voice of Women was formed. Within a few months, there were several thousand members, including a large Quebec membership headed by Thérèse Casgrain.

Ann Gertler, who was in at the beginnings of VOW, says she first saw the name Voice of Women in the United Nations Library – it was the title of an African magazine. Sometime later, she met Helen Tucker and asked her if that was where the name came from and Tucker, though a little sheepish and a little defiant, agreed it was.

During its first years, VOW grew rapidly. Women across the country, in cities, small towns, and rural areas, sent in their $2 fee, and often more. Financial contributions included baby-bonus cheques, one woman's 'money I was saving for a washing machine but peace is more important,' and the old-age pension cheques from a Saskatchewan couple who wrote, 'We are fed up with all this war talk. It won't matter to us if this world is blown up, as it well may be, but it matters to our grandchildren.' There was great agreement when Mrs L.B. Pearson, one of VOW's founders, declared, 'Mankind must find another way than war to settle international differences.' VOW's early slogan was Construction, Not Destruction.

Hundreds of the first members of VOW had never joined an organization in their lives. Most were mothers who felt they must do something to make the world a safer place for their families. They saw the potential for appealing to women all over the world who cared for their children and families to put an end to fighting and violence. Other women had already been working for peace in their church, community, or political group, and they welcomed any movement to swell their voices.

Some were asked by the VOW central office to set up meetings. In Victoria, half a dozen women, who had joined after reading an article in *Maclean's* but who did not know each other, were asked to arrange a meeting to hear Dr Gordin Kaplan from the Radiation Hazards Committee, speak on the dangers of radioactive fallout. None of them had done anything of this kind before but, learning on the job, they booked a hall, made all the arrangements, and got a big crowd to hear him. Other women put a small notice in the local paper, inviting women to meet and talk about their hopes for peace. They were amazed at the response. It was often the busiest women – like Peggy Hope-Simpson and Muriel Duckworth in Halifax, with husbands and young children to take care of – who responded and set up an organization, study group, or other activity.

At its beginning, VOW's structure was modelled on the typical Canadian organization: national, provincial, and local presidents with their officers and executives, councils and committees, constitutions and annual meetings. VOW held its first annual meeting in 1961 at the YWCA in Toronto (now 21 McGill), where much of the time was spent in approving the constitution and statement of purpose. The procedures followed Robert's Rules of Order and members conformed, more or less, to these rules and regulations. Eventually, this complicated structure gave way, in 1971, to the national coordinating committee, later with a paid coordinator. Over the years, trust built up between VOW members across the country, and this allowed the less formal system to flourish. Women who happened to be willing and accessible for meetings joined the national coordinating committee, taking responsibility for their geographic regions or using the particular expertise or ability they could provide for VOW's work.

There were, in the early days, almost no grant-giving arrangements with governments to finance women's organizations. Some travel-expense money came out of members' or their husbands' pockets. It was said that Thérèse Casgrain would sell a piece of her jewellery when she wanted money to attend a conference or peace meeting. And often VOW groups banded together and raised funds for one of their members to attend some important gathering and to speak in their name. They did this by means of bake sales, jumble sales, theatre nights, dinners, and other enterprises thought up by imaginative women.

For an organization that raised all its own money, we certainly believed in travel. 'Join the army and see the world,' they used to say; we updated it to 'Join VOW and see the world.' Certainly I've been lucky in seeing quite a bit of the world on account of my association with VOW. (The rest is due to the connection with the 'distinguished visiting professor' half of my family.) I used to be able to work out where I had been in what year by the place that Voice of Women had held its annual meeting.

VOW was already in full swing when I was lured in to help plan for and organize a world conference of women for peace, to take place in 1962. I went to VOW's first annual meeting, in 1961, but, because of the large number of local members, I was only allowed in as an alternate delegate for the afternoon session. It was all very different from the Association of Women Electors. In AWE, we had had specific objectives and tasks. We observed, studied, and recommended, and we were listened to. Voice of Women's agenda seemed to be boundless, its activities unconventional and without precedent, and often it was not listened to by governments. During the meetings, the president, although knowledgeable about rules of procedure, was not always interested in following them. However, I did get used to operating with a world perspective; indeed, I think it was the enormity of the task before us and the world figures involved which made it daunting.

I think it was at this 1961 annual meeting that I first met Muriel Duckworth. Muriel Duckworth is my best friend. She is also my role model. She once, in a crisis situation (I was being stopped at the US border), called me *her* best friend. This made me feel pretty good, although I suspect at least twenty other people call Muriel their best friend, which is not in the least surprising. I used to say, and I still think, that what is so remarkable about Muriel is that, besides being kind, non-violent, and a perfect grandmother, she is also a dangerous subversive with world-shaking ideas and ideals.

Who else do I remember from that first meeting? There was Jo Davis, who with Helen Tucker had founded the Voice of Women, telling us how exhausted she was from working for peace. And I remember Ann Gertler from VOW in Montreal, who had worked with Helen Cunningham on drafting VOW's aims and purposes, standing up and insisting we put the words No Nuclear Weapons in Canada into our policies.

And of course there was VOW's president (1960–2), one Helen Tucker, of whom I had never heard. She was so enthusiastic about everything that she seldom finished a sentence and was often well-nigh incoherent, yet she taught *speech* to architecture and dental students at the U of T. She was also addicted to a series of extraordinary hats, which of course led to my family calling her Helen the Hat, like all those Dylan Thomas characters, Jones the Milk and so on.

She was dynamic, tireless, and infuriating, a quite extraordinary woman I was to see much of in the coming months and years. Her persistence and toughness irritated many people, but she got things done, often over odds that would intimidate lesser mortals like us, and she has a remarkable list of achievements about which she would be the first to blow her own trumpet. It went as far as putting her own (studio portrait) photograph on the cover of the special edition of *VOW News* devoted to the 1962 conference. Happily, one of Helen's saving characteristics was that she could laugh at herself, her reputation for hats, and the unquenchable enthusiasm people remembered her for.

Helen was full of joie de vivre. In 1964, celebrating her sixtieth birthday, she jumped off a tree into a lake, landed in a foot of water, and broke her ankle. Determined not to miss a meeting, she attended in a cast with crutches. She also sported a huge black cloak and a hat that looked rather like a witch's bonnet, and a bystander was heard to remark, 'Gee whiz, I just saw the Witch of Endor.' In Dorval airport, wielding her crutches as she sat in her wheelchair, going up in the food lift of the Air France jet, she looked as if she was flying off on her broomstick.

Before she turned her hand to peace, Helen was an organizer of groups travelling to exotic foreign countries. She knew, or got to know, everyone who counted anywhere, so VOW had contacts such as Margaret Mead, Nehru, Philip Noel-Baker, and Mrs Bandaranaike (prime minister of what was then Ceylon). Helen was particularly adept at gathering together high-level and distinguished women to take part in the Voice of Women's conferences and activities. When Helen's VOW and international activities lessened, she was active in the National Action Committee (she was NAC's first secretary), and she's still organizing. In the early 1980s, she took a busload of Grandmothers for Peace to present a plaque to Pierre Trudeau for his peace initiatives.

I realized quite suddenly, when I first met Helen Tucker, that this moment in my life was significant. I didn't know why. I couldn't foresee some of the most stormy, controversial, and satisfying hours of my life which would follow during the next years. But meeting Helen and working with Voice of Women changed my life, and somehow I knew then that this was going to happen.

My mini-part in VOW's global strategy was to help set up a meeting in Eaton's Auditorium in Toronto, where some well-known American women would meet with VOW's leaders to plan the 1962 world conference of women for peace. That was the first time I met Thérèse Casgrain, and I fell completely under her spell. She arrived by train looking as though she had just stepped out of a Paris couturier. A black suit, basic black, a string of pearls, and a velour hat of a glorious cherry colour which was big but not flamboyant like Tucker's. She spent all day at the meeting and captivated many of us. Overwhelmed by her charm and charisma, we became her devoted slaves, and took her out for a sandwich at lunchtime, since the big shots had forgotten to include her. Later on, Thérèse sat patiently on the platform, waiting to speak. But the other speakers went on so long that her train time came. One shrug of her shoulders was more expressive than all the words that had gone before. She made more friends with this gesture than any speech could have done and took the audience away with her in her hand.

The other moment I particularly remember was when Otto Nathan, the revered peace worker from the US, contemplated this gathering with Helen's and Thérèse's colourful hats in high profile and asked me in a mild and friendly voice, 'Would you describe the Voice of Women as a middle-class organization?' He may have had a twinkle in his eye. I replied solemnly, 'Yes, at present, I think that is an accurate description,' and we were firm friends from then on.

In September of that year, just as planning for the 1962 International Women's Peace Conference was hotting up, a notable day-long event was organized at Hart House by the CBC, entitled 'The Real World of Women,' and I believe this was where I first met VOW stalwart Ella Manuel, soon to be a good friend, who attended along with her good friend Muriel Duckworth. Ella had bright blue eyes, which made you think of the blue sea and mountains she knew so well. When she grew older, her weathered-looking face was covered with tiny wrinkles which somehow made her look even more beautiful. She grew up in Newfoundland and had just enough Newfie accent to give full flavour to her expressions and wonderful stories. As a teacher, writer, and broadcaster, and in her many campaigns for the environment and for peace, she often tangled with the authorities. At the time of the 1962 conference, she was doing commentaries and broadcasts from Newfoundland and Halifax.

Soon after that CBC conference and before the main conference in Montreal, a group of some thirty-five women met in the Laurentians. They included Indian, African, South American, Japanese, British, European, and North American women, as well as the first women from the Soviet Union and other communist countries to visit Canada officially. There were: the American Margaret Mead; Margaret Ekpo from Nigeria; Diana Collins, wife of Canon John Collins of Britain's

Campaign for Nuclear Disarmament; the writer Jaquetta Hawkes ('Mrs J.B. Priestley'); Olga Tchetchetkina from *Pravda*, USSR; Mirka Hrubasova from Czechoslovakia; Sofia Dembinska from Poland; Mira von Kuhlmann from West Germany; and Mary Clarke of the US Women Strike for Peace, to name but a few. They addressed the question of nuclear war and what women could do to prevent it, then took their findings to the larger conference, VOW's second annual meeting. Although the two conferences were separate, a number of VOW members attended both.

A number of us packed ourselves into a car and drove down to meet some of the renowned women at the Montreal conference when they joined the bigger gathering. Several hundred women met at the University of Montreal for the AGM, where the general membership could have a say in VOW's policies. And it was at this conference that the idea of a UN-declared, worldwide international peace year was born. A delegation took this idea to the UN, where it was supported by Prime Minister Nehru of India, and 1965 was proclaimed International Cooperation Year (rather like International Women's Year, which followed ten years later).

The Montreal conference was an ambitious affair. I have no idea how it was funded. Margaret Ashdown, the VOW treasurer who was also, I believe, treasurer of the Coleman Company, must have been a financial wizard. The conference included a reception by the Mayor of Montreal in the chalet on top of Mount Royal, at which our international guests had fun demonstrating their various national dancing styles. Tucker was good at recording every occasion with her camera and still somehow managed to get into every picture. Slides and photographs provided colourful documents of our friends from the Soviet Union, Nigeria, India, and the rest, and were later sold by VOW in the form of 'hasti-notes' (greeting cards). The music and conversation live on in memory only, since it was still five or six years before cassette tape-recorders came into their own.

Two of the younger women at the conference were upset by their first experience of being cut off by the chair as time ran out (a frequent conference occurrence). It was while we were comforting them in a nearby bar later on that I met a woman who said, in response to my question, 'I'm Hilary Brown, and I come from Hornby Island.' 'Where's Hornby Island?' I asked and so opened up another contact which changed my life. I next met Hilary at VOW's 1963 meeting in Winnipeg, where she provided solid support for me against all sorts of slings and arrows hurled at my head by the 'less radical' (meaning, I think, less 'red') members. Then we went to Banff in 1964 (our PR woman wanted our theme to be 'High in the Rockies,' but we had to veto that), to Ottawa in 1965, and finally to Vancouver in 1966, providing me with my first chance to visit Hilary at home on Hornby.

As the 1962 conference drew to a close, a new group, the Women's International Liaison Committee, was formed to continue linking women around the world by efforts to bring about peace and international cooperation. This committee, which eventually added 'for ICY' (International Cooperation Year) to its name, continued its liaison activities under Helen Tucker for several years after the conference.

Although Helen Tucker naturally wanted to head this committee, she also wanted to continue as president of VOW. At this prospect, however, the membership became obstinate and voted to have Thérèse Casgrain as president. Thérèse was in many ways the antithesis of Helen (not surprising that they were not the most compatible pair). Thérèse was French, she was elegant and charming, but she also had a sharp and acute political sense, having moved in political circles all her life, since her father and husband were both politicians and she herself ran nine times for office (although never successfully). Her achievements include helping obtain the women's vote in Quebec in 1940 and persuading the government to make family-allowance cheques payable to mothers.

Thérèse was enchanting to listen to, and she had a feeling for other women which came through wherever she went. She had a bracelet which was the perfect conversation piece in meeting women all over the world. There were thirteen charms on her bracelet, one for each of her grandchildren. Meeting someone for the first time, Thérèse might not know a word of the woman's language, but after a minute or so there would be smiling, nodding of heads, finger counting, showing of snapshots, and firm friendships cemented. That, along with a hug and a kiss, became a common language.

Thérèse had organized La Voix des femmes, the Quebec branch of VOW, and when she became national president in 1962, the office was moved to Montreal. Ann Gertler remembers being sent to Toronto to do the moving. She also remembers that she and I had a tug-of-war over the membership list (then on three-by-five-inch cards) and that they eventually stayed in Toronto. So, after two years as a Toronto-based organization, VOW made a major switch in location and learned more about the bilingual aspects of being a national association.

Ontario VOW continued in the old building at 341 Bloor Street West until, after a spectacular auction/house-closing party, we moved out to make way for Teperman's demolition and what was to become Rochdale College.

Among the notable actions that followed Thérèse's becoming president was the women's peace train. Quebec VOW chartered a train, and four hundred women set off to make their voices heard in Ottawa. They were joined by a busload of Voices from Ontario all set to address the Diefenbaker government, which was undecided about whether Canada should acquire nuclear weapons. Together, all the women walked up Parliament Hill, carrying between us a laundry basket filled with telegrams, letters, and petitions from all over the country demanding No Nuclear Weapons In Canada. We had no brief or prepared statement that I remember. An English-speaking Cabinet Minister came to hear from this predominantly French-speaking delegation, and the women were insulted and said so quite forcefully until a French-speaking Minister was hastily substituted.

The press made much of the 'hysterical women screaming at the minister.' In fact, press coverage of the whole occasion gave us a vivid example of how news reporting can distort and falsify events. This lesson is still being reinforced today. At that time, though, the press reports horrified the more timid and stay-at-home Voices, who thought even going to Ottawa was a bit unladylike. They didn't question the accuracy of the reporting. We had a long way to go and a lot to learn in those days.

A sequel to this story began on the train returning to Montreal. Writer Solange Chaput-Rolland was being volubly hurt and resentful, and she received sympathy, expressed in perfect French by an English-speaker from Westmount, who turned out to be author Gwethalyn Graham. Their subsequent friendship created the book *Dear Enemies*, published simultaneously in English and French. And that was one of the forerunners of the Royal Commission on Bilingualism and Biculturalism, given its nickname, La Commission Bi-Bi, by Ghislaine Laurendeau, wife of the Commission's co-chairman, a VOW vice-president and close friend of Thérèse Casgrain's. Ghislaine chaired VOW's foreign-policy committee, known variously as International Affairs or International Relations until, at one meeting, bowler-hatted Aunty B – Beatrice Brigden, a sprightly seventy-year-old stalwart from Winnipeg – solemnly asked whether we preferred having relations or affairs.

In the fall of 1962, the Cuban missile crisis hit the world. VOW members called in or wrote from all over the country, making proposals, asking for information, and calling on the world's leaders for sanity and an end to the confrontation. The VOW office was a scene of frantic activity: press releases, statements, appeals, letters – everyone was active. Thérèse wanted to lead a group of women to Cuba to act as hostages to prevent a war between the US and the USSR. Helen Tucker wrote a stirring appeal, sadly still relevant: 'We are meeting here today under similar conditions of crisis that gave birth to the Voice of Women following the failure of the Summit Conference in 1960. On that occasion Mr Kruschev walked out; on this he walked in – and so did Mr Kennedy – into Cuba. In 1960 our feeling was anxiety and despair; today it is anger and terror. The chances that nuclear war will be unleashed on our doorstep are very real. We are confronted with the most colossal brinkmanship in international politics imaginable. How do we women cope with this situation?'

Finally, it was the Soviets who took the initiative and saved the day by withdrawing their missiles. The tension eased, VOW members heaved a sigh of collective relief, and went back to their plans for long-term cooperation and nuclear disarmament.

Later, I sat in on a local meeting of the United Nations Association where members felt that their group had not responded adequately to the Cuban crisis. After a long discussion, they decided that the best way to ensure that they could react promptly was to initiate Sunday evening fireside chats whenever the need arose. Remembering the round-the-clock activity of VOW members, I figured that this showed the difference between the new group, Voice of Women, which responded to events by action, and the older established groups, which responded by study and discussion.

During the Casgrain reign in VOW we travelled to Montreal for council meetings. One was held on the day President Kennedy was shot. At another, we received letters from women in Vietnam describing the atrocities and hardships inflicted upon them during the time just before the Vietnam War, when the effect on Vietnam civilians of the continuing fighting between the Saigon régime and the National Liberation Front was appalling. In 1963, we had to find out where Vietnam was.

During the meetings Thérèse put a couple of us up for the night, and we remember with delight being turned out of our bedroom one morning because that was the day for her 'little seamstress' to come.

Solange Chaput-Rolland recalls that when she dropped in for a cup of tea she might find Prime Minister Nehru or Madame Vanier, the governor-general's wife, or a prominent politician having a quiet chat. Or perhaps Thérèse was giving advice to one of her children or grandchildren. An enchanting mixture of grand dame and peacenik, Thérèse enjoyed shocking her family, who often thought their mother's activities very embarrassing.

When she became president of VOW in 1962, Thérèse had announced that she had no plans for running for election again, but she was unable to resist the call to stand as a candidate in the federal election of 1963. The Liberals were elected and Pearson declared he was going to accept the Bomarc nuclear missiles. Mrs Pearson resigned from the Voice of Women, and Thérèse was besieged by interviewers. Not having seen Thérèse's earlier encounters with the press, we were somewhat apprehensive. Thérèse, however, was more than equal to the occasion. 'Of course, I can understand poor Mrs Pearson's dilemma,' she said silkily, and reminded them that her own father was a cabinet minister and her husband the speaker of the House of Commons. 'Certainly Mrs Pearson would want to be loyal to her husband, and naturally I can sympathize with her position. Of course we understand.' Radiating charm, she graciously dismissed the press.

Thérèse made a glorious figurehead for VOW but, in general, she left organizational details, paperwork, and things like minutes and daily business to lesser mortals. I was one of the Toronto ones, having been elected a vice-president at the Montreal meeting, largely on the basis, I suspect, of my admitting that I was a busybody. I enjoyed a number of escapades, visits, conferences, and travels with Thérèse, all of which taught me a great deal. I wouldn't have missed one of them for anything. I remember one occasion, strolling along the Avenue de l'Opéra in Paris, window-shopping with her, when she bought a couple of diamanté-studded peace doves for some young relatives.

By the time she reached her seventies, however, Thérèse was sometimes grumpy and dissatisfied, also more establishment-minded. In 1970, Trudeau appointed her to the Senate (just in time, some months before she reached the age of seventy-five and had to retire). She described to me how he had phoned her, and they discussed the property requirements for entering the Senate. Muriel and I went to visit her in her new office overlooking the front lawns of the Parliament Buildings, where, to her disgust, she beheld the pickets from the mail carriers' union who were striking (the Lapalme boys, I think they were called). Thérèse was the daughter of a Conservative and had married a Liberal. Her point of view now sometimes matched that of the current Liberal government, so we weren't surprised to hear her say, 'Oh, these strikers, if only they'd listened to us. We [sic] could have had the strike settled by now.' In spite of Thérèse's nine campaigns for the CCF/NDP, party policy lines were now getting a little blurred in her mind.

10

VOW, Part Two

In 1963, when Thérèse stepped down as president, no other nearby vice-president could be found and I was left 'acting' in her place, even though I was married to a Marxist professor and was myself thought to be very radical at the time! After her electoral defeat, Thérèse was undecided whether to stand again, and Helen Tucker even considered coming back to save the day. But eventually they agreed with the general meeting that someone new was needed. I remember sitting between these grandes dames, each wearing an enormous hat. I was dressed in whatever scruffy outfit I could muster, totally eclipsed by the one's presence and the other's flamboyance, and luckily (in the light of potential collisions) without a hat myself. In those days, I was the equivalent of a blushing violet. However, at the 1963 annual meeting in Winnipeg, after soul-searching, inquisitions, and some wonderful songs, I became VOW's third president.

My four years as president (1963–7) were crammed with exciting and challenging activities. Even when the family was on holiday at Gananoque or visiting our friends in their summer hide-outs, I managed to write innumerable letters keeping in touch with members or combining social visits, to BC for instance, with VOW meetings and get-togethers. I learned that one seldom creates a brief, press release, or statement without expecting it to be modified, edited, discarded, amended, and rewritten a dozen times. One must not be possessive or hurt when one's creative writing is changed. This process produces more of a consensus document and represents our common perspective better than any single-handed masterpiece. I learned, I hope, to listen to others' opinions and to try to reach compromises and syntheses and to work towards an atmosphere more creative than confrontational and competitive.

Being president considerably stepped up my education in politics, as well as in public and international affairs. Meeting the press, doing radio and television interviews, and making up delegations to politicians and officials became part of the almost daily routine. I was new to it then and vividly remember one telephone interview which took place in a hotel room. Happily, I had Ann Gertler at my side – every time my mind went blank, she would feed me information, an invaluable activity she has continued on many occasions since.

The 1963 Winnipeg AGM was one of the most gruelling weekends I can remember. Rosamund Truelove (daughter of E.M. Delafield, an English author to whom I had been very partial some years before) was the current Winnipeg VOW president. She told us how she had moaned to her family at breakfast, 'What am I going to do with two hundred Voice of Women members?' 'You could put them in a silent vigil,' suggested her 12-year-old son.

Helen Tucker attended the meeting, although she was on the eve of leading a delegation of twenty-eight women on a peace mission to a number of European countries, including the Soviet Union. She was in fine fettle and full voice and brimming over with ideas for International Cooperation Year. Helen's resolution in favour of ICY was a masterpiece. Every 'whereas' clause contained Helen Tucker's name and spoke of her prowess. 'Whereas the VOW was founded by Helen Tucker ...' and 'whereas the conference organized by Helen Tucker ...' and so on. It went on for quite a long time. I was chairing this plenary session and suggested mildly that perhaps the resolution could be a little shorter. Up jumped Betty Nickerson, a sharp-tongued Winnipeg television hostess and no friend of Tucker's (prima donnas recognize their competitors, and VOW had many of them), 'I agree with Mrs Macpherson,' she said, 'Cut the commercial!'

On the last day of the meeting, we bade farewell to the delegation setting off on its travels. Helen, of course, had bought a beautiful new hat for the occasion, a spectacular one covered with flowers. Solange Chaput-Rolland, meeting the hat for a second time as they said goodbye, clapped her hands and exclaimed, 'Oh Helen! They grew in the night!' Helen was delighted.

But in fact the meeting had been something of a nightmare, because the previous winter had been fraught with suspicion and internal upheavals. Jo Davis, co-founder of VOW and a tremendous organizer and fund-raiser, had become convinced that radical militants were taking over VOW, and she did her best to combat this threat. I was one of the threats, and so were Ursula Franklin and Diana Wright. I was definitely put on trial at the annual meeting before some of Jo's followers could bring themselves to accept me. I was grilled by the BC delegation for a couple of hours. I had to assure them that I was in favour of positive, constructive policies (peace-building, international cooperation, exchange visits with women of other countries) rather than being totally dedicated to such militant activities as banning the bomb and going on marches and demonstrations.

Jo Davis had circulated a mimeographed letter to every member of VOW, and a day of study had been held, chaired by Solange Chaput-Rolland and Diana Wright. An early VOW member, Diana was the daughter of Admiral Sir Charles Kingsmill, so she grew up amongst Ottawa's élite, and her family owned Grindstone Island in the Rideau Lakes near Ottawa. Diana eventually left it to the Society of Friends (Quakers) for use as a conference centre, and VOW members attended many weekend study sessions there.

The day was intended to present every side of the questions raised by Jo: Was VOW too militant, too radical, too far left? Should it be less politically oriented and more for cooperation between women all round the world, speaking Esperanto, and not talking about banning the bomb? (Mr Pearson was about to defeat Diefenbaker on that precise issue, and many of our 'ladies' were good Liberal supporters.) Jo asked the membership to choose between two alternatives: 'moderate peace-making' such as discussions, letter-writing, and exchange visits, or 'radical political action,' including ban-the-bomb campaigns, and so on. This conflict confused and divided a great many VOW members.

The discussion raged all day, and at the end the feeling was against Jo Davis' point of view. She promptly said she had not had adequate time to present her case. Since she had provoked the meeting by sending a seven-page letter to the entire membership, without any executive authorization, VOW members considered she had had more than equal time. So she resigned.

The question of reds and radicals was not the only one to thin out the ranks of VOW. Moderation was supposed to apply in all things, and Charlotte McEwen's excessive and obsessive energy, along with the effects of some of her public actions, succeeded eventually in turning away or burning out a number of hardworking and dedicated (but not that dedicated) members of VOW. It was sad, but Charlotte had that effect on people. Her enthusiasm was infectious, and newcomers would be impressed by her knowledge and energy, but then ... All we knew was that, when some harassed mother was getting kids off to school, making lunches, and all the rest, Charlotte would be on the telephone with some urgent task that must be done immediately, or some dreadful catastrophe, if not all-out nuclear war, would overtake us.

Charlotte had been one of VOW's early members and helped organize the Ottawa group. She was married to a civil servant and had four school-aged children. She also had a small apron-making business and a room filled with cardboard cartons stacked to the ceiling, which were her files. The numbers on her telephone dial were almost completely worn away from the hard use it had received. Always smiling and peering through her large glasses, Charlotte would become so involved in the discussion on hand that she left her belongings all over the place. Yet her energy was unbounded, her analysis astute, and her ability to retrieve every piece of pertinent information quite remarkable.

Charlotte's talents as a sleuth were prodigious, and she applied herself to finding out about the organization known as Moral Rearmament, which was, in her view (more than likely correct), a right-wing, semi-fascist movement. She tracked down the origins of the group in the States and infiltrated their training school. She also found members amongst our Members of Parliament. During a VOW annual meeting once, someone found an anonymous briefcase lying around. Looking inside for the owner's name, she found a stack of moral-rearmament propaganda. 'Have we got an infiltrator among us?' she asked in a horrified voice. She calmed down somewhat when told that this was Charlotte's file of evidence.

On one occasion, when Paul Hellyer was Minister of Defence, he had ordered new arms, or endorsed some armaments program, which was counter to VOW's efforts for peace. That Christmas, he was singing in a church choir in Ottawa, and the program, naturally, included a number of 'peace on earth' hymns. As he emerged from church, there, with the press photographers, was Charlotte armed with a large placard. HOLY HELLYER THE HYPOCRITE, it proclaimed, and made a nice scoop for the newspaper.

Although her goals usually coincided with or preceded those of Voice of Women itself, some of Charlotte's actions appeared to other VOW members to be dangerously radical, dragging our good polite name in the political mud and spoiling our ladylike image. Meetings and discussions took place on how to control Charlotte, even to the point of trying to expel her for unconstitutional behaviour or whatever acting on one's own was called. What a hope! She wouldn't go away, let alone stop being a member. Charlotte had a genius for hitting the political nail on the head and for getting press coverage when she did so.

The trouble with VOW at that time was that many members were scared. They were new to this public life, talking to the press, asking questions or making speeches, writing letters to officials, and – perish the thought – marching and demonstrating. And it was still only 1963; the letter to Jo Davis from VOW's corresponding secretary reprimanding her for unauthorized use of the mailing list is addressed to Mrs Fred Davis and signed 'Raymonde Roy (Mrs Georges).' I remember spending hours debating the difference between a march and a walk. (The first time VOW indulged in this unladylike pursuit, we held a Walk for Peace from our Toronto office on Jarvis Street to the Metropolitan Church for a peace service, all wearing our best Sunday outfits, with children and baby carriages and only one banner.)

The word 'militant' was perilously near to 'dangerous radical,' if not 'terrorist,' or so it seemed to some more timid newcomers. Also, we must remember that the McCarthy era had still many hangovers, including a paranoid attitude to any thing or person labelled communist or red. So many of VOW's early crises concerned militant versus other more ladylike (and often less effective) actions, and many women left because they felt VOW was becoming too radical, if not downright pink. It was in this atmosphere that the story burst that Thérèse and I had been flung into a Paris jail.

Thérèse had arrived in Paris late in 1964, having attended a women's conference in Israel. I was already there, at a conference in the UNESCO building, which resulted from the 1962 peace conference in Montreal and was to plan events for International Cooperation Year. It was organized by Helen Tucker – she had a broken ankle at the time, but that didn't stop her. Thérèse and I then went on to a NATO protest. Some six months earlier, NATO had proposed a Multi-Lateral Force (MLF) whereby any NATO naval commander would be able to press the nuclear button whenever he deemed it necessary. This appalling prospect had brought together 1500 women from western Europe and North America at the NATO headquarters in The Hague. A conference was held, and letters (and flowers) were presented to the NATO officials. Incidentally, the Hague conference provided me with my first experience of being stopped at an international border. The Dutch police were so horrified to realize that 1500 women were descending on them that they tried to stop some of them. The organizers explained our peaceful mission and we were allowed in when we came back the next day. The conference also gave me the opportunity to meet George Ignatieff, Canada's NATO ambassador at that time, later president of Science for Peace.

Then, in Paris, we arranged with the authorities that we would present a statement to the Secretary-General of NATO, Sr Manlio Brosio, and we agreed to send only one woman from each country (one English- and one French-speaking from Canada), so that we did not appear to be a demonstration. The French police were very nervous. There were other peace groups protesting NATO's actions, and the streets around the NATO building were filled with police cruisers and baton-brandishing gendarmes. There were fifteen or sixteen of us, all from NATO countries, and we walked quietly up to the building, where, after some parleying, were told that only one woman could enter. This wasn't good enough. We wanted a minimum of two, preferably more. While we were talking to the guards, an enormous uniformed giant came stumping out, swept us all up in a gesture, and ordered that we be removed – for daring to deliver a letter to the Secretary-General of NATO.

We were hustled into a police paddy wagon, and I shall never forget the delighted look on Thérèse's face as she was rudely pushed up the steps. There was a wonderful cartoon later in the Montreal paper *Le Devoir*, captioned 'Thérèse Casgrain à Paris,' in which she is stepping daintily into the paddy wagon brandishing a peace sign. We were driven halfway across Paris and taken to what later turned out to be a police barracks or training college. There, a group of (I think) police recruits were ordered to search and record these dangerous criminals. The two French women in the group had, by this time, been hustled off to some unknown fate of their own. We were foreign agitators, so our handbags were searched for dangerous weapons. They took my scissors and pocket mirror and, when I asked why, the official vividly demonstrated how I could break the mirror in two and cut my throat with it. The idea had not occurred to me.

We were finally escorted under heavy guard to a large cell with wire netting for walls and a bench around the sides. Thérèse dubbed it a salad-shaker. All this was much too exciting, and we were already plotting, first, how much of a nuisance we could make of ourselves and then, more important, what we could do with the press. The Belgian woman had an appointment with her ambassador and raised the roof about missing it. One by one, we asked to visit the washroom, a primitive place if ever I saw one, and this meant an individual escort across two courtyards, with doors to be locked and unlocked and police time to be wasted. Then, to our delight, we discovered that one of our women was pregnant. How could these brutal police treat a *femme enceinte* in such a callous way, we asked. Paris in December was anything but tropical, and it was very cold in our unheated 'salad-shaker.' Thérèse put her long and elegant gloves over her feet to keep them warm. One of the British women discovered the searchers had overlooked her small flask of scotch, so we all had a thimbleful to cheer us. I even tried the heat of a cigarette to warm myself (and then took five years to stop smoking again).

Finally, after about five hours, during which our demands to see our ambassadors never ceased, we were visited by an important-looking group of officials. They read us a severe lecture and explained in threatening tones that we would be released if we promised *never* to demonstrate, or march, or do several other things, on pain of never being permitted to enter France again – or it might have been instant deportation. I forget. (The next time I was in a demonstration in Paris was about five years later. I wasn't deported.)

As soon as we were released, off we went to make the most of our experience with the press and our embassies. Our Canadian ambassador in Paris told Thérèse, who had known him since childhood, that she really must warn him when she was planning more of these escapades, so that he could protect her! Thérèse, of course, had dandled most of the embassy staff on her knee when they were youngsters. Official notes were sent. Voice of Women and its 'two distinguished representatives' (I liked that) were on the front page of *The Globe and Mail* and the Quebec papers for three days. More important, when all the fun and games were out of the way, the real reason for our protest did get through. We were opposing the highly dangerous escalation of nuclear force by NATO. Sounds familiar, doesn't it? Months later, NATO dropped its plan for the MLF. We will take credit for some of that decision, although it was probably due to all kinds of other reasons.

On our return Thérèse was fêted. Jean Lesage, then premier of Quebec, meeting her by chance in the main dining-room of the Windsor Hotel in Montreal, rushed up and embraced her. 'Let me kiss my jailbird!' he exclaimed. My treatment was rather different in Toronto. I faced a mini-inquisition of Voices for my behaviour in Paris. 'Drinking in a Paris jail! Was that fit behaviour for the President of Voice of Women? And who were you consorting with? Were there any communists in the group? What will our members think?' The (paid) secretary resigned, and the office was left to look after itself.

But, as Solange Chaput-Rolland said à propos of the Jo Davis debate, 'When the wind blows hard, some of the leaves fall off the tree.' This occasion effectively divided the sheep from the goats. We did lose quite a few of our local members, especially our more timid and inexperienced women, but on the other hand most VOW members were tremendously supportive, and they showed it in their telegrams and letters to Thérèse and me. Two or three of our wonderful sixty- and seventy-year-old members came into the office and worked their heads off typing letters, answering the telephone, and filling the loopholes until things got back to normal. And one day, as I was sitting rather forlornly at my desk, Moira Armour appeared and proposed to take over the production of the newsletter.

I had first met Moira one day in the early sixties, at the O'Keefe Centre. It was a fund-raiser in aid of something or someone. The woman sitting next to me introduced herself, Moira Armour, and her friend, Judy Lawrence. I then forgot about them, but they turned up again at the sale and auction we were holding when Voice of Women moved from Bloor Street West, and I learned that Moira worked at the Board of Education as 'Visual Aids' and Judy was the CBC's puppeteer for a show called 'Butternut Square.' Both became valued friends.

The newsletter was a major link between VOW's several thousand members, and Moira's offer came at a crucial time. For the next seven or eight years she was responsible for the production of most of our printed material, including the newsletter. She had a printing press in her basement and all the resources for production through her connections at the Board of Education. Moira was our photographer, archivist, film expert, and, many times, our press officer. She is still the ever-ready expert for running films, taping lectures and speeches, and recording the activities of VOW (also of NAC, and, in their times, Women for Political Action and the Feminist Party of Canada).

For several years these activities kept Moira, Judy, and me in constant communication. We coupled VOW meetings with holidays and combined serious political lobbying with hilarious fun-making. I expect this is when we coined the slogan: Every Meeting A Party – Every Party A Meeting. This is part of the joy of the women's movement: what starts as a formal reception or a fund-raising event can evolve into deep and serious political discussion or, just as easily, into dancing and singing, or both.

One summer, when Judy was in Australia, Moira and I drove, laden with camping equipment we never used, through the New England states to Halifax for a brief stay with Muriel, and thence to Newfoundland to see Ella. We had a wonderful time. This was when we heard, in a store, 'No, we haven't any fish, but there's plenty of salmon if you want it.' One day, after a few rums, Ella said she would drive us 'over the mountain' to Trout River. Moira and I swear that she was so busy talking to us that she never even looked at the unpaved road of hairpin bends.

It was in 1964, too, that I first met Terry Padgham, when she came to a VOW council meeting in Winnipeg. During the meeting the temperature rose, and Terry pulled off her big woollen sweater to reveal a black silk-and-lace slip covering a more than ample bosom. This behaviour startled some of the older council members. Terry, cool and comfortable, continued to play an active part in that and probably hundreds of subsequent VOW meetings.

Since both she and her first husband were geologists, work took them to mining centres all over western Canada: Saskatchewan; Campbell River, BC; Flin Flon, Manitoba; Yellowknife. After a stint overseas Terry changed partners, acquiring an archaeologist doctor, and lived in Edmonton before moving back to her birthplace, Victoria. In every place she lived, Terry joined or established a VOW group and actively promoted handicrafts, often setting up a workshop or store, with many Third World connections. Besides her professional interests and a very astute political sense, Terry's accomplishments ranged from the theatre to weaving and other handicrafts. She has, as do many effective VOW members, an excellent sense of humour and a touch of the prima donna, which enables a woman to step easily into the breach when required.

In the NWT, she was involved in running a craft store that provided an outlet for the local women. Once when I was visiting, I went with her up to the tree line, where she gathered moss for making dyes for her wool. During our travels she speculated whether she would be admitted to the DEW line station (Distant Early Warning, NORAD) if she took a group of children to look at the 'weather station,' which was how it was billed locally.

In 1969, in Campbell River, Terry set up meetings to hear from me about Vietnam, which I had visited the previous year. My visit coincided with the visit-in-his-yacht of the macho star of US Vietnam films, John Wayne. Some of the local women who were helping with supplies for his yacht reported that his bath towels and linen were all woven in stars and stripes. Antiwar VOW members did whatever possible to show their displeasure during his visit. I gave a couple of radio and newspaper interviews to try to counteract his new movie. For visiting the young radio interviewer, Terry wore her 'work clothes,' a loose, low-cut sweater, which boggled the poor man's eyes.

I remember we were in Ottawa in 1965 and went dashing off to listen to the foreign-policy debate in the House of Commons. Lorraine Bates was there, the young (thirty) president of BC VOW. She had come all attired in very high heels and a hat for her first official VOW visit to Ottawa. She was so thrilled that in her excitement she broke the heels of both her pairs of shoes. When we finally gathered to go to the House of Commons in the pouring rain, she had lost her hat too and was wearing a pair of my running shoes and someone's old raincoat. 'I never dreamt I'd be doing this,' she said, pointing to my sloppy old shoes, 'but' she added triumphantly, 'it doesn't matter!' Solange Chaput-Rolland wrote a furious column in *Le Devoir*, as she had counted only fourteen Members of Parliament in the House for a foreign-policy debate which VOW, at least, considered important.

The Vancouver conference in 1966, which provided me with my first chance to visit Hilary Brown at home on Hornby, combined provincial and national meetings, which meant a great deal of activity and very little sleep. I remember there was one woman who gave a seminar that included discussion on something we knew nothing about at that time. She called it self-actualization. We had another workshop on visual facility: how quickly we could read the printed word on a screen. I was abysmally slow. Just how all this fitted into peace work I cannot now remember. I can remember bringing down the wrath of the local members on my head for innocently asking one of them, known to her not-too-kind associates as the earth mother, to tell us briefly about her experiences in Asia. Black looks nearly killed me as she started on her familiar (to them) dissertation on the life of a peace protester in the Far East. After dinner on the Saturday night, we saw some of the first gruesome films to come out of Vietnam. Though it had been going on for years, VOW was just becoming familiar with the brutality of that far-off war.

To cheer us up, we were then treated to a puppet show by Judy and Moira. The curtain came up on Finnegan explaining to Casey (of the 'Mr Dressup' show) what he just had been observing at this extraordinary meeting. 'You've no idea what strange things they chatted about,' said Finnegan in his silent way, shaking his ears and whispering to

Casey. 'What did they talk about?' asked Casey disbelievingly. 'Self act ... what? Self act-u-al-iz-ation?? Well, don't let your mother see you at it,' said Casey and brought the house down.

Later on, the noise of our partying woke up dear old Luella Schneider, aged about eighty, who came tripping in with her pink nightgown and bedsocks, complaining of the racket, and stayed to have a twenty-minute conversation with Finnegan (who was draped over Judy's hand and quite willing to chat with this nice old lady). The rest of us sat around in awed silence listening to this beautiful, childish, and enchanting conversation between the silent puppet Finnegan (interpreted by Casey) and the little old lady whose short legs hung down like a small child's, unable to touch the floor.

After the conference, I was ferried around to do radio interviews and press conferences. I do remember doing an interview with one of the Vancouver regulars, who settled me down and started the interview by saying, 'Now, what is the Voice of Women?' Fifteen minutes later, he just had time to say, 'Thank you very much, Mrs Macpherson.' Very polite we were in those days. At least, that's how the story goes.

Then it was time to go on the ferry to Vancouver Island. Hilary bundled me into her car, and we set off for the ferry at Horseshoe Bay which would take us to Nanaimo. When we were started, she confessed that dear Mrs Fagan in Parksville had gathered all the Voices there together and please could we just drop in, between ferries, for a cup of tea. Hilary added that Mrs F had a garden that was famous all over the island. How could we refuse, even though I was beginning to feel that one more speech or handshake and I'd keel right over. Anyway, we made it, although it was a bit of an ordeal. I think this may have been the occasion when I gave a long and (I'm sure) fascinating talk, all about what VOW had done, was doing, and planned to do. Afterwards, a dear little old lady came up to shake my hand and confided, 'I'm a little deaf, dear, and couldn't quite hear all you said. Could you just tell me what was in the talk?' I refrained from swatting her.

Finally, we got into the car for the last leg of the trip up the island, past Bowser and Fanny Bay, and boarded the Buckley Bay ferry for Denman Island. Twenty minutes later, we were off and racing to make the Hornby Island ferry, seven miles across Denman. When we landed we took the road, which has since been washed down the mountain because of the effects of logging. After negotiating a small precipice, we arrived at Heron Rocks, the Brown's cleared and cultivated space just up from the beach.

I was introduced to HB, Hilary's husband – opinionated, short-tempered, and bullying, or so he would have everyone believe. Harrison Brown was a wonderful ex-newspaperman who, after having travelled all over the world, had seen the war clouds gathering in Europe in 1937 and brought Hilary here to make a life with him, clearing the land and building their house on this beautiful point jutting into the bay, with the sand and rocks, the huge pine and fir trees, oysters on the beach, and birds everywhere.

I forget whether I did more than just say hello to HB, because Hilary firmly led me to the beach, with the words 'You need a rest.' It was true. Most VOW annual meetings took me a week to recover from, but I remember being totally exhausted by this one. Hilary sat me on a log, saying, 'I'll call you when supper is ready,' then left me to the quietness of the place.

That was one of the most beautiful moments. Hilary had guessed exactly what I needed. I sat and looked – at the sea, the rocks, the birds, the fishing boats. I smelled that wonderful salt and ozone and rotting seaweed smell that I had missed for so long amongst the lakes of eastern Canada, and I listened to the calls of the gulls and the herons, the crows and the sandpipers. I began to relax and to stop thinking of anything beyond the sights and sounds of the seashore. Peace, quiet, and absolute contentment began my first evening on Hornby Island. I felt I had come home.

That night, I slept a glorious uninterrupted sleep until woken by the birds singing. Judy and Moira joined us the next day, having arrived too late for the last ferry, and Hilary took us exploring the island. Later, we lay in the sun, drank HB's home-brewed beer, ate salmon, oysters, and clams, and felt that the world was a wonderful place and the Voice of Women a wonderful organization for having such friendly and hospitable members. Sadly, we had to leave, because Moira, Judy, and I were due for a meeting in Victoria. We drove down the main island looking for shrimps, the only shellfish Judy liked, but had to settle for other delicacies as we picnicked our way to Victoria, Jim Lawson's house, and more VOW meetings.

Moments like that one on the seashore are magic, and I am grateful to VOW for many of them. I particularly remember a moment in the Winnipeg airport where I had been bidding farewell to a whole series of VOW members and seeing them to their planes. (It must have been after that VOW council meeting in 1966.) It was one of these moments of personal revelation. It seemed that these women really liked me, and I realized that, although there were women present who could not get along with each other, somehow I had managed (unwittingly, I think) to be on friendly, humorous, and even affectionate terms with almost all of them. I remembered, too, that on the occasions when I had not taken the time or trouble to be diplomatic and kind, disaster usually resulted. But, I thought, I was able to get along with almost everyone. And it struck me that perhaps this was something that not everyone else was able to do, and I was very thankful for it. I remember thinking, 'Maybe that's why I seem to be doing all right as president. If that's so, I'd better just be grateful that I've got that quality and try not to abuse it or manipulate them because of it.' I have a nasty suspicion that, ever since, I've been getting away with more than I should.

I was also lucky enough to visit the Soviet Union later that year, along with five other women from VOW. We had been invited by the Soviet Women's Committee as part of a series of exchanges with Voice of Women designed to further understanding and mutual desires for peace. In 1962, Soviet women had attended our peace conference and the first group of Voices, including Nancy Pocock, went to the Soviet Union for a return visit. In 1963 Helen Tucker had visited them with a VOW delegation. Then in 1964, four Soviet women visited us in Canada and VOW members raised enough money to take them from coast to coast, meeting with as many Canadians as possible. That same year, Thérèse Casgrain from Montreal, Nancy Pocock from Toronto, Beatrice Brigden from Winnipeg, and a VOW member from Saskatoon visited the Soviet Union. After their return, Beatrice Brigden, who was probably over seventy by then, gave over fifty talks about her trip to native and women's groups all over Manitoba.

When we visited the Soviet Union in 1966, we were shown schools and farms and met politicians, children's groups, and many women. We were taken to all the show places – the opera, the ballet, the Hermitage in that beautiful city Leningrad. We saw wonderful scenery, the sea coast, and tea plantations in the south. We even visited the Chinese embassy in Moscow at a time when the Soviets and Chinese were barely talking to each other. We also visited the Canadian embassy, which was almost bereft of attractive material about Canada – but perhaps they didn't need it, being the only embassy we visited in Moscow that kept its doors locked so no one could enter.

I was succeeded as president by Muriel Duckworth. There were two versions of what the Voice of Women was in the 1960s, directly attributable, we decided, to whether Muriel (1967–71) or I was president at the time. One version went, 'Oh, I thought they were a temperance group,' and the other, 'Oh, I heard VOW had drunken parties and drank up their membership money.' It is true that I am directly responsible for placing the Duckworths on the road to perdition by introducing alcohol into that teetotal household. Muriel was an easy pushover for the little nip of sherry, though as a courtesy to Jack we put the bottle under the kitchen table when he came into the room. But on one memorable occasion at Magog we were having a cosy supper, with sherry, and Jack said, 'What does that stuff taste like anyway?' After he'd had a few sips, he conceded that it was quite good, and my dastardly deed of subversion was completed.

An effective and serious speaker with nice touches of humour, Muriel gave up her job with the Nova Scotia Department of Education to become VOW's fourth president. She represented VOW at conferences in Moscow and Paris, as well as at meetings across Canada. At that time, we were dealing with the seven-day war in the Middle East, the Colonels' coup in Greece, government upsets in Africa and South America and, of course, the war in Vietnam.

In 1967, we held the International Women's Peace Conference in Montreal during Expo. We had raised over $17,000 to bring in women from thirty-five countries, and over three hundred women attended the dozen or more workshops. Hélène Kazanzakis was our main speaker. Since the Greek coup that April, she had been living in exile in Geneva. We heard also from Jewish and Arab women (the Arab-Israeli war had just broken out), from Constance Cummings-John, mayor of Freetown, Sierra Leone, who could not return home because the government had been overthrown since her departure, and from a Bolivian woman whose family life was interrupted by early-morning visits from the secret police. Several women had come from countries which had revolutions or from which they were refugees. 'The last conference I attended,' reported one delegate, 'we all had to lie on the floor – they were shooting through the windows.'

The conference organizers nearly had an international incident on their hands when they inadvertently sent an invitation to the Chinese embassy in Ottawa, which at that time represented the Chiang Kai-shek régime in Taiwan, as opposed to mainland China. We were expecting Soviet guests, and at that time they recognized and were friendly only with the People's Republic of China. So the 'wrong' Chinese had said they would be delighted to attend and were about to send Madame Chennault, wife of the American general, a 'fascinating public speaker and militant anticommunist.' We had a gruelling discussion with our guests from the Soviet Union, who eventually agreed not to walk out of the conference, but just not to be there, should Madame C arrive. Then we waited in fear and trepidation but, fortunately for us, she never came. Think what the press would have made of it if we'd barred someone from a peace conference! Think what might have happened if she had let her militant anticommunism loose on our guests!

We finished the conference by taking some of our overseas guests to talk to Donald MacDonald, then Minister for External Affairs. We talked, but felt we had made little progress. On the occasions when we met with officials, politicians, and bureaucrats, we seldom received a positive response. We were usually greeted with polite indifference, and little action followed. On the other hand, the meetings with women around the world brought us together in a way that established long-term friendships and renewed energy to cooperate on a number of projects and actions. We hope these meetings will dissolve the national, social, and economic barriers that have, in the past, come between us and prevented communication and cooperation.

After our polite meeting with Mr MacDonald, we set off for Grindstone Island in the Rideau Lakes, where the Canadian Friends Service Committee ran a wonderful summer camp. We were distributed round the island in various cottages and all ate together in a big dining-room. There was a definite 'girls' dorm' atmosphere about the big bedroom where six of us slept, and we kept asking who was bringing the cocoa for our midnight feast. We made costumes, dressed up, sang and danced, and Maria from Bolivia taught us a new dance. It was the perfect ending to one of the most exhausting and exciting weeks VOW members could call to mind.

At the start of that conference, I had played the rottenest trick on Muriel. We started off with a big press conference with all the important overseas delegates present and lots of press. I was outgoing president at the time, so I did the introductions, then turned the meeting over to Muriel to give the assembled dignitaries all the details about the workshops. Then I fell asleep! (I really did have an excuse, as I doubt whether any of us had had more than three or four hours sleep each night during the week before the meetings began, but that didn't help Muriel.) We were sitting on opposite sides of a big circle of press and delegates, and there was I, fast asleep. What to do? Muriel could tell you her thoughts: to scream suddenly? to have a strenuous paroxysm of coughing? to shout at me? to fall off her chair? She went on with her explanation, and eventually I came to, gathered my wandering thoughts, and brought the meeting to an end.

In the midst of all the storms and tribulations that VOW went through over the years, Muriel had one ultimate weapon. Muriel cried. It may have been misery, rage, frustration, or sheer despair, but no one could continue the argument (or battle) when that happened. I remember one dreadful evening when Muriel was subjected to a kind of inquisition, all documented, dated, quoted, and supported by a naïve group of women, new to VOW and the circumstances. (Moira will remember this; she kept nobly supplying us with drink to help cope with the bombardment). Finally, Muriel could stand the battering and bullying no longer, and she began to get tearful. That stopped it. It also probably stopped some of us from losing our non-violent and peaceful principles and tearing out a few hairs from the persecutors.

Many a time has the silver tongue of Muriel Duckworth persuaded committees or conferences to her point of view. And it was always Muriel, that sweet, innocent, grey-haired grandmother, who would stick her neck right into the lion's mouth and let them all have it. What was the point we women were all (silently) boiling about at that 1975 Social Science Research Council of Canada conference, when Muriel got up and castigated them for leaving out women as participants? We had been asked to attend as 'citizen observers,' but there was little chance in the rigid conference structure for us to speak, let alone for groups of people to talk to each other. We were used to being token women; I think this was our first go at being token citizens. I wrote a very stern letter to them afterwards (well, they had *asked* for comments and suggestions), but Muriel did all the thinking on her feet.

When Muriel became president of VOW, she couldn't or wouldn't type, in spite of my giving her *Teach Yourself Typing* for a summer holiday task. So she got hold of some of that fancy paper that has about five carbon copies attached, and proceeded to write letters to the executive so we would all keep up to date. It was a lovely idea, and she sent reams of fascinating information to us and nearly drove us out of our minds. Muriel's handwriting is not known for being legible, not by me anyway. Faced with carbon copy number five, only a clairvoyant or mind-reader could have had a clue as to the contents. It was at this point in our beautiful friendship that I decided that my glorious role model had at least a very small Achilles heel. She also sometimes (only very infrequently) would forget to do things, just like us ordinary mortals. I was saying something along these lines (I'm afraid it was in pub-

Pat Boulding, Lorraine Bates, Judith Lawrence, Robin Sears, and Moira Armour at Toronto Airport, after Voice of Women Annual Meeting (1965)

Voice of Women Annual Meeting: Kay president (1966)

Brough (centre) with Frank and Nora Toole, in Toronto for Vietnam 'Teach-In' (mid-1960s)

Voice of Women delegation in Moscow: Ruth Kettner, Ann Gertler, Lydia Sayles, Kay (1966)

Suffield: Claire Culhane, Director, Thérèse Casgrain, Louise Lipell (1968)

VOW members in anti–Vietnam War demonstration, 1968, Toronto (includes Win Hall, centre, in light-coloured coat; Muriel Duckworth, carrying VOW sign; Kay, extreme right)

Kay in Vietnam at Medical University, with Hetti Vorhaus and Mickey Murray
(left and right, holding flowers) (1968)

VOW members in BC at time of Amchitka explosion: Kathleen Ruff, Kay, Deeno Birmingham, and Mary Cox (1971)

'Women Walk Home' – Cyprus: Margarita Papandreou (back to camera), Lady Amalia Fleming (carrying Greek flag), Melina Mercouri (behind and to the left of French flag–bearer), and Kay (carrying Canadian flag) (1975)

National Action Committee on the Status of Women Lobby of Parliament,
meeting with NDP Caucus: Ed Broadbent (2nd from left), John Gilbert
(centre), Stanley Knowles, Kay (president of NAC) (1977–8)

NAC Executive members meeting at time of AGM: Lorenne Clark (back to camera), Cathleen Morrison, Lorna Marsden, Kay, Jean Woodsworth, Brigid O'Reilly, Lynn Kaye (1978)

VOW delegation to Ottawa (1979)

'Persons Day' Dinner, Toronto: Ceta Ramakalivalsingh, Anne Johnston, Kay, Judith Lawrence (1980)

Family photo (1981)

Kay on telephone (1980) (Photo by Pamela Harris)

Ella Manuel, Newfoundland (1983)   Kay in Newfoundland (1983)

lic, I hope not at the CRIAW Duckworth Award gathering), when someone wailed, 'You mean she isn't perfect? Oh, oh dear!!'

There have been many times when I have stayed with Muriel at her wonderful home in Halifax, known to us as the 'group home,' and many are the rooms and beds we have shared, in Canada and the States, New York, and Paris. On one occasion, in 1968, Muriel and I were in Paris as part of the women's delegation meeting with Vietnamese women (including Madame Binh, who was appointed Foreign Minister after the war) from both the North Democratic Republic of Vietnam and the southern National Liberation Front. The Canadian and Australian delegates were billeted in a special municipal apartment kept for guests of the mayor of a northern Paris borough that had a communist council, and we went for runs together during the rush hour before attending the sessions with the Vietnamese women.

Muriel, then in her seventieth year, spent a glorious night on the town searching for 'soul food' with a gorgeous young black woman from Watts (Los Angeles) and a stunning blond Australian from Melbourne, both at least thirty years her junior. Off they set to sit drinking outside the Café de la Paix and generally paint the town until the early hours. (I later spent a night with Muriel's Australian at her home right on the beach in Melbourne, when Brough was being a visiting professor at the Australian National University in Canberra.) That evening in Paris I spent with Mary Clarke and others from Women Strike for Peace, making a tape about the conference – it turned out to be a very funny take-off. Mary had been to the press conference at which only one reporter (from *L'Humanité*, the Communist newspaper) had turned up, so we had interviewed *her*. It was all quite scurrilous and reduced us to near hysteria.

In 1980, Muriel and I again shared rooms in Connecticut, at a conference of the Women's International League for Peace and Freedom. I seemed to spend my time waiting for Muriel to finish fascinating conversations with women, old and new friends, who wouldn't let her go. I've decided that Muriel will eventually be late in arriving in heaven, because there will be hundreds of people who want to talk on the way.

11

Vietnam

The situation in Vietnam had been a concern of VOW's since the early 1960s. Thousands of peasants and rural workers were living in terrible conditions, often as refugees trying to escape the intensifying hostilities. The northern leader, Ho Chi Minh, had been responsible for the defeat and ousting of the French at Dien Bien Phu in 1954, when Vietnam was divided. Now the American government was supporting the south against the north. Canada's officially neutral stance seemed to reflect the US position far more than any true neutrality.

For roughly ten years, VOW's major efforts were centred on trying to end the Vietnam War and Canada's support for US aggression. We worked closely with American women, particularly Women Strike for Peace (WSP) and the Women's International League for Peace and Freedom (WILPF), and with other antiwar groups in Canada. VOW called for an end to bombing, use of napalm, burning, and devastation, and kept up constant pressure on the Canadian government. We had some success. Mr Pearson had his knuckles rapped by President Johnson for suggesting, of all things, a 'pause' in the relentless aerial bombing of North Vietnam. When Pierre Trudeau was coming to the end of his term as Prime Minister, he went to the UN's first special session on disarmament and made a strong speech proposing specific and practical measures for disarmament, such as 'suffocating' the arms race by taking away its financial and diplomatic fuel. But support dwindled away after the session ended, and the unremitting build-up in armaments increased dramatically under Ronald Reagan in the 1980s, with enthusiastic support from Canada's Conservative government.

In early 1963, when we started receiving reports from the Women's

Union of Vietnam about the dreadful situation of women and children there, we set about verifying the stories. The records eventually showed how true they were and how the increasing US military involvement was adding to the suffering. Everything possible was being done, particularly by Quaker, church, and medical-aid groups to provide much-needed supplies for the Vietnamese civilians.

One need in particular made the concerns of VOW members concrete, or rather woollen: the need of Vietnamese babies for clothing and blankets. Hiding can be very cold. Families had to live underground, in caves and dugouts, sometimes floating the babies in baskets when trenches were flooded. At first, some VOW members doubted the validity of expending so much effort on an aid project, but the consciousness-raising effect was tremendous. The garments had to be knitted in dark colours only. Asked why she was knitting baby clothes in dark green or brown, the knitter would explain that in Vietnam babies couldn't afford to have light colours, which could be seen by American bomber pilots. Hearing this, women were shocked and horrified. They wanted to know more and they offered to help. Many joined VOW to work for peace.

This project involved hundreds, not only in Canada but also in the States where it was against the law to aid and abet the enemy. During the next ten years about thirty thousand of these woollens crossed Lil Greene's kitchen table. They were packaged and sent to Vancouver, where Kay and Alan Inglis of Canadian Aid for Vietnamese Civilians sent them to Haiphong via free shipping they had obtained in Soviet ships. With them went medical equipment and money to purchase additional medical supplies.

Every knitter was thanked, personally or by letter. Lil Greene called it a full-time after-hours job in which her whole family and many friends were involved. In addition to compiling the knitting instructions and sorting and packaging the incoming knitwear, there was much drafting of letters and leaflets, holding of meetings, giving of speeches and interviews, and of course the fund-raising that supported the project. Lil is still in contact with many of the women who worked on this massive project, as help is still needed in Vietnam.

Out of the antiwar effort grew the support of VOW members and other Canadians for the draft-resisters and deserters from the US, and later from the South Vietnam army, who came to Canada to escape fighting against the Vietnamese people. Many of these young men have stayed on and made their homes in Canada, as have many of the

Vietnamese refugees who were helped and sustained by women such as VOW member Nancy Pocock. (Nancy and Jack Pocock were the coordinators of Grindstone Island's summer programs for several years.) Nancy subsequently put in years of committed service on behalf of refugees from Vietnam, Central America, and elsewhere, and is still up to her neck in peace activities. When she received the Pearson Peace Medal from Governor-General Jeanne Sauvé, a former VOW member, Nancy noted the irony of the fact that her first protest as a peace activist had been against the Bomarc missiles being brought into Canada by the Pearson government.

Also active in the Vietnam campaign was Claire Culhane, one of VOW's more colourful members, who had a great knack for getting publicity. She it was who camped out near Parliament Hill in the middle of the winter and who chained herself to one of the seats in the House. She had served in South Vietnamese hospitals earlier in the war, has since written a couple of books, and is at present in the forefront of the efforts to reform the prison system and women's prison conditions in particular.

My part in these endeavours, which covered the time I was VOW president (1963-7), gave me added responsibility and involvement. It helped immeasurably to have a husband who gave time, money, and encouragement to all these campaigns. Our long-suffering children also supported our exploits and fended for themselves whenever necessary. When the RCMP arrived at the door to search the basement for drugs or weapons (we had a draft-resister staying with us, whom they picked up), it was daughter Sheila who grasped the situation in a flash while I was still blustering on the doorstep, warned the resister's wife to disappear and, having checked all the rooms, innocently showed the RCMP around.

As president of VOW, I became a travel agent, tour organizer, conference manager, press agent, and would-be diplomat. All this was priceless experience, filled with crises, emergencies, hilarious situations, some very worrying moments, and some very moving ones. I won't easily forget standing with the Vietnamese women during their 1969 visit to Canada, gazing across the Niagara Gorge at the overwhelming power of the United States. Or examining the sophisticated surgical and rehabilitation equipment at the Hospital for Sick Children, seeing through the eyes of these women who were used to dealing with the crushed bodies of Vietnamese children without any such equipment. In fact, in one of those flashes of introspection that occasionally hit me, it occurred to me that, probably more than any other VOW member, I have been given incredible opportunities and experiences, for which I am seldom sufficiently grateful. One of these was my visit to Vietnam.

VOW had originally invited Vietnamese women to attend the International Women's Peace Conference held in Montreal during Expo '67. At the time, they were 'too busy' with the war, but I, as president of VOW, and two other women were invited to visit Hanoi. I will never forget the two weeks we were in Vietnam and Cambodia. Before I went, I wrote (from Cambridge, England, where we were spending Brough's 1967/8 sabbatical):

In case I get to Hanoi and end up with a bomb on top of me, I want to put down one or two thoughts beforehand ... Not many people are invited to go to Hanoi. To have earned the trust of the Vietnam women is a very great honour, though many people in the west might not think of it this way. We cannot treat such an honour lightly, nor, however reluctant I felt, would I dream of refusing to go.

I hope to be able to explain to other people how it must feel to be a woman in Vietnam today. Perhaps, if we can understand this better, it will make it impossible for us to forget, to ignore, or to stand aside while these terrible things are happening to people like us.

We waited almost a year to make the trip. The invitation from the Vietnamese Women's Union first came to us in May 1967. It was renewed at a conference in Prague in October, and we planned to go the following month. But because of heavy bombing at that time, the invitation was cancelled. Next spring, renewed letters of invitation went out. At an international conference in Paris in April we met women from both North and South Vietnam and planned the details with them.

My companions on this two-week visit were Mickey Murray, a stalwart member of the Congress of Canadian Women and long-time peace worker from Thunder Bay, and Hetti Vorhaus from London (England), whom I had met on our exploits over NATO with Women Strike for Peace. For years the Vorhaus home in Hampstead was a base for itinerant peace women, and all VOW's returning Moscow delegation stayed with her in 1966. Later, Hetti's home was the London refuge for the Greenham Common women. The whole Macpherson family had at different times been welcomed by Hetti and her husband Bernard. They knew all the good theatres and restaurants in London, which was wonderful for Canadians on sabbatical leave.

While waiting in Cambodia for our plane going into Hanoi, we spent a day at Angkor Wat, the extraordinary temple built about the twelfth century and for a long time almost hidden in the jungle – an incredible and beautiful series of buildings whose walls are covered with designs and pictures in stone. Cambodia was then a peaceful and beautiful small country, as yet untouched by American bombs. The first sign that we had come into a country at war came when the plane touched down at Hanoi airport and taxied over to the terminal. The landing strip lights winked off and at the same time all the lights inside the plane were turned out. Immigration men came aboard and examined our passports by flashlight.

As we deplaned, a group of women wearing exquisite silk dresses were waiting to greet us with flowers and embraces. We were welcomed in a mixture of English and French and Vietnamese – not that any of us spoke Vietnamese, but some of our hostesses spoke English and French and one was a professional interpreter. Then we got into two large, black cars of some antiquity and drove in the dark down a narrow road so crowded with people, on foot and on bicycles, that it seemed miraculous our drivers avoided hitting anyone. A long and bumpy detour took us to the Red River, spanned by a triple-pontoon bridge.

Our hotel, built in the French colonial period, had originally been called the Metropole, but was now named Unification. Its manager was a woman. I had an enormous room to myself, with plenty of hot water, both for washing and in a Thermos for making tea. A big fan whirred in the ceiling, and mosquito netting covered the bed. It was very hot and humid, but there were actually fewer mosquitoes to be seen than in Toronto at that time of year.

We were very struck by everyone's courtesy and consideration. Our waitress in the hotel was distressed when we protested that three four-course meals a day was really too much, even for westerners. She was an enchanting young thing who looked like a fragile piece of porcelain. I was quite startled during my first air-raid alert to see her, complete with pellet-proof hat and rifle across her shoulders, marshalling the hotel guests into the shelter. Later we met girls who had shot down planes with these same rifles.

The day in Hanoi began before 5:00 a.m., and rush hour was in full swing outside the hotel by 5:30. Trucks and cars would hoot their horns continuously, and pedestrians, bicycles, pedicars, and oxcarts would move to the side in a leisurely fashion. By far the most frequent method of transport was the bicycle. Both cyclists and pedestrians often carried huge loads, such as bags of rice and parts of machines. We saw small, slim militia girls who, during the heavy bombing, had carried boxes of ammunition weighing 20 kilos (44 lbs, the weight of luggage allowed on an overseas flight) to the anti-aircraft units.

In downtown Hanoi, there was little evidence of bomb damage, since much of it had by this time been cleared away or rebuilt, but it was a different story in the suburbs, and especially in the towns and villages farther south, below the twentieth parallel, where the bombing had been greatly intensified. Casting my mind back, I don't remember seeing any sizeable building outside of Hanoi which had not suffered bomb damage. Yet a month or two before, while watching on television the US Senate hearings, I had heard Dean Rusk assure the world that the US was only hitting military targets in North Vietnam and that no civilians were being bombed.

We saw towns and villages where almost every single building had been destroyed. We climbed over craters and walked down silent streets where birds flitted in and out of the remains of artisans' workshops in the small stone or brick houses. Some buildings had been near railways, which were acknowledged military targets, but many houses, schools, churches, and hospitals hadn't been near the railway at all. In a military museum, we saw 3000-pound bombs with US markings on their cases.

As we continued to walk about, we became aware that this was not, after all, wholly a place of death. Life was going on under our feet. The warning and shelter systems had saved many people, who were carrying on their daily lives underground in factories, engineering shops, and even restaurants. We visited parts of a now-dispersed textile factory, where women were producing thousands of yards of cotton material. We saw some of the small engineering shops, built half-underground, with sleeping quarters right in the shelters beside the machines. In spite of the walls being cracked as a result of nearby bomb hits, the restaurants reminded me of those exclusive Parisian 'caves,' but the meals were rather cheaper and the raison d'être definitely different. The meals were not simply emergency hand-outs; the customers had several choices. Speaking of French restaurants, in the countryside some of us picked up snails which looked very similar to escargots, but they never appeared on the menu. When I asked why, they said, 'Oh, we don't eat those, we feed them to the ducks.'

'How can your people continue to produce enough food for everybody?' we asked. 'Oh, we have better methods now, better organization,' we were told. The food producers were organized into co-ops. Every man and woman could own a small section of land for individual use, but the total amount of privately owned land, including land held in trust for men fighting on the various fronts, was only a small portion of the total held by the co-op; the rest (about 95 per cent) was cultivated cooperatively. Government agricultural experts provided advice about crops. For instance, one group we visited was experimenting with a low-growing rice that was not so liable to get knocked over by storms. The importance of fresh green vegetables to supplement the staple diet of rice, fish, poultry, bananas, and other fruits was emphasized. We saw patch after patch of rau muon, a spinach-like vegetable which is easily grown.

Even on my first trip outside the city, I got the impression of a land bursting with fertility. As we travelled further, we saw endless rice paddies that now produced two or more crops a year; we also saw bananas and other fruits, coconuts, corn, and many water plants, including the orchid-like hyacinths that are one of the most nutritious pig foods! There were flocks of ducks and chickens, turkeys, and geese. What looked to us like muddy pools proved to contain quantities of fish. It is true that in these agricultural areas there were frequent air-raid alerts when planes went over and some actual bombings. But thanks to the efficient alarm system and prevalence of shelters, few civilians were hurt (except of course in case of a direct hit in the area.) We were told that the transplanting of rice, a lengthy process, was often done during the hours of darkness as the peasants were then safer from air attacks.

It was during the visit in Hanoi that I met Phan Thi An, vice-president of the Vietnam Women's Union and a member of the national assembly of the Democratic Republic of Vietnam. Phan Thi An was a serene, middle-aged, competent-looking woman who had grown up during the French colonial era in Vietnam. She had received a good education and trained as a teacher of literature. Then she wanted to study law, but the French president Pétain had decreed that there were to be no women advocates. Phan Thi An and her husband joined the partisans. After the war in the South was won, the women's union had developed their 'three responsibilities' campaign for women:
– to replace men in both agricultural and industrial production;
– to care for their families and relieve the men of family worries while fighting for liberation;
– to form their own militia and defence force to defend the country-side whenever they had to.

By 1968 these priorities had changed. Phan Thi An quoted from Ho Chi Minh: 'If we want to liberate the people, we must liberate women first.' One of the first priorities was education, especially for older women and those in the south who had been denied even primary education under the colonial régimes. School hours were staggered until enough schools were built for the children. Women were working to obtain qualifications and were moving into managerial and leading positions in all fields. We saw women in the factories, some of them in their forties and fifties, studying grammar and geometry beside youngsters of eighteen. Several members of the Women's Union were learning a second or third language. There was still a dearth of books, printed matter, and paper, yet practically every adult was going to night school. But attitudes were changing only slowly. The law against polygamy was not passed until 1960, and many women could remember the days when men could take and discard wives.

Meanwhile, women were turning to other uses the skills they had gained in the militia. Bomb craters in the countryside were filled in and put to use before they could fill with water and become breeding-grounds for mosquitoes. Buildings, roads, and railways were needed, as well as much medical and rehabilitation work, but supplies were still very scarce. The burden of health care was eased by political decisions made under Ho Chi Minh, who decided that education for prevention and the involvement of all people on every level of society was the only hope. Thousands of cadres trained in the basics of medicine and hygiene were pledged to pass on their knowledge to every village and hamlet. They formed networks of peasants and workers, learning as they worked, to promote basic hygiene and simple health routines.

People learned how to filter water to purify it for drinking, how to prevent sewage contamination, and how to process and use human and animal waste for fertilizer. They also learned about basic cleanliness in cooking and preserving food (such as eliminating flies). Gradually the wisdom of this decision became apparent. In the fourteen years since the French régime ended, the changes had been almost incredible. North Vietnam's infant mortality rate dropped from 30 per cent to 2.5 per cent, one of the lowest in the world. Plague, cholera, and smallpox were eliminated. Malaria almost disappeared. Spectacular change took place, and the people themselves felt responsible.

Health concerns were now integrated into the general life of the country. The students at Hanoi Medical University (2000 of them in the first three years of their six-year medical training) were expected to build their own place to study and live in, to grow much of their own food, to help the local people grow theirs, to work with them for better sanitation and health, and to inspire and even entertain them, as well as 'getting their academic year.' And they were doing so with enthusiasm.

The university was established in the 'dispersed area' in 1965. To get there, we had to drive a long distance into the country in jeeps. The road became an unpaved track, like some of our Canadian logging roads, and we got into the foothills and jungle. We passed villages where the houses were almost hidden under the palm trees, whose leaves were woven to make the roofs. We found four hundred buildings scattered over a wide area, often hidden by the dense jungle foliage. All had been built by staff and students. The students had dug miles of communication trenches and hundreds of wells, had built latrines and wash-houses. Classrooms were often sunk below ground level for protection from bomb fragments.

Half of the students were girls, and quite a few of them came from the ethnic minority groups. Their enthusiasm for their new life was even more understandable when they explained that up until fourteen years previously there had been no opportunities for education or social advancement of any kind. A woman's lot was to be a household drudge or, if she became one of the wives (up to four were allowed) of a rich man, a piece of property, a symbol of conspicuous expenditure. Now those from the minority groups, both men and women, were given extra attention in special classes, and their pride in even simple achievements was touching. They sang us beautiful songs of their mountain regions and asked us about the students of our countries. 'Give them our greetings and wishes for success in their studies.'

These young women, like Phan Thi An and the women who came with their delegation to Canada in 1969, were sterling examples of the determination and will of the Vietnamese in their struggle for liberation. As Phan Thi An said, Vietnamese women can be both fierce and gentle; they can both struggle and love. We left Vietnam with warm feelings, many friends, and a determination to do everything we could to end the war. And indeed, going back over this material has brought back many details of that unique experience and renewed my deep admiration for the bravery and endurance, humour, and friendship of the Vietnamese women. On my return, I spoke to many groups about the situation in Vietnam, and showed pictures, films, artifacts, and gifts I had been given.

VOW had the good fortune to host visits from women from Indochina in 1969 and 1971, while Muriel Duckworth was president. The second delegation included women from Cambodia and Laos, then also in the war. VOW raised the money for the expenses of these two visits while the delegations were in Canada. (When we went to Vietnam and to the Soviet Union we raised our fare money, but everything was provided for us once we were there.)

I think it was during the 1971 visit that Muriel and Jack Duckworth (baggage master par excellence) went across the country with the group. What an experience! VOW had planned a conference in Vancouver, which was intended to be a peace conference, to work towards liberating Vietnam, but through a misunderstanding many women thought it was a women's liberation conference, and we were talking at cross purposes. We experienced women's liberation rampant, a pregnant American who had to be sent home, Black Panthers, and so on. Another conference was held in Toronto, at the end of the trip, at which some members of Women Strike for Peace stood in the middle of a Toronto meeting proclaiming, 'In this country, we ...' We dubbed them American Imperialists of the Left, and we became more and more Canadian every minute. One group of Americans installed themselves as the bodyguards of the Vietnamese, a totally unnecessary routine in Canada at the time. As we had suspected, they weren't too efficient. Muriel described how all the guards had stationed themselves on the porch of the Duckworths' Magog cottage, as night-watch women but, when Jack went out for his early-morning swim, he stepped over completely unconscious bodies, oblivious to any invasion or infiltration.

There were two international women's conferences in Paris on the situation in Vietnam, and VOW was represented at these, as were Vietnamese, American, European, Australian, and other women. VOW members attended many other conferences, and visited in Moscow, Zagreb, Prague, Helsinki, and other capitals whenever we had the opportunity. We spoke, wrote, or gave interviews about our experiences and tried to make our opposition to war and violence known. Yet often, especially during the war in Vietnam, it seemed that no media or government people were listening. But eventually the war did stop. The American government was beaten, though they have never admitted it and have been trying to make up for it ever since.

When the Vietnam War came to a halt in 1975 and the Americans started pulling out, Vietnam, especially the south, was a devastated country. Tons and tons of bombs (many unexploded), miles of farm land wasted, burned, and rendered useless by chemicals and napalm, and thousands of wounded and impoverished civilians remained. Little or nothing was offered to restore the country: no reparations, no aid, no loans or financial support, no diplomatic contacts. Voluntary organizations around the world continued support, but nothing was done by governments, except those in socialist countries, themselves confronting economic troubles. Voice of Women continued helping with aid. Some supplies were sent but not enough to make a dent in the needs of the destroyed countries, which were still affected by war in Cambodia.

Nowadays, other situations demand help and attention, but our links with Vietnam, our consciousness of the damage, and our memories of the friendships still remain.

12

VOW, Summing Up

During the 1970s and 1980s, the Voice of Women had a lower profile than during the somewhat spectacular sixties. The reduced number of members required VOW to organize differently, and the increasing influence of feminist ideas led to a different approach in the structure of groups and the procedure for meetings and decision-making. After presidents Tucker (1960–2), Casgrain (1962–3), Macpherson (1963–7), and Duckworth (1967–71), the National Coordinating Committee was established. Working by means of a series of stalwart helpers (Lilian Zaremba, Connie Gardner, Lyn Center, and Sylvia Porter), this committee made policy decisions and set priorities. Then, from 1974 to 1979, Donna Elliott was our paid national coordinator.

During Donna's period a great deal of time and effort went into making submissions on the future of Ontario's nuclear-power production. In 1977 and 1978, Donna spent the best part of a year covering the Porter Commission on electrical-power planning. In the 1990s, this question is still a very hot one, although most of the world's nations are gradually recognizing the dangers, not to mention the catastrophic expense and misuse of the world's resources, that the nuclear industry has perpetrated on today's world.

In 1980, Dorothy Smieciuch volunteered to act as national office coordinator, an unpaid position which held the Voice of Women together for six years. She did a magnificent job. Amongst other things, she totally reorganized our filing system, sent material to the national archives, compiled the annual calendar of meetings, wrote financial reports and the newsletter, and generally kept communications going between members from coast to coast. We should all be eternally grateful for the effort she put into this work. In 1986, at the Montreal

AGM, we reorganized with a board of directors (president, Martha Goodings) and, courtesy of Nancy Jackman, a paid secretary (first Vera de Jong, and currently Carolyn Langdon).

VOW has sometimes lurched and sometimes bounced forward in its progress as an effective national women's peace organization. Even at times when VOW's profile was less public, significant steps were taken. VOW's original plan had been to get the blessing of the leading politicians and then to work towards making contacts with women round the world, so that women would say, 'Stop making war. We want peace and international cooperation,' and the power of women would stop war. It was a beautiful and unrealistic vision, which gradually changed to cope with the real world and real politicians.

None the less, we carried on the practice of seeking to bring officials and politicians into discussion to press for new non-violent ways of settling the world's disputes. Voices went in delegations to UN, NATO, and other meetings to advocate cooperative discussion and the setting of common, non-violent goals rather than the frustration of confrontation and threats.

In 1979, Halifax VOW member Marion Kerans and I went to Brussels for the December meeting of NATO defence ministers. For the first time in twenty years, NATO was planning to install ground-based nuclear weapons in Europe, although Holland refused outright to take them. NATO wanted to locate Pershing and cruise missiles in five NATO countries. These 'small' 'tactical' weapons, easily hidden in a truck, have ten times the power of the bomb that destroyed Hiroshima. There was much opposition and dissent, and Canada's Defence Minister said he wouldn't make his mind up until he got to Brussels.

Marion and I joined a disarmament demonstration of fifty thousand people marching three miles through the streets of Brussels in the pouring rain, shouting slogans, carrying banners, and singing. It was dark by the time the demonstrators reached the city square, where a youth group was fasting in protest against the missiles. They listened to speeches from Belgian politicians, union leaders, and 'foreign personalities' (that was us). We made our speeches in French, and from a balcony, like the Pope or the Queen! 'Nous parlons au nom des femmes du Canada ...'

After the demonstration, we met with the Belgian women from the Rassemblement des femmes in a restaurant. We got warm again and had some good discussions before returning to the Youth Hostel where we were staying (no discrimination against the aged there, which was fortunate, given the astronomical prices everywhere else!). The Norwegians, whose bus was leaving the next morning, wrote a message for the NATO ministers and sent fond greetings via Marion to Berit Ås, their feminist parliamentarian, who was visiting Halifax.

We met with the Canadian delegation, all men except for Flora MacDonald, who arrived at lunch-time on the day of the meeting. We all agreed that our aims were peace and disarmament, but VOW disagreed fundamentally with the NATO stance that we can only negotiate 'from a position of strength,' that is, if we have a bigger stockpile of nuclear weapons than the enemy. Both sides already had enough nuclear weapons to 'overkill' the world's population between twenty and forty times.

We found their notion of 'the enemy,' a necessary item in military strategy, totally unacceptable. It was also a little too flexible. In Europe, at the end of last world war, 'the enemy' had been switched rapidly: the Russians, our wartime 'gallant allies,' became almost overnight 'brutal communist hordes' who threatened us, although the Soviet Union, devastated and with twenty million dead, was hardly in a position to overrun Europe, which was in any case already in ruins. NATO had been established to counter this perceived threat, and NATO's assumptions and policies had changed little since it was formed in 1949.

It is always difficult to talk in terms of alternative non-violent solutions, collaboration rather than confrontation, and so on. The military men and the politicians who are supposed to make the decisions cannot comprehend any language that does not include concepts of threat and force, good guys and bad guys, us and them. Our suggestions that 'the enemy' (the Soviet Union) might not be about to overrun Europe and attack the United States, and that NATO and the Warsaw Pact might be disbanded in the cause of peace, met with a shocked silence. We later met with the NATO Chef du Cabinet, a dapper and experienced diplomat from Holland, Mr Van Campen, who greeted us with impeccable assurance and said, 'Where we are now is quite satisfactory.' He credited nuclear weapons with the 'peaceful' state we had enjoyed for the past thirty-four years. During the three hours we spent in NATO headquarters, we saw only one woman, and she was the receptionist in the Canadian section.

After that 1979 NATO meeting, I wrote: 'If ever there was an area where women are invisible, out of place, *not wanted*, it is in the NATO, Warsaw Pact, SALT, and so-called disarmament discussions. So, what better place for women to intrude, when the NATO ministers are discussing their plans for the future? There is a whole perspective that they never consider.'

We have to replace the use of the threat system (Ursula Franklin calls it the 'do as I say or else' system) with a new agenda (as Marion Dewar says, 'What is our common bottom-line objective?'). Women have developed some of these methods round their kitchen tables and in dealing with their children, as well as in their communities and workplaces. It's time for them to be used in public and international life.

In 1981, women met at a conference in Amsterdam to work again on strategies for opposing nuclear weapons in Europe. Huge demonstrations had taken place in many countries, and most of the women present at the five-hundred-strong Amsterdam meeting that November took part in a torchlight march of ten thousand women at The Hague, ending in speeches and singing in front of the legislative buildings.

Besides women from the NATO countries, there were women from the Warsaw Pact countries, the Soviet Union, Poland, Hungary, and Czechoslovakia. Their presence gave an added dimension to the discussions, and many women discovered for the first time that in spite of differences the major concern of women everywhere is that a way be found to end the threat of war and nuclear destruction. During the first day's presentations, we heard from two British women from Greenham Common in Berkshire where, since the summer, a group of women had been camping in front of the air-force base where it was thought cruise missiles would be placed. Their first action had been a march, which started at the Cardiff nuclear station and progressed through Wales and England to Greenham Common. And the rest, as they say, is history.

The Amsterdam conference was held in the ornate Institute of Tropical Medicine with its elaborate staircase, tall pillars, and marble rotunda, which we used for displays, discussions, and song sessions, and also for coffee, snacks, and the reception given us by the Burgomeister of Amsterdam. Much of the work was done in nine workshops, where a small number of women could get to know each other and work on their chosen topic. These included examining the policies and strategies of the nuclear powers, the history and strategies of peace movements, education, media action, and the conversion of industry to peacetime production. All aimed to come up with proposals for action.

I went to the workshop on international treaties and the laws governing the conduct of war, where I was impressed by the wisdom of Yvonne Sée, veteran French peace woman, active with the WILPF (Women's International League for Peace and Freedom). 'If conflict can be solved peacefully,' she said, 'then it can be positive and constructive.' We also heard from a Dutch air-force captain who had made an exhaustive study of the laws relating to weapons that cause cruel and unnecessary suffering, and had concluded that the use of such weapons violated all the laws of war and was, in fact, a war crime. Since the laws of war are already in place, he was campaigning for his country and NATO to enforce the laws by renouncing nuclear weapons.

Since 1981, a series of VOW groups has attended the UN, Geneva, and Vienna disarmament talks and many special meetings in North America and Europe, speaking for VOW whenever possible. Voice of Women's UN and international connections have been continued and expanded by Janis Alton. VOW has also profited from Madeleine (Mady) Gilchrist's involvement with WMS (originally Women for a Meaningful Summit, now Women for Mutual Security), which has concentrated on having women present at NATO, Warsaw Pact, and summit meetings. In fact, when she wasn't acquiring a BA, doing an almost full-time nursing job, and being a mother of two, Mady has given all her time to building feminist connections around the world.

As part of WMS's activities, sixty women from thirty-five countries met in Athens in November 1986, at the invitation of Margaret Papandreou and the Women's Union of Greece, to plan for the next summit meeting of US and USSR leaders. The proposal that women from NATO countries meet with their permanent NATO representatives was followed up that winter. Then, the next June, the women met with the ambassadors of their respective countries and the whole group of some thirty women met with Lord Carrington, Secretary-General of NATO, in Brussels. Mady and I represented the Voice of Women and, at that time, both of us were part of NAC's Survival Committee too. We met with NATO ambassador Gordon Smith. 'No one would be better pleased than I,' said Mr Smith, 'if we could reach an agreement with the Warsaw Pact Alliance ... but both sides must agree on this process.'

We wanted greater NATO accountability, fewer secret military decisions, fewer unilateral US decisions, and more attention devoted to non-military conflict resolution. In particular, we asked for: (1) the adoption of an immediate nuclear-force agreement; (2) the acceptance by NATO of the Warsaw Pact's offer for discussions; and (3) the establishment of a nuclear-weapons-free zone in Central Europe.

'It is doubtful,' I wrote for *Broadside* that July, 'whether any NATO staff members are occupied with examining non-violent, trust- and confidence-building means of negotiation.' When reporting to the press, Papandreou and women from other countries made the point that NATO is an obsolete monster, that its decision-making is unclear, and the Secretary-General, as he told us, has no power. ('Je n'existe pas,' Lord Carrington had said.)

The WMS work culminated in the precedent-setting event in 1988 when women parliamentarians, peace researchers, and activists attended a meeting in Sofia of all the Warsaw Pact foreign ministers, including the Soviet Foreign Minister Eduard Shevardnadze. The VOW UN group had been to Geneva that year for the disarmament talks, where they had lobbied ten delegations. Then Margaret Papandreou had asked Mady and the others to a WMS meeting in Athens to speak about the Middle East, since they had been in contact with the Israeli women. After that, Mady et al. went on to Sofia to the Warsaw Pact meeting, which they followed up with a meeting with NATO ministers. Their reception at the former was much more productive and positive, involving all the ministers; also they were invited to make use of the press conference already planned by the ministers for themselves. The NATO encounter was much less satisfactory.

From the beginning, Ann Gertler has been constantly on the alert for new situations with which VOW should concern itself: NORAD, OAS (the Organization of American States), Namibia, test-ban treaties. She it was who obtained observer status for VOW at the United Nations, where she was our official observer for many years. I remember once, after a gruelling day of lobbying, arguing, persuading, and debating with politicians in the House of Commons, Ella Manuel and I were lying totally exhausted on two beds in a hotel room in Ottawa. In came Ann Gertler, a question on her lips: 'What are we going to do about NATO?' A whole vista of brief-writing, discussion, and lobbying arose before us. We could happily have thrown something at her.

Our members have been at meetings on the South Pacific and the Arctic, as well as the three UN Decade for Women meetings (Mexico City, Copenhagen, and Nairobi). I didn't go to any of these three congresses. I heard about Mexico City from Muriel Duckworth and Jean Woodsworth, and they told me how Mary Two-Axe Early's case and Canada's discriminatory Indian Act were brought before the congress there. In 1980 in Copenhagen, Maureen O'Neil of Canada's official delegation contributed significantly to the final conference document. At Nairobi in 1985, our good friend Margaret Papandreou of Greece was an outstanding speaker, and many Canadian women contributed to the peace and other activities of the non-governmental Parallel Congress.

For the Nairobi Congress ending the Decade, the Canadian Department of the Secretary of State wanted to assist women from across the country to attend. They provided a limited amount of funding for this purpose and set up a selection committee on which I served (the only other selection committee I've served on was the Persons Award committee). We were assisted from time to time by other women with detailed knowledge of specific groups and categories of women, but it was a mind-boggling task and I'm not quite sure how many of our recommended groups and individuals were picked in the end. But at least the government tried to help a good many women to get to Nairobi.

At other government-organized meetings in Canada, however, there is often a lack of broad-based representation. In November 1986, I was invited to attend the first of the Department of National Defence's informal consultations, hopefully intended to lead to a new defence policy. The meeting included about forty individuals, with the military and big business well, if not overwhelmingly, represented by various high-level executives, some of whom were former admirals, generals, and high-ranking officers in the Forces. It was difficult for me to distinguish these from representatives of strategic-studies programs and veterans' and reserve organizations. The peace movement there consisted of four people: I was there from the Voice of Women, George Ignatieff from Science for Peace, Ernie Regehr from Ploughshares (for the United Church), and Father Lombardi from the Catholic Church. There were only three women present (plus Mady, who was kindly admitted to help me read through the agenda and recognize faces).

One after another the participants expressed their concern for the decline, as they saw it, of Canada's military forces, for the low defence budget, for the lack of up-to-date equipment, and for Canada's not making an adequate contribution to the military alliances or 'pulling our weight' with our allies. Canadians, they said, are freeloaders depending on the Americans for our defence. With our poorly equipped troops we have no adequate armaments for surveillance or defence of our borders. No one spoke of the possibility of disarmament, the nuclear freeze, a test-ban treaty, or seeking different ways of solving international problems without threats and deterrence. This was a language that seemed completely unfamiliar in that company.

And, though Father Lombardi reminded the meeting of the effects of the arms race on the people of the Third World, the general feeling seemed to be that peace people are dupes and traitors, lavishly funded either by Moscow or by the Canadian government. We were told that the huge contributions given by the government to the peace movement starve and undermine our Defence Department. Many of these points were carried to the extreme by the three advocates of Peace through Strength. When I spoke, I said that I represented this dire threat to Canada's armed might and expressed what Perrin Beatty later referred to as 'Mrs Macpherson's idealistic notions.' (Later, former MP Ronald Ritchie chivalrously denied that I was a threat, except when I ran unsuccessfully against him in the 1979 federal election.)

But, whether or not the government seeks our participation, VOW has kept up the pressure on our elected representatives. I couldn't begin to count the number of occasions when Voice of Women met with federal ministers or presented briefs or statements to parliamentary committees or other bodies. I remember the indignation of VOW members in 1965, after being given a verbal run-around by Paul Martin, then Minister of External Affairs. Said one, 'He's a master of double talk – in two languages.' Another time, meeting with a different Minister of External Affairs, VOW member Ester Kulak was so indignant at the smooth talk that she exploded, in her Brooklyn accent, 'Oh for Christ's sake, Mr MacDonald!' (Later, in Winnipeg, I remember celebrating with Ester when she was let out of jail, after a peaceful antiwar demonstration, just in time to receive her Canadian citizenship.) On yet another memorable occasion, we sat around on the floor outside the PM's office with Ann Gertler's two-year-old running up and down. And then there was the time when two small demons set off stink bombs in the MPs' wives' sitting-room, which they had kindly allowed us to use. And the time when one of our more excitable members had a tantrum in the corridor because she had been left out of the delegation ...

In 1979, twenty or more VOW members met with a number of specialists from External Affairs. I arrived at the meeting in characteristic fashion. I had left my writing class in a rush, then dashed into the liquor store for a couple of bottles of sherry and into the NAC office to see how the news-sheet (my responsibility) was progressing. 'Don't worry,' said NAC secretary Pearl Blazer, 'we won't have finished it all by Monday. You can bring in the last two pages then.' I rushed into the bank for some cash to use in Ottawa for any penniless Voice of Women members in need of instant funds, and thence to the grocery store to provide for one lonely husband and any visiting Voices returning from Ottawa with me. That left one hour in which to gather up papers for our presentation to the government, food for extra snacks and nibbling (necessary when twenty-five members meet all day), and, last but not least, some clothes. On the way to the bus station, we lost Nancy Pocock, but found her on the street corner, and arrived to find the bus full and ready to leave early. In Ottawa, we took a cab to our 'anchor-woman's' house, where we found peace-minded women from all over the country and settled down to prepare ourselves for the four-hour meeting. On the next day, we were first to arrive in the room with the big tables arranged in a hollow square, so we strategically seated ourselves in alternate chairs, thereby splitting up the departmental colleagues. The result was good, if not always productive, discussion.

Recent meetings have been less satisfactory or non-existent, although Joe Clark and Jean Chrétien took time to discuss matters seriously. Our confrontations with Perrin Beatty as Defence Minister were not productive, and we found Ursula Franklin's comment very true: 'We used to think governments were badly informed but well intentioned. We now know that they may be well informed but very badly intentioned.'

Nevertheless, it slowly becomes apparent that much of VOW's philosophy and many of the policies we have been advocating for years have gradually penetrated the obsolete and inappropriate thinking of those in so-called high places. The Secretary-General of NATO spoke in Toronto in 1989 about cooperation being better than confrontation. The general public is aware of the threats to our environment, even if the politicians are not. It is comforting to have anyone (apart from VOW and the 'idealist dreamers') question the acceptance of nuclear power, or nuclear deterrence, or MAD (Mutual Assured Destruction), or Star Wars, as national policy, but it is never enough – and always too slow in coming.

Now the emphasis on women's situation, the environment, and the threat of nuclear power and waste has created more areas for concern. People sometimes ask why a peace group tackles such varying issues as threats to the environment and nuclear power, but as a 1982 VOW statement points out, 'the nuclear age has changed the nature of war, and a nuclear war could result in the destruction of all life on this planet.' Survival, as Helen Caldicott says, 'is the ultimate conservation issue.'

We recognize that all these crises and situations are connected, indeed interdependent. We know now that deteriorating or non-existent social services and diminishing aid for development are connected to the loss of resources and to funds spent on armaments and wasteful megaprojects. Violence against women is directly related to the arms race. Greed, misuse of power, and domination are at the root of the world's problems. All these questions have become more easily understandable, but finding solutions has posed yet more problems.

The slogan 'Think globally, act locally' has guided many of Voice of Women's actions, consciously or unconsciously. From the beginning each member could find actions she could undertake, alone, with a group, or as part of a larger effort. 'If you can't find a group, found one' led to all kinds of enterprising combinations. The national newsletter, started in 1960 and soon augmented by local bulletins, set out weekly tasks – campaigns, actions, targets for letter-writing, fund-raising suggestions, and countless other projects – which were taken up by enthusiastic women. Women exchanged letters all over the world, learned Esperanto, participated in phone-in shows, and lobbied their MPs, as well as studying subjects and situations, programs and possibilities for the achievement of world peace.

In Nova Scotia, Betty Peterson mobilized support for the Innu, and in New Brunswick VOW members took action against the nuclear power station at Pointe Lepreau. The nuclear activities of the US and Canadian armed forces at Comox and Nanoose Bay off Vancouver Island provoked opposition ranging from demonstrations to questions raised in the House of Commons. In Halifax, VOW members dealt with visits from nuclear submarines. In Labrador, members contended with the devastating effect on human and animal populations of NATO low-flying jet planes. In Saskatchewan and Alberta, Voices demonstrated against cruise-missile tests and chemical- and nerve-warfare research at Suffield. Nancy Pocock from Toronto went to investigate the devastating effects of pulp-mill mercury emissions on native people in Northern Ontario.

When I look at the work done and the energy expended by VOW members, I am overcome with admiration. VOW presidents and members have met with the Pope, with bishops, and with the women's unions/committees representing most European and Soviet bloc countries as well as Vietnam. We have attended international conferences and meetings dealing with NATO, the Warsaw Pact, the UN and disarmament, human rights, South-East Asia, and Central America. We have mounted three major international women's peace conferences

(1962, 1967, and 1985) and hosted cross-country visits for one Soviet, one Vietnamese, and one Vietnamese/Cambodian/Laotian delegation. In 1963, a VOW delegation visited several European countries and attended a Soviet women's congress. Two delegations have visited the USSR, invited by the Soviet Women's Committee, and all four VOW presidents went there at one time or another.

VOW's first campaign, fund-raising for Dr Norman Alcock's Peace Research Institute, raised something over $200,000. Then we worked to support the test-ban treaty, which resulted in the partial test ban in 1963.

One of VOW's most successful campaigns, the collection of children's baby teeth (1961–2) provided over 5500 teeth for the Faculty of Dentistry at the University of Toronto, where Dr Murray Hunt was researching patterns of radioactive fallout across the country. The findings of his research forced the government to undertake more comprehensive monitoring procedures in detecting radioactive fallout in Canada. Nuclear fallout from testing in the atmosphere led, via the food chain (from the atmosphere to the soil, from the soil to vegetation and animals, thence to human beings), to strontium-90 deposits in bones and the increased likelihood of later cancer and leukaemia. Apart from their publicity value, baby teeth were the most readily available kind of bone sample.

It was a typical campaign for VOW, in that local action was combined with top-level political pressure. VOW members took up the challenge with enthusiasm. We had a booth at the CNE in Toronto, with a barrel for children to put their teeth into. Boards of education, dentists' offices, libraries, and hundreds of women spent hours collecting, sorting, and documenting the specimens (where conceived and born, breast- or bottle-fed, statistics about the mother and child, and so on). In 1985, at the VOW twenty-fifth anniversary party on Hornby Island, women reminisced about the rows of documented teeth on their living-room floors.

The final brief was prepared by Ursula Franklin and presented to the government. I was lucky enough to go along with her to lobby officials in Ottawa. The increased national and international concern eventually resulted in the partial (still not total) test-ban treaty.

When I first heard about Ursula Franklin, I think she was called Director of Research for the Voice of Women. A professor at the U of T, her reputation as a scientist and teacher grew steadily. She was and is consulted and quoted frequently by individuals and by government.

She has, thank goodness, always been available and ready to give advice and help, and her patience and practical advice seem inexhaustible. 'Let's see what Ursula thinks' is often heard amongst VOW members, who are thankful that she has so often spoken on our behalf.

As well as the baby-teeth project, Ursula was responsible for landmark statements and briefs such as those on the involvement of Canadian manufacturing in US military production, Canada's nuclear-power production, and many aspects of feminism and technology. Her paper 'The Effects of Canada's Defence Production Sharing Arrangements on Canadian Foreign Policy' has drawn attention to the collaboration between Canada and the United States, as well as the profound effect of the US on Canada's policies and economy. She showed how military manufacturing arrangements have locked Canada into the ever-increasing militarization of the economies and policies of both countries.

Ursula was awarded the Dawson Medal of the Royal Society of Canada which is given for bringing together two disciplines in scientific work. (Of the three people to receive the award since it was established, she is the only woman.) This, of course, is only one of more than a dozen awards and degrees she has been given. In 1989, she was invited to give the Massey Lectures – her admiration for Brough and his work led her to follow his example and name her lecture 'The Real World of Technology,' and she gave him a moving tribute in the opening lecture.

Another popular campaign that began in the sixties is VOW's campaign against war toys and violence on television, children's shows in particular. This has paralleled our efforts towards disarmament and opposition to all forms of nuclear weapons, violence, and war, including war in space. Preparation for and threats of war are all part of this horror. At one time, Eaton's had fourteen pages of war-toy ads in its Christmas catalogue. Women all over the continent tore out the pages and mailed them back with a few well-chosen words – and no purchase orders. During the height of the campaign in the 1960s, a mother dashed into our Calgary toy convenor's living-room. 'One of our kids was playing with a war toy, and he's scratched his ear.' 'Wounded by a war toy!' exclaimed the convenor, 'What a headline! Quick, smear ketchup on his face and take a picture – we'll rush it to the press!'

One positive effect of this campaign is the promotion and support of toy firms manufacturing and promoting constructive and non-violent toys. Women leafleted street corners and picketed stores. When the

Lionel toy company had a Christmas ad in *The New Yorker* which read, 'This train does not shoot, kill, or stab. It just goes round and round its track,' the peaceful point had been well and truly made. But there is still a long way to go before violent films and TV cartoons and shows are curbed, although their influence in promoting violence has been proved again and again. As well, hundreds of letters appealing to the CBC not to discontinue the children's show 'Butternut Square' resulted in over twenty years of 'Mr Dressup,' the award-winning non-violent children's delight. This show produced a whole generation of young fans for Judy Lawrence's puppets Casey and Finnegan and Ernie Coombs' 'Mr Dressup.'

For a while, maybe ten years, peace women decided that promoting peace and opposing war were more important than the emphasis on oppression of women, day care, equal pay, and the rest of the concerns of the women's liberation movement. Meanwhile, the 'women's lib-bers' were immersed in day-to-day crises, providing women's centres and services and campaigning for change. By the 1980s, all these objectives were seen to be a part of the whole, with environmental issues requiring as much attention as the arms race. What we have been saying for decades, that military budgets take money from 'equal-ity, development and peace' (the watchwords of the Decade for Women), is finally out in the open, and governments know that the electors know it.

Indeed, we now have new respect for the foresight of the women who wrote VOW's objectives and constitution emphasizing the power of non-violence, the value of cooperation, opposition to military alli-ances and to threats of force, and the responsibility of women to take part in decision-making. With the thinking and development of the women's movement we have become more explicit in defining the patriarchal system and militarization of our society, which lies at the base of many of the problems we face today. What is encouraging is that the public, the unofficial opposition, is now recognizing and speaking up about it.

None the less, membership in VOW dropped significantly. VOW reached its peak membership within a couple of years of starting up, though estimates vary from 6000 to 10,000. From the beginning, VOW had attracted women from many different backgrounds and interests. Although many were trained as professionals, the great majority were housewives with young children. One of VOW's strong points was the means it provided for women with time but little money, often tied to their homes and children, to *do* something constructive and effective. Indeed, a favourite flyer of VOW's, 'What Can One Person DO?,' set out all sorts of ideas and information about how to write letters, interview officials, and so on. Taking action in connection with other women lessened feelings of isolation and made the weight of women's concerns felt in the places where decisions were being made.

Sometimes this was disruptive of home life. Some men, coming home to find children parked with the neighbours and a note saying, 'Hot dogs in fridge. Please bath Johnny. There'll be 20 women stuffing envelopes at 8. Love, B,' found it a bit hard to cope with. Though the women were increasingly involved, effective, and happy, some men just couldn't take this unconventional, independent type of wife, and some separations and divorces ensued. Others, finding that the 'little woman' was off interviewing the local MP, simply got on with the household chores, forming what we called the men's auxiliary.

I have a letter from Betty Nickerson in Winnipeg that begins, 'I'm writing this the morning after a long, exhausting annual meeting. I should, of course, be at work removing the debris of a household left in the custody of three children and a husband.' But she goes on to add, 'I'll go to my meeting with a notebook filled with upwards of 50 ideas to extend and strengthen our work in many directions ... I wanted you to know these things because you are part of that strength. But now, adieu. I have two days' dishes to wash, and then I'll phone my friend up the street. She should be in Voice of Women too.'

It's true that there were some resignations during the first two years on ideological grounds, because of conflicts of interest, like Mrs Pearson, or because VOW was supposed to be 'too radical' or under communist influence. And after these first hurdles, membership declined because women who had learned all kinds of skills in VOW turned their attention to other causes: the women's movement, specific campaigns, Chile, Quebec, and later Vietnam, draft-resisters and refugees. But above all, VOW members, even while they had young children, joined the workforce.

In 1961, 65 per cent of Canadian families were headed by a married couple only one of whom held a salaried job. Like many other women, after I was married, I gave up my paid work and everything subsequently was voluntary work, other than payment for attending Ontario Physio Board meetings and, rarely, for writing an article or for being on television. By 1985, the picture had changed: a mere 16 per cent of couples had only one partner in gainful employment; in most couples, both partners worked for pay. The percentage of women in the work-force had increased enormously.

This completely changed the numbers available for volunteer work and has affected all those organizations run by volunteers, including VOW and the peace movement, as well as the women's and later the environmental organizations. They could no longer depend on day-time hours from women with children at school or looking after babies at home. Not only are there no longer the volunteers for attending day-time meetings, staffing the office, and licking the stamps for mailings, but creative and policy-making positions now have to be paid for or performed by volunteers outside their working hours.

In addition, the number of voluntary-service and socially oriented groups has enormously increased. In 1961 and even as late as 1971, there were no or very few groups working to better the situation of women. Now we have these and also many special committees to support Third World countries and medical concerns such as Alzheimer's and MS (multiple sclerosis), as well as ratepayers' and neighbourhood groups, and they all have called on women particularly to help with their work. Many women who had never joined any group before VOW are now working actively in two or more organizations and hold memberships in several others.

These groups fill important needs, some of which should be the responsibility of governments. Many provide the groundwork for what subsequently becomes a government agency. Others are formed specifically for pressuring reluctant community or government authorities. Many of these situations have led women into entering the political arena. I believe that more women than men follow this route, because women want to see social change, whereas men tend to see politics as an enticing career. So we see former members of VOW currently in politics and in positions where they hope to influence public policy.

Looking back on thirty years with the Voice of Women, I have been reading reports and talking with new members and old friends. The enthusiasm, ingenuity, and energy that VOW members put into their actions is reflected in many verbal and written accounts from and about early VOW groups. I realize how new and exciting the organization was for women in 1960. Very few had been involved in political and social action of this kind. Certainly, there had been the suffragists, organizations of business, union, and farm women, Women's Institutes, and so on, but VOW was dealing with powerful national and international forces, indeed with the whole patriarchal system which dominates our lives. An extract from the statement of the VOW 1985 Halifax conference sums it up: 'Militarism is an addiction that distorts human development, causing worldwide poverty, starvation, pollution, repression, torture, and death ... We reject a world based on domination, exploitation, patriarchy, racism, and sexism. We demand a new order based on justice and the equitable distribution of the world's resources.'

VOW (with a strong push from Moira Armour) got me into the women's movement, feminism, and politics. My continuing thanks go to VOW and the Voices for all this and for the lifelong friends they have given me.

13

Women's Liberation

In the late 1960s, there were no advisory councils or committees on the status of women, no NAC, no 'Minister Responsible.' There were no women's centres, rape crisis services, or interval houses, no women's counselling or health services, and few consciousness-raising groups. *Ms Magazine* and other publications were yet to emerge. Words such as abortion, affirmative action, harassment, assertiveness, and lesbian were almost unknown or at least were never mentioned. *Chatelaine*, under Doris Anderson, was getting attention, not all favourable, by discussing some of these topics and by asking why so few women entered the political field.

Women in the peace and civil-rights movements were beginning to see their roles in these movements as subservient, and they were becoming dissatisfied. Groups of women came together to talk about their situation, to hear each other's stories, and to discuss action. Many women discovered that they could talk to each other instead of competing for the attention of men or devoting their lives to looking after the needs of men and children. They began to think about women as sisters, not rivals. Sisterhood is powerful, they discovered. In 1970, the first national women's liberation conference was held in Saskatoon.

At meetings, everyone was very polite and 'sisterly,' hearing each other out with no interruptions. When, on one occasion, a couple of men wanted to observe, they were politely told that it was for women only. There were, however, many subsequent debates about this policy and some interesting meetings ensued. I remember one time when a group of couples had gathered for a discussion. Linda Ryan Nye suggested they meet again, sitting the women together in a circle with the men listening from outside the circle without interrupting. Some of the women had not spoken to each other before, but after a few minutes they were airing all kinds of subjects, from husbands to health, sex, children, and discrimination. The men's minds were boggled. Some wished they could do the same thing – and recently some men have been trying to do just that.

I used to sit in on some of the bigger meetings held by women around the U of T campus. I usually went with one of my contemporaries, since we were about thirty years older than most of the participants. I was not particularly good at consciousness-raising. My friend Vi Thompson later remembered: 'We attended consciousness-raising groups where women talked about their personal experiences of sexism. You were silent when it was your turn to speak. You havered. "No. Not me. Go to the next person." I remember your face, bright, interested, but somehow embarrassed, pushing the matter away. Why? Didn't you feel any sex discrimination? I didn't, so I talked about how it feels to be on the lowest rung of the social order. But we were both there knowing that women were not treated equally.'

But, though I was quiet in meetings, I too was having to think about sex roles and conditioning and the effect they had on my life. I mentioned earlier how naïve we physiotherapy students were and how Brough and I relied on our good friends to help us give parental advice to our offspring. In addition to my slow awareness of sexuality, my education was slow in other areas too.

Members of the British middle class were (are) snobbish about feeling superior to the working class. When I was growing up, we despised the 'board school' children, with their accents and untidy clothes, because that was the attitude we learned from family and friends. We knew few Jews or Catholics, but since we saw them as middle-class, we accepted them more or less as equals, and I knew nothing of racial discrimination as such until I came to Canada. When I started work in Montreal, one of my colleagues had a sister who lived in Washington, and she gave me a lesson in the danger one might run into if confronted by black men. I was impressed but had no relevant experience.

Another colleague talked about Jews in a disparaging way, as being somehow different from and inferior to us, but since, again, I had little experience, this didn't impress me very much. I must have absorbed some of the attitudes and disparaging talk unwittingly, however, because Val and I, sometime in 1939 or 1940, went for a weekend to New York to stay with a couple of delightful young men we'd met on the Laurentian ski slopes. As the weekend went on, we couldn't understand their growing alienation and coolness until after we had returned to Montreal and one of them wrote us a letter. We had by our conversation shown them our anti-semitic attitudes. He explained in his letter, 'You see, I am a Jew.' Both Val and I were totally devastated, horrified at ourselves and the hurt we had inflicted, unknowingly. They did later forgive us and became good friends with Val when she lived in the United States.

Along with other subjects that were either unmentioned or unmentionable in my family and those of my friends was homosexuality. There were famous cases, such as Oscar Wilde's, which were generally deplored and probably avidly read about, but homosexuality (male, of course) was one of those things Not Done in the best circles though it could be passed over if the proponents were talented artists or actors. I had all the stereotypical reactions of one brought up assuming heterosexuality was the normal state and homosexuals were queer oddballs and a bit scary.

However, I remember from my high-school days how many of the teachers paired up with other women on friendly and affectionate grounds, and perhaps I was the naïve one. This was after the First World War when thousands of husbands and potential mates had been massacred, so in our communities there were many professional women on their own who shared homes and may or may not have been sexually attracted to their partners. I remember, much later, hotly debating with a lesbian friend the possibility of two women living together without a sexual relationship. I thought it quite possible, given my own and other English women's inexperience of sexuality. My friend couldn't believe such circumstances could exist.

I didn't get into discussions like that until a long time after I was a student. But I do remember my intensely affectionate and potentially lesbian (I suppose) relations with my inseparable friend Beth, and how our mothers worried about us spending so much time in our bedrooms discussing who knows what for endless hours. I was sent to Paris during one Easter holiday period, ostensibly to learn French, but essentially to get me away from Beth for a month. I spent a great deal of time writing daily letters to her. I wish I knew what they contained as it might give me a clue about what we felt.

For me, there was a long, slow process of getting to know many lesbian and gay people and making many wonderful friends. I was helped a great deal by getting to know so many of Susan's friends, dancers and others, and my friends in the women's movement. It was a very long time since those schoolgirl hand-holding days before I felt any sexual attraction for another woman. I can still remember the moment. Much of this went along with the growing awareness of women and their potential power to change things.

For a long time I clung to the conviction that a married woman who had a relationship with another woman wasn't really being 'unfaithful' to her husband. When I learned that my husband had occasionally shown that sometimes he was attracted to other young men, I was immensely relieved. This state of affairs (no pun intended) was normal and comforting. I discovered that old friends had faced this kind of situation and coped with it. I now have the conviction that my lesbian friends knew far more about my attitudes and feelings than I did myself, and treated me with a good deal of tolerance and understanding. What I have come to believe is that we can all, women and men, be attracted to both men and women and that no one is locked into one or the other role.

By 1977, I was writing, in an article in the October *Chatelaine*:

When I say that some of my best friends are men, I must also admit that most of my best friends are women. When I go on to say about men that I wouldn't want my daughter to marry one, I should also add, at least until the present legal system ceases to regard a woman as a man's dependent, not because of the housekeeping and childcare service but simply because of her sex. I must also make it clear that I am as happy to see my children living with members of the opposite sex as I would be if they were living with members of the same sex. That is their choice, and I am delighted if they find a partner, or a group of people, with whom they can live happily and compatibly.

My marriage worked well, but only because we had always considered marriage a partnership. By the time I got married, in 1943, my ten years as a physiotherapist had changed me from a naïve English schoolgirl into an independent Canadian woman who was beginning to be socially conscious. Brough and I pooled our finances, which were available for separate or joint needs, with few differences of opinion. Responsibility was mutual, chores were shared, each had areas of special expertise. I concluded the *Chatelaine* article: 'I wouldn't want any couple to be denied the delight of marriage. Marriage can be the most fulfilling and satisfying and creative human experience, provided that both partners understand the hazards and combat them.'

So all this mental and emotional turmoil was going on in the late sixties and into the eighties, and I'm still working things out, slow learner that I am. I get worried about intolerance towards lesbians and gay men, yet can still feel uncomfortable at too much public display of affection between individuals of either or both sexes. Perhaps it's still the British 'don't show your feelings' edict, which has plagued me for years.

Whether it was due to the consciousness-raising or whatever, things began to happen all over the country. At the time of VOW's 1964 annual meeting in Banff, Robert Pritty, an MP from BC, was introducing a bill in the House of Commons to have the Criminal Code changed to permit the advertising and sale of contraceptives. VOW passed a resolution urging the passage of this bill, from which VOW's Quebec delegation, being predominantly Catholic, abstained. However, several Quebec delegates told us they personally were on the recently introduced birth-control pill, and, at the following AGM in Ottawa, it was the Quebec delegation who introduced our resolution on the grounds of human rights and a woman's right to choose.

Women staged a sit-in at Hart House, U of T, against its men-only policy; beauty competitions were questioned (noisily); in night-time raids, advertisements were labelled SEXIST. The most successful campaign was against the Benson and Hedges 'The Longer, the Better' ad, which showed a woman displaying long nylon-clad legs being ogled from a man-hole by a leering construction worker. This ad was actually cancelled by the company, which was said to have cost them $60,000. At McGill University in 1968, two medical students produced the *Birth Control Handbook*. By the time the Criminal Code was changed in 1969 (amendments introduced by Pierre Trudeau as Minister of Justice), two million copies had been sold.

Altogether, there were various significant developments pointing to the need for investigating the situation. Increasing numbers of feminist books such as Germaine Greer's *The Female Eunuch*, and US President Kennedy's women's commission, all focused on the current situation of women, and it seemed time to look at how Canadian women saw themselves.

14

NAC, Part One

In 1966, Laura Sabia, at the end of her term as president of the University Women's Club, called a meeting of the leaders of a number of national women's organizations to discuss the status of women in Canada. They were to consider the situation of Canadian women and establish whether, as they suspected, women were in fact being treated as second-class citizens.

I was still president of the Voice of Women at the time, and we were involved in the situation in Vietnam as well as preparing for a centennial international women's peace conference. But when Moira Armour, always alert to new happenings in women's activities, phoned me to say she thought this would be an important meeting for VOW to attend, we went along. She was right, of course. This was the second time in my life (the first being my meeting with Helen Tucker) when I felt that an occasion was somehow significant. It was the first time I had seen Laura Sabia in action. It was a landmark meeting, and led to the demand for a royal commission on the status of women.

The meeting was held in the basement of the University Women's Club on St George Street in Toronto. We found there about twenty women, with Laura in the chair, and Helen Tucker acting as secretary. We met women representing the National Council of Women, the YWCA, the United Church Women, Business and Professional Women's Clubs (known to us as the Bs and Ps), the Catholic Women's League, the Imperial Order Daughters of the Empire (IODE), the Federation of Women Teachers' Associations of Ontario (FWTAO), and several others. These women were part of the group which became the Committee on Equality for Women, later the National Ad Hoc Committee on the Status of Women, then finally NAC, the National Action Committee on the Status of Women.

Laura called the meeting together, and we discussed the signs and symptoms we could see in society, with examples of discrimination on the basis of sex: differences in pay, in promotions, in the family, in law, and so on. Many women could speak from personal experience, but no one felt we had enough information to start any kind of campaign for improving the status of women without more facts. Various ideas were suggested, and the best seemed to be to call on the government to set up a royal commission.

A small group, including well-known lawyer Margaret Hyndman, Peg McLellan of the Bs and Ps, Harriet Christie of United Church Women, and Dorothy Martin (FWTAO) got in touch with government leaders, and the committee's brief calling for a commission was presented to the Justice Minister in November 1966.

When the press asked Laura Sabia what she would do if the request was not granted, she jokingly replied, 'Oh, I expect we'll march a million women to Ottawa.' The next morning, to her horror, there were the headlines: A Million Women To March On Ottawa. Nevertheless, it was not too long before Prime Minister Pearson announced the Royal Commission on the Status of Women (RCSW), to be chaired by Florence Bird, better known as writer and radio commentator Anne Francis, and referred to by the press and in the government terms of reference as Mrs John Bird (remember, this was 1967.)

One of the Commission's most active members, and later the continuing architect of NAC's organization, was Elsie Gregory MacGill. Canada's first woman aeronautical engineer, she had designed the wartime Hurricane fighter plane, and she was still a leading member of the Bs and Ps. Elsie worked tirelessly on the hearings, travelling all over the country with her crutches or wheelchair (needed because of the disability caused by poliomyelitis earlier in her life). She played a major role in writing the Commission's report, which is still an important milestone in women's progress in this country.

Three other women and two men made up the Commission, with Monique Bégin, later to become a Liberal cabinet minister, as secretary. They travelled from coast to coast, listening to women from all walks of life, as well as commissioning many studies and reports. The organization providing most briefs and statements was the Voice of Women. Members described women's experiences from outposts in

Newfoundland to farms in Alberta. Ella Manuel wrote about the women of Trout Creek, near her home in Newfoundland, of their hard lives and their need for more education and social services. This was said to have made the women in the isolated area somewhat resentful, since, whatever their struggles, they didn't like to see themselves as needy. In Edmonton, Betty Mardiros and Nellie Peterson, two women who both led lives in which they shared burdens and rewards as equal partners with their husbands, finished having dinner one evening, and Betty said, 'Tony and Roy, you do the dishes; Nellie and I have to write the Royal Commission about how deprived we are!'

In all, the Commission received 469 briefs and some 1000 letters, heard 890 witnesses, visited 14 cities, including Whitehorse, Yellowknife, Churchill, and four settlements in the Keewatin district. They completed their report in 1970, and it was tabled in the House of Commons that December. The report was extensively read by women all over Canada, who studied and circulated it. Provincial status-of-women groups sprang up across the country.

Sharp-eyed Ontario women examined the 167 recommendations as they applied to provincial legislation, and in 1971 the newly formed Ontario Committee on the Status of Women (OCSW) began to meet. I joined them for actions, and for their regular meetings which were often held in Lorna Marsden's home. I felt I played a very minor part in their activities, but I realize now that, with many of my friends, I spent quite a bit of time in OCSW activities. The talents of the women involved were phenomenal. We held forums, lectures, and conferences. We supported striking women at Dare, Radio Shack, Fleck, Puretex, and Blue Cross. We lobbied for changes in laws affecting matrimonial property, citizenship, and equal pay. We protested sexist advertisements, displays, and beauty contests, lobbied against men-only policies, and monitored the media. From 1971 to 1981, OCSW produced 33 briefs, 31 leaflets, and 27 newsletters to keep members informed and active. And let us not forget the hilarious OCSW Follies, where remarkably accurate impersonations of our politicians were mixed with hilarious comments on their behaviour, and we awarded the Harriet Martineau Ear Trumpet Award (motto: Am I Hearing This?) for outstanding sexist statements, which were obligingly provided for us by politicians and other public figures.

While all this was going on, we were still awaiting the government's response to the Royal Commission report. In spite of the growing public awareness of women' rights, the report was almost completely ignored by Prime Minister Trudeau. Towards the end of 1971, women were getting tired of the silence. Still led by Laura Sabia, the Committee on Equality reorganized as the National Ad Hoc Committee on the Status of Women. The women studied the Commission's report and started placing priorities on the 167 recommendations. They picked out seven or eight of the most urgent recommendations the Commission had made at the federal level. They commented on and supported recommendations on equal pay, abortion, child care, and other matters. The Committee called meetings and obtained approval from member groups to take their statement to Ottawa. Their Ottawa presentation ended with a request for federal money to hold a conference to study and recommend on the whole report in detail.

To our surprise, this request was granted. The province added some money too, and the Ad Hoc Committee (Thérèse Casgrain always said 'haddock committee') set about organizing Strategies for Change. Chaired by Laura Sabia, the conference was held in Toronto at the King Edward Hotel in the spring of 1972, and seven hundred women came to Toronto from all over Canada. The National Ad Hoc Committee on the Status of Women dropped the 'ad hoc' from its name; this was to be no ad hoc committee.

The conference was exciting and stimulating and was recorded by Moira Armour in her film *Strategies for Change* made at her own expense. Among the well-known women were Helen Tucker, Muriel Duckworth, Madeleine Parent of the Canadian Textile and Chemical Union (she and Laura had gone to the same convent), and many others. Moira and Judy Lawrence coached Rita MacNeil for her first major public appearance – Rita overcame her nervousness, and her audience loved her. Liberal party member Jan Steele spoke of how hard it is for women working in the established party structure. Thérèse Casgrain mentioned her nine attempts to get elected and the years of struggle before Quebec women got the vote; her watchword 'I desire peace, and I've been fighting all my life' was greeted enthusiastically. RCSW member Florence Bird reported herself 'deeply moved' by the progress that was being made. New Feminists member and sculptor Maryon Kantaroff warned us not to make the mistake of aping men and not to sacrifice our principles to expediency. 'Don't let fear take over,' she urged, 'If you know you're right, then fight for the right. And please fight!'

There was an incredible mixture of main-line women's organizations and radical 'women's libbers' groups. These latter sat up half the night compiling a list of complaints about the organization of the conference, which can be found on page 23 of the Strategies for Change report. I sat in on some of their discussions and saw Madeleine Parent there too, but we both decided we were too tired and went to bed before they had finished.

The next day they (the radical women's caucus) picked Charlotte McEwen to make their report to the plenary session after the regular resolutions had been dealt with. A good choice: nothing will stop Charlotte. Even when told over and over that her time was up, she still clung to the microphone. Finally, we all applauded so long that we drowned her words and she had to stop. I was sitting between Helen Tucker and Muriel Duckworth, both of whom had already had experiences with Charlotte in VOW. Muriel was practically in tears because VOW's reputation was at stake, and I nearly had to restrain Helen from rushing up to the platform and dragging Charlotte off bodily. It was all very entertaining for the onlookers.

But the discussion ranged over a wide area: Should there be a women's political party? Should a council be established to continue the work of the Commission? Should we protest Mr Trudeau's appearing at the Men's Press Club, when he had declined our invitation? Can we support women in the armed forces? Do we want to fight for women to get into an exploitative system? Are we asking for the right things?

Throughout the conference, Elsie MacGill, who later designed and organized the system by which NAC's annual resolutions can be consolidated and catalogued, worked solidly on addressing the resolutions. She had been one of the strongest feminist powers in the Commission, and she knew what was important. I remember that Elsie and psychology professor Esther Greenglass then guided the plenary session through the recommendations made by the Royal Commission and the resolutions coming from the conference itself. As far as I can remember, the only one that the delegates could not agree on was the one recommending the establishment of advisory councils. Opinions differed on whether these would act as a cushion between the government and the pressures from women or whether they could serve a useful role in providing research and support for women's needs. There have been occasions when both these predictions have come true.

It is interesting to note the ten issues raised by NAC in its first presentation to the federal government: day care; family planning; divorce; immigration; citizenship; women under criminal law (prostitution and vagrancy); appointments to boards and commissions; equal pay (this was already stipulated in Convention 100 of the International Labour

Organization, which was already twenty years old, but Canada did not sign the Convention until later that year); inclusion of 'sex' and 'marital status' in human-rights codes; federal status-of-women council.

NAC's demands on the abortion question, indeed Elsie MacGill's separate recommendation in the RCSW report, that abortion be completely decriminalized, could have been written today. When the pro-choice stand of NAC had become clear, the Catholic Women's League withdrew, but apart from one other withdrawal (the Fédération des femmes du Québec resigned over a procedural dispute at the 1981 annual meeting, but they only stayed out for a year), I do not think any other groups have resigned on policy grounds, unless this has happened recently.

Coming from my work with Voice of Women, I was used to operating with a world perspective, and it wasn't until Laura Sabia and status-of-women questions came on the scene that I had to change gears and revise my approach. Laura was very knowledgeable, very bright, and quick to grasp and respond to situations and problems. She was cheerful, outspoken, and fearless, just the person for putting women on the map. She made good copy for the press – witness the mythical march of a million women to Ottawa – and she knew how to get on with politicians.

So NAC embarked on this new voyage, with Laura at the helm, until she was scooped up, first for the federal Advisory Council and then by Ontario to head its Status of Women Council. She did an excellent job, methodically taking up the necessary issues, subjecting them to public scrutiny, getting laws changed when she could, and passing on to the next item. The changes in Ontario's matrimonial property laws resulted from Laura's digging the Law Reform Commission out of its long-term comfortable hole and forcing it and the government into action.

In the early days of NAC, while Laura was still president, FWTAO, the Federation of Women Teachers' Associations of Ontario, was of considerable benefit to the organization. All the office work and reproduction of documents was undertaken by Dorothy Martin and her colleagues, particularly Kay Sigurjonsson who took care of publicity and public relations.

In 1974, when Laura was appointed chair of what is now the Ontario Advisory Council on Women's Issues, Grace Hartman took over as president of NAC. Helen Tucker kept the records straight, and Aline Gregory, treasurer for the 1972 NAC conference, continued as treasurer. I also remember federal civil servant Freda Paltiel, and later Katie Cooke, president of the federal Advisory Council, visiting NAC for discussions and combined actions on women's issues. Grace remembers wage and price control being a big issue for NAC during her term of office. At the AGM, Madeleine Parent had made a forceful and eloquent speech against the legislation as being detrimental to women.

Grace performed a holding operation from Ottawa, where she was secretary-treasurer of CUPE and preparing to try for the presidency there. She used to come in to Toronto to chair our somewhat disorganized executive meetings. For the first few years of its existence, NAC's executive-committee members tended to represent either the established women's groups or the growing number of Status of Women committees. (Grace was one of the few union women.) A more varied representation followed as member groups and government funding grew. This funding allowed delegates from outside the Toronto-Montreal-Ottawa triangle to attend meetings. Having executive members from as far afield as the Yukon and Newfoundland, from prairie farms, women's centres, and other varied backgrounds, gave a better perspective and increased the number of issues and problems for NAC's attention.

From my point of view, NAC's increasingly diverse membership gave me a wonderful chance to learn about and understand the difficulties and situations facing women in very different circumstances from my own. Young women trying to find money for training, education, and housing while supporting themselves and sometimes a whole family made it very clear what a struggle they faced if they wanted to contribute to improving women's status. Many could serve on the executive for only one year and even that entailed sacrifices for their families and careers.

But in fact we did not spend a great deal of time talking about family life, and one could go for quite some time without knowing much about a woman's age, work, family, or background. I remember, some time later, an executive meeting where one member was sketching in her somewhat colourful and nomadic family background, including the fact that her three children were at home being cared for by the current house-husband. Her story boggled the mind of one of our more conventional members, who drew me aside in wonderment to ask, 'Does this happen to many of our members?' I said that this was perhaps a bit unusual, and that my own background was pretty routine. We agreed that it was a very useful and 'broadening' experience to work on the NAC executive.

By 1975, it was generally thought that it was time for a change of executive. There had been preliminary talks, and I had struck a bargain with Helen Tucker, who had been secretary since the beginning. I was (again) considered 'a dangerous radical,' and I persuaded Helen that neither of us would stand for office when NAC met in Winnipeg that summer. Lorna Marsden took over as president, with OCSW's Cathy Morrison as secretary. Lorna had been the first woman appointed to the board of Air Canada. At the same time the equilibrium of the staid board members was shattered by the appointment of the first Jewish person, a man who, to Lorna's delight, turned up wearing a velvet jacket and bow-tie. A woman and a Jew at the same time was almost too much for the grey suits of the day.

With the election of Lorna Marsden in 1975, NAC had had as president a prominent member of each of the three major political parties. Laura subsequently ran as a Conservative candidate in the 1981 federal by-election; Grace, as president of a large union, was closely allied to the New Democratic Party; and Lorna, from being a vice-president of the Liberal Party, was appointed to the Senate by Prime Minister Trudeau in 1984.

In the fall of 1975, NAC was about three years old, and we were established in a rather dusty office on the main floor, rear end, of St Paul's Church on Avenue Road in Toronto, the home at that time of a number of struggling groups devoting their efforts to promoting human rights, peace, and social justice. We paid a minimal rent, since our financial resources were very limited, and we employed a part-time secretary who held the organization together. When Ruth Herman Chud announced that she was going back to law school, NAC advertised for someone to take her place. Pearl Blazer was chosen by the search committee and moved into the scantily furnished, noisy, friendly environment she shared with visiting mice and the occasional pigeon that wandered in through the open door. The office contained left-over and donated furniture, a not-so-new typewriter, and a filing cabinet. Xerox machines and electronic equipment were unknown in our organization, and our files and record books were embryonic. Lorna maintains that the role the telephone played in the women's movement was, and is, a major one, and cites Elsie's daily calls when she (Lorna) was president of NAC. I too remember the value I placed on the calls of both Elsie and Lorna when I succeeded Lorna as president. Lorna remembers Brough answering the phone and patiently asking, 'Are you a Voice or a NACer?'

Lorna was a very good president for NAC: well organized, friendly, diplomatic, and very efficient. Pearl used to marvel at her having drafted and delivered all the mail and documents for typing before she went off each day to teach at the university. NAC itself wasn't that developed and organized, and when it came to the annual meeting, I remember Lorna in the chair, trying to cope with resolutions presented at the last minute, verbally or on scruffy bits of paper. Remember, NAC's membership had grown from 40 to 140 member groups in a year or two.

With Lorna's and Pearl's efficiency, NAC began to expand, to get its act together, and to become much more of a representative national organization than it had been able to manage previously. Increasing funding meant that Wendy Williams from St John's and Ruth Bell from Ottawa were no longer our only two outside-Toronto executive members, attending meetings when they could afford the trip or piggyback a meeting with some other commitment.

Lorna was president during International Women's Year, when all sorts of things were going on. This was the year of the International Congress in Mexico City where Canadian women brought up the case of Jeannette Lavell, who had lost her Indian status under the Indian Act by marrying a white man (this case later went to the International Court of Justice). It was at this conference, too, that Mary Two-Axe Early spoke of the plight of Canadian native women and, ironically, herself received the news that she had been evicted from her own reserve for marrying a non-Indian.

In 1976, we held our first national annual meeting in Ottawa and began our annual lobbying of cabinet ministers. The evening before the meeting proper, we met with parliamentary assistant Robert Kaplan, sent by his minister, Marc Lalonde, to answer questions posed by the assembled women. Pensions for homemakers was one of the burning issues, and this puzzled Mr Kaplan greatly. 'But,' he said, 'housewives don't work.' We met with him at the hotel where we were staying, a less than elegant establishment, chosen for its affordable prices. I remember Lorna standing in the lobby to greet arrivals. She was intrigued to see one respectable gentleman dropping off his IODE-type wife for the NAC meeting in this less-than-impeccable venue which, from the look on his face, he already knew better than his wife did!

Having as president an influential member of the Liberal Party made things easier for our budding organization, but it gave us no additional clout if Marc Lalonde or John Munro refused to accept our beautifully reasoned recommendations. We held workshops, we elected a far-flung executive and, after a chaotic process of debate, we passed a number of important resolutions. The individual responsible on this occasion for all the organization of support services, the agendas, everything from name tags and ballots to travel cheques, was Pearl Blazer. No one counted working hours. She was just there all the time.

By 1977, Pearl's niece Maxine Hermolin became a permanent and invaluable part-time staff member, and we actually got around to discussing staff salaries, holidays, and raises. Then in 1978, a young woman, relatively fresh from New Zealand and very diffident at first, came in from the typing pool to help out as an office temp. She got hooked very quickly and soon became Pearl's right hand and a general support for all the executive members, each one of whom tended to consider her own letters and reports the most important piece of work the staff must address. That diffident young woman was Janet Port.

Increased operational funding was received from the Department of the Secretary of State. During the following years, with committees beginning to function on a regular basis and the executive coming together more frequently, the work expanded, the office moved and increased its space, and the staff increased to three part-time workers who managed to accomplish the amount of work usually undertaken by a large corporation.

At the beginning of 1977, I was being sounded out as to whether I would be a suitable successor for Lorna. Presumably, after two years, either I was less radical or NAC was more so. I remember a meeting in Halifax, which must have been a CRIAW meeting or some 'consultation,' because I was cornered (was it in Muriel's house at a party?) by Lorenne Clark and Lynn McDonald. They asked me about policy and my 'intentions' for NAC. I had the impression that this was to be an interim period. Maybe this is hindsight, but that is the memory I have.

15

NAC, Part Two

Ten years after ending my presidency of VOW, I became president of NAC. It felt quite familiar to be signing letters and talking to the press again, and of course I had Pearl, then Maxine, then Janet too, in the office. I abused them, wasted their time, and worked them to death, but we had fun and wonderful experiences. Maxine's number-three baby was a frequent visitor. The staff vividly recalls my having baby on knee while arranging appointments with MPs, and lawyer Mary Eberts, then on the executive, used to leave her daughter Alex sitting on the table when she had a nearby appointment. ('I taught you to say "yellow,"' said OCSW's Lee Grills, when she was later reintroduced to a sophisticated nine-year-old young woman.)

In fact, through all the changes – office moves, expansion, reorganization, and the incredible increase in workload – our staff members, Pearl, Maxine, and Jan have been the rocks on which coming and going presidents and executive members have learned to depend, often to exploit, and above all to love. As one of the worst exploiters and most unorganized of their trials and tribulations, I can say this with affection. I want to thank them, and all our past and present volunteers. Over the years they have built up our confidence and strength and have given time and effort far beyond anything that was expected. They have built NAC and the women's movement on a mixture of devotion, efficiency, and love which we, the lucky ones, have experienced, and for which we are abundantly grateful.

The *Status of Women News* had been started by Moira Armour in 1973. She had managed to assemble material, devise illustrations, do layout, and print the publication as a volunteer, one-woman project. In 1977, I started writing an interim message between newsletters which became the *MEMO*, a summary of recent developments, announcements, and suggestions for action. This was mimeographed at first, later photocopied, and eventually printed.

Around this time, some of us started having the coffee parties which eventually, under the next president, formally became the Friends of NAC. NAC was an organization of member groups, and the Friends was established as a way for individual women to get involved. It also provided an opportunity for fund-raising, since we were again discussing the pros and cons of government funding.

The debate about government funding was a hot one during NAC's early years, and it still continues today in NAC and many other women's groups. Some members believed that the organization would tend to compromise itself by being beholden to the government and thus possibly swayed by government policies. Others were convinced that women had every right to use taxpayers' money – their own money – for furthering the rights and progress of women and for other social causes. NAC received government money for the first conference in 1972, and again in 1975 to hold its AGM in Winnipeg instead of Toronto. Until 1984, government funding contributed substantially to NAC's growth and progress, and to public awareness of women's needs.

Since 1984 there has been steady reduction in government funding, not only to women but to every voluntary social-action agency, to research, education, housing, and health, and to most of the efforts being made by native people and other citizens to improve their lives. As a consequence, all these groups have had to emphasize their fund-raising efforts, which has used up campaigning energy and, in some cases, led groups to distort or disguise their objectives and work in order to conform with the criteria for getting grants or charitable status. This reduction in government funding was a part of the move to the right which grew more marked as the 1980s came to an end. NAC has documented this trend in its 'Rise of the Right' paper and in its parallel report to the government's 1988 UN Status of Women report.

One of the things I most enjoyed as president was travelling around Canada talking about NAC and women's concerns and incidentally having a wonderful time. I learned a great deal about how NAC's member groups operated. We all faced the same problems: funding; finding volunteers; helping women with legal, job, family, and other problems. Women suffer from isolation in cities as well as in rural communities. The services and counselling that can be offered by a large city women's centre, such as that provided by the Vancouver Status of Women Council, are needed not only in Vancouver but also in smaller towns such as Prince George, Nanaimo, or Nelson. The life of women's centres was often short, usually because of funding cuts. To counter these and other problems, women needed to know the techniques for political action. This prompted the Whitehorse group to set up a workshop with a discussion leader from the Prince George centre.

In Terrace, BC, the Status of Women Committee was well established in the community. Some women had run for municipal office and been elected, and all had gained experience in working in and observing the political process. One of their successful projects was setting up a child-minding service in town, so that women could have a few hours free. In contrast, many of the women at the Victoria Faulkner Women's Centre in Whitehorse had lived in the Yukon only a short time. They worked in traditional jobs, but also on construction projects, as fire-fighters or members of road gangs, and in the media.

Up north, in the Territories, one got a feeling of being close to the frontier, even though the towns were actually well supplied with city amenities. The Yellowknife Status of Women Committee, aided and abetted by Terry Padgham, had organized the Northern Homecrafters Society, which had a workshop and store. Prospectors and geologists, women and men, came and went by air, water, and land-rover from the barrens, from gold and other mining claims, and from the high Arctic. Roads were still largely unpaved and treacherous in wet and winter weather. The winters are long and dark, and temperatures can drop to 50 below. ('Carry an axe, matches, candle, kindling, paper, chains, sleeping-bag ... block heater and battery warmer,' advised a government leaflet.) Extreme temperatures, blizzards, and grizzly bears are very real dangers. Women and men all learn to do their own mechanical work if at all possible. In the summer nights, darkness lasts for only three or four hours, and flowers and vegetables grow quickly in the long hours of daylight.

In the Territories, women often feel that their governments are lagging behind in providing funding, services, and the necessary legislation. In BC, the government was cutting down on social and educational services; the Alberta government seemed to be unresponsive to women's needs; but the women in Manitoba seemed to be faring a little better, with new family-property legislation passed just before the election. In Edmonton, I met with our members from Indian Rights for Indian Women, a group which had organized in the late sixties under the leadership of Mary Two-Axe Early and which regularly attended NAC meetings. They were planning research, conferences, and a national meeting and lobby in Ottawa. They were still dealing with the thorny problem of that section of the Indian Act which deprived Indian women of their status if they married non-native men.

I met with Kathleen Ruff in Victoria and Carole Geller in Regina, both directors of their provincial Human Rights Commissions, which were beginning to have real impact as cases came before them and were followed through. Meeting the Saskatchewan Action Committee, I discovered that their executive members represented all areas of the province and their funds allowed for regular meetings, a policy NAC hoped to be able to follow on a national scale. Back in Toronto, at the meetings of the Ontario Committee on the Status of Women, we were learning more about the mechanisms of government, with their attendant power plays and manipulation. Sometimes we wondered how to make any impact at all. So we worked to get women elected, and we organized workshops as well as legal and other kinds of training, both locally and provincially.

From the travelling, I had a strong sense of an active women's movement in Canada. There have, however, been times when 'sisterhood' was severely strained. At the risk of stirring up a whole bunch of hornets' nests, there is perhaps a need to fill in some of the background to the 1978 NAC annual conference and the general concern over the press coverage and actions of the Wages for Housework group.

Just before the annual meeting, the membership committee received a number of applications, several of which had the same addresses and/or signing officers. One group was Wages for Housework and at least one other was affiliated to it. It was by then too late for the applications to go through the usual admissions procedure, so NAC's membership committee recommended, and the executive supported, rejecting them. Letters came back from the groups asking to meet with the executive, although only three days remained before the annual meeting.

The discussion made it clear that we did not disagree on short-term goals: day care; job-training programs, and so on. But our long-term goals still did not seem to be compatible. NAC had already had a large debate on the subject in 1975, and we were agreed that we did not support the concept of wages for housework. We were working towards equal opportunities, the freedom to choose, and liberation from sex roles for both sexes. And it seemed to us that pay for housework, even the housework done in keeping oneself clean and fed, would ultimately reinforce the stereotype of woman-in-the-home and the current division of labour by sex. In addition, we mistrusted some of the tactics employed by Wages for Housework groups. It was always difficult to get a clear-cut statement from them, but the discussion ended with the agreement that these particular women would be present as observers at the conference, and in fact one was to be a resource person.

The WFH women had received notices about the registration procedure, so we assumed that they had registered. But they hadn't, and they claimed that this verbal exchange constituted a registration, which it did not. Many WFH women turned up at the meeting and tried to register on the spot; some wanted to pay, most did not, and many wanted to be present for only part of the proceedings. Space at the meeting was limited, and delegates from the approximately 160 established member groups had to have priority, since they had come from all across the country and were officially representing their organizations. We had decided against pro-rata registration fees, since even the full amount didn't begin to cover our expenses.

The conference finally agreed to let the women in and to set up extra discussion groups in some of the delegates' rooms, since all workshop space was filled. However, few of these women took part in workshops or discussions; they sat around in the passageways and blocked the halls with display tables and video machines. As a result, NAC's own delegates – some of whom, like the squid-fishing women from Newfoundland, had raised their own funds with bake sales and the like – did not have space for their displays.

The press, of course, made the most of the 'élitist,' 'well-off' women keeping out the 'poor' workers, although various of the NAC delegates and observers had been helped financially by other women. The sensationalistic 'poor women kept out' reporting, running a close second to press coverage of Margaret Trudeau's private life, obscured the objective of the conference: to obtain specific and concrete changes in government policies directly affecting poor and working women and their families. But reports reached as far as the US west coast, a feat not even achieved by the news of our federal election.

Such methods of grabbing publicity, obscuring major objectives, and appealing to public sympathy through sensationalism are some of the reasons for NAC's concern. These tactics are counterproductive in that they divert attention from important issues and bring ridicule and divisiveness to the women's movement.

This was one of the more distressing episodes to occur while I was president of NAC. But there was never time to brood. In this period, there were so many meetings, conferences, and so on that a free weekend was an oasis in an otherwise endless frenzy of activity. Free long weekends – which had dragged in Birmingham, brimmed with social activity in Montreal (with Rosie Brewin's help), and been full in Toronto when the children were little – now became something precious, to be savoured throughout each minute, so that one almost gloated at the prospect of parcelling out the time in the way it could best be used. I had the feeling of hugging these unique moments to myself, thanking heaven for being alive.

It wasn't all work, of course. There were birthday celebrations and festive office parties. A Christmas party was Nancy Jackman's first introduction to NAC in Toronto, when she returned from BC at the end of the 1970s, and she maintains that, by inviting her to that party, I launched her into the women's movement of the day. I had first heard about Nancy while we were discussing the pros and cons of government funding. Someone mentioned this millionaire feminist who had returned to Toronto, bought a huge Rosedale mansion, and offered to match the contributions of all those present at a coffee party she had attended. So we invited her to the party, and she did offer to help with Friends of NAC. I had always been wary of people with lots of money; I think they made me feel inferior. And here was someone who was rich, who was given to awful language and questionable table manners, and yet she became one of my closest friends. She had all kinds of generosity and understanding and loveable characteristics. My family accepted her with all her reactionary-mixed-with-radical-feminist ideas and outlandish behaviour. Brough would explain and reason, I would argue and fight, and the Ss took her in their stride.

Other celebrations included the festivities around the fiftieth anniversary of women becoming 'persons' in Canada back in 1929. The Governor-General of Canada presented the first Persons Awards, which consisted of a medal designed by Dora de Pedery Hunt. NAC marked the event with a fund-raising project coordinated by Betsy Carr which sold hundreds of bronze and silver medallions, designed by the same artist, to anyone wishing to join in the celebration. The first silver medallion struck was reserved for the first woman to be appointed to the Supreme Court of Canada, and was eventually presented to Madame Justice Bertha Wilson in 1982.

Also memorable, though for different reasons, were visits from

David MacDonald (soon after he had been appointed Minister Responsible for the Status of Women) and a wonderful grade-five class from an alternative school, who came in to quiz us about equality and abortion legislation. The knowledgeable leader of the group, aged about ten, admitted she had an aunt who was a lawyer. The lawyer turned out to be Rosalie Abella, a former NAC executive member later appointed youngest judge of the Family Court. And Rosie's son, whose father was a history professor, was later heard stating firmly that men are professors, women are judges.

And there was the following memorable occasion, reproduced here as I recorded it at the time.

The telephone rings. I pick it up.

'Hello. It's Pearl.' Pearl is our secretary. Though frequently plagued by problems and interruptions to do with the heat, the cold, the generally erratic temperatures and draughts in the office, her health, the interruptions, and her family, she is the most efficient person you could wish for in any office.

'How would you like to meet the Queen?'

'What queen?'

'Don't be silly. *The* Queen. You know, Her Gracious Majesty Queen Elizabeth.'

'Pearl, dear, explain yourself,' I say patiently.

'You have received an invitation, addressed to Ms Kay Macpherson, from the Prime Minister. He requests the pleasure of your company at a gala concert in honour of the Queen and the DOOK. Of course, it doesn't say she'll *be* there. But it says 'and guest,' so you can take someone along. Can I go?'

'Well ...' I'm slightly stunned. 'Isn't that nice of Pierre Elliott. He must be inviting the presidents of every organization in the country. No, they couldn't possibly fit into the Arts Centre. Oh well. We'll never be able to fathom the inscrutable workings of the federal government.'

Pearl continues, 'It says at the bottom, 'RSVP,' and then 'Ottawa. Black tie and decorations or lounge suit.'

'No!'

'Yes!'

'And it's addressed to *Ms* Kay Macpherson?'

'Correct.'

'Oh, how wonderful. The male orientation of our esteemed government is enchanting. How will I ever decide? Black tie and decorations or a lounge suit?'

My imagination runs on. A simple black tie? and nothing else? Or perhaps the Victoria Cross and the Order of Canada as pasties, one on each breast? Enough. I shall borrow my daughter's beautiful, long, brocade dress made from an old curtain. The other Macpherson 'and guest' for the occasion loves to dress up in academic gowns and things, and will be enchanted to wear his decorations and a black tie. So everyone will be pleased, including, I hope, the Queen.

It is very difficult to remember what one actually *did* in the hours and hours that were spent, first housekeeping and caring for children, and then in voluntary groups and organizations. There were years when I was in the Voice of Women office, or acting for it, almost daily. The same thing happened throughout the ten years I was most intensely involved in NAC. So when I ask myself what did I *do* in the NAC and VOW offices, I guess it boils down to reading (letters, articles, speeches, and press releases) and writing (letters, articles, speeches, and press releases). Then there were executive and committee meetings, conferences large and small, and lots of useful activities, some learned on the job: making posters; designing announcements; putting bulletins and newsletters together; taking pictures; making up skits and songs; packaging literature; and all kinds of errands and pick-ups.

I couldn't have managed it without a car, and one of the worst hardships I later had to face was giving up driving my car, because of failing eyesight. At least I wasn't ordered to do so; I realized myself that I was becoming a danger to the public. But *revenons à nos moutons*, as one of my favourite phrases has it. Looking back on those two years as president of NAC, I feel that the atmosphere was usually friendly. I considered our staff members part of the family, so to speak, and probably the general impression was that I was easy-going and positive, but not too well organized.

All that changed when Lynn McDonald was elected president in 1979, in NAC's first contested election (Jean Woodsworth also ran). Then we moved to larger premises, the president had her own office, and NAC was conducted in a strictly business-like way, not as an informal women's centre. Lynn was president during the Canadian Constitution repatriation period, when NAC submitted a brief to the parliamentary hearings. She and various executive members were at odds over the 'entrenchment' of the Canadian Charter of Rights and Freedoms. Whether it was over this or over pensions, there was a good deal of tension on the executive. Some of the regional members remember feeling very much left out of the decision-making, and there were one or two confrontations with the president. I remember acting as some sort of mediator and going to visit Lynn to talk it over. We ended up drinking a glass of sherry together, but it was not a happy time.

Jean Wood eventually succeeded Lynn McDonald as president. She is a brilliant and lively Scot whose insurance-company employer had transferred her to Toronto in the late 1970s. She and her husband took turns in following the other to wherever each was transferred, so they set up house in Toronto and Jean soon appeared in the women's movement. First elected as treasurer of NAC, she contributed a great deal to the then current debate about housewives and pensions.

Jean was a fantastic organizer and planner. She could cheerfully point out all the things one was doing wrong and was thanked and loved for doing so. She was no conventional president, either. An early riser, like her predecessor Lorna and her successor Doris Anderson, she used to leave letters, memos, and drafts in the office long before the staff arrived. Pearl remembers unlocking the door to find at her feet the first of a series of arrows which led under tables, up bookcases, along walls, and over doors and filing cabinets until the trail came to rest in some unsuspected spot and the day's work was discovered.

At one meeting, Jean was being given a hard time on the pensions issue. There were some in the executive who felt that, because she worked for a private insurance firm, she must have divided loyalties and be in a conflict-of-interest situation. Jean was holding her own but was liable to tire under the hostile barrage. Pearl went up and whispered, could she get her anything. Jean's reply was brief, low-voiced, and to the point: 'A drink!' Pearl went off, filled a coffee cup with neat scotch, and handed it to Jean who expected it to be coffee. By the time the meeting was finished, she was definitely on top and feeling absolutely no pain whatever.

She was the first president to institute a personnel policy for NAC staff, and she called for more accurate job descriptions so that, as she put it, Pearl was not left juggling plates (executive requests) and Janet poised to catch any that fell. She will be remembered as introducing pensions and other protective measures for the staff. Those women still mourn the day she left to follow her husband back to the United Kingdom, after only one year as president. (Later, on one of our trips to London, Jean came to have breakfast with us. Another time, we went out together for dinner in a country pub and later visited their enchanting Huntingdon village.)

When Jean stood down, NAC had no potential president waiting in the wings for 1982. Doris Anderson of Advisory Council fame was persuaded to stand for election, and Chaviva Hošek moved from secretary to vice-president. Nancy Jackman had wanted to be treasurer, and she would have been a good one, but unfortunately she was not elected and was very disappointed. The new treasurer was young and inexperienced, which meant that Doris had to help her, thus adding to her own workload. (Doris, of course, also had to adjust to working with our very limited resources after working with the superior budgets of *Chatelaine* and *Maclean's* magazines.) Moira and I were elected members-at-large. Some old blood was required, I suppose, since Doris as president had at least twelve new executive members to cope with.

The 1982 annual meeting was prey to all sorts of conflicts, manipulation, and hidden agendas about resolutions, though it didn't turn out too badly in the end. Because of my interests and the increasing number of VOW members involved in NAC, NAC was, for the first time, formally considering the subject of global survival and the need to demonstrate the link between Canada's ever-increasing military budget and the decline in funding for social programs and women's needs.

We organized a workshop and showed the Helen Caldicott film *If You Love This Planet*, with a few distractions provided by the hotel staff noisily clearing away the lunch dishes while we tried to hear the script. Subsequent discussion included proposals by Sister Rosalie Bertell as to how women might, on the sixth day of each month, work only for peace and non-violence, thereby downing tools and in effect going on strike. This suggestion did not receive wholehearted approval from the whole conference, some of whom had not seen the film and missed the urgency for action that gripped the workshop participants. But I was very happy to be the chair of the Survival Committee we started up, later called the Survival of the Planet Committee. In 1986, the Committee put together a Peace Kit which was circulated to all member groups and updated as needed.

When we came to planning the annual lobby that year and the questions to ask the three party caucuses, there was great interest and many women worked on making the most effective presentation. When Judy Erola, who led the Liberal caucus (we've never yet had our lobby attended by the PM or any other major minister), heard the questions about negotiation and disarmament, she made the mistake of saying she would pass the questions on to the appropriate ministers, for Defence and External Affairs, because, she said, 'these are not women's issues.' She brought the roof down on her head. Angry women stated in no uncertain terms that they thought it was time they were women's issues. As the last of the NAC speakers appealed for greater action on the government's part towards disarmament and peace, the whole group of over a hundred women rose and applauded their delegate.

Throughout Doris' term (1982–4), a fierce debate went on as to whether the national office should move to Ottawa. The first time this was debated at the AGM we ended in an incredible tie vote, the three hundred delegates' votes split exactly in two, and the motion to move was lost. This is the only dramatic split vote I can remember at NAC. The second time, a year later, the vote against moving increased, and the office is still in Toronto.

Chaviva's presidency (1984–6) was noted for the national television debate on women's issues held during the 1984 federal elections. It was also said that Chaviva had done a great deal to make 'feminism' a respectable word. There were fundamental office changes when she became president, and eventually NAC employed a full-time coordinator.

As time went on, pressures between the executive and the staff had escalated. NAC's agenda became more ambitious and, as always, funding remained limited. Communication between executive and staff was a low priority compared with what appeared to be more urgent issues. Jean Wood had started the process of putting our staff on a business-like footing, with decent pension and salary arrangements, but later on more difficulties arose over the terms of their employment and the unionization of the staff (including a disagreement as to whether the executive coordinator was union or management).

The reputation of women's organizations for treating their paid staff abominably was probably deserved, at least during the 1970s and early 1980s. At the beginning, the NAC executive and what staff we had just worked their heads off, because we were breaking new ground, trying to establish an effective women's movement. We were used to being exploited, overworked volunteers and working with other exploited, overworked volunteers. We considered our staff members as friends and equals and forgot that our volunteer work was their livelihood. In an article in the labour paper *Our Times*, the staff listed their complaints as 'overwork, an out-of-date wage policy, stress, lack of respect, and contradictory instructions.' Before the situation was resolved it was necessary for the staff to resign en masse at the 1988 AGM to highlight labour-relations problems.

However, the staff eventually formed CUPE Local 3380, with all staff being members, including the coordinator. NAC then began its third decade in a more stable and amicable state. All this upheaval served to highlight for us, as the staff pointed out in their article, 'the importance of appropriate models for feminist labour relations for the long-term health of active feminist organizations.'

NAC's only francophone president to date was Louise Dulude, a lawyer and pensions expert (1986–8). Lynn Kaye(1988–90) took over from her at a time when the government had cut NAC's budget in half, and Judy Rebick began the 1990s with further debates on how to cope with restructuring and reduced budgets, though determined to continue to strengthen NAC's regional and visible-minority representation.

Time has marched on. NAC has been described as the 'most powerful lobby in the country.' Would that it were true! We have lobbied our MPs, then the party caucuses, then the cabinet, and assorted ministers. We have held regional conferences and a series of meetings called 'Feminist Visions of the Future.' We have produced studies and briefs on every conceivable subject to do with women. Our membership grew from about thirty groups to over three hundred in less than ten years. We can no longer be called a Toronto-based group since our executive members come from every part of Canada.

Our lack of money meant that NAC's first executive committee was composed largely of women from the Toronto area and the 1973 and 1974 annual meetings were held in Toronto. The next year, with government help, NAC managed to hold an annual meeting in Winnipeg. After that it was decided that, for a national organization, the place to meet was the nation's capital, where we could speak face to face with our politicians. Since for many of NAC's delegates a visit to Ottawa was a new experience and the chance of seeing parliament at first hand something not to be missed, this choice has continued.

So in 1976 the AGMs were moved to Ottawa and an annual lobby was established. During my time on NAC's executive, the lobbying process evolved substantially. In 1976, members of the executive met with the ministers responsible for NAC's priority issues, with delegates observing the process. The next year, we tried to lobby as many individual MPs as we could and asked them to meet with our delegates. We were helped by CARAL members Jean Forden and Ruth Miller, who had tried this approach quite successfully the year before. Although very popular with delegates, it proved immensely time-consuming (each MP's office had to be phoned three or four times to set up an appointment) so that we eventually settled for the format of meeting with the party caucus members, each for one hour and strictly timed for fairness.

The lobby has now become a question-and-answer meeting between NAC delegates and the party caucuses, and it has often been the high point of the whole annual meeting. The exciting thing about all this is the change in what women have learned during the years since 1972 about lobbying, negotiating, and presenting their case to powerful and not-so-powerful officials and politicians, usually but not always men. If we note the issues dealt with at recent NAC lobbies, we can see that women are now clearly articulating the details of their oppression and the underlying causes of it. We have become better informed, politicized, and sophisticated in our dealings with officials and politicians. In turn, governments and politicians are now more wary in their dealings with women's groups, and with NAC in particular.

But in some areas little headway has been made, and there have been occasions when women have let their anger show. Then, of course, MPs and reporters were quick to voice their indignation and castigate the women for their justifiable despair and fury. Indeed, in 1988, the Mulroney caucus used the spirited behaviour of the previous year's delegates as the excuse for not attending NAC's lobby. 'Women must be ladies, even if politicians are not always gentlemen,' we learned. All the same, something had to be done. Delegates wished to protest the government's position without doing anything to stop our own agenda from going forward. 'When in doubt, do both,' I doubtless encouraged them. We chartered a bus and fifty delegates volunteered to try to deliver NAC's note to the Prime Minister. Some members wrote individual letters to the PM while the regular agenda went on. Later, other NAC members attended question period in the House of Commons where they suddenly stood up, revealing T-shirts with slogans demanding that women be heard.

In 1989, when the PC government still refused to meet with NAC, NAC substituted its own government, represented by the Ministers of Child Care, Disarmament, and so on, who answered appropriate questions. In 1990, the delegates questioned an empty chair and spoke with the other two parties.

This reluctance on the part of the government was, perhaps, not so surprising. Even though she had already had the experience of chairing one of these sessions as president of NAC, I remember Lynn McDonald saying that, after she became an MP, she really felt intimidated when she had to face two hundred women and their questions as a member of her party caucus. It is natural that NAC's relations with opposition parties are better than with the government of the day, but they had never before been at the abysmal level that they reached in 1988.

Such is the growth and turnover in NAC membership that each year about 50 per cent of delegates have no knowledge of our earlier history and some believe it is the first time we have lobbied the government. An orientation session now precedes the other business of NAC's annual meeting.

In fact, NAC's annual meetings were usually a lot of fun, including the celebrations that went with them. We had a picture auction one time, the Nellie McClung players from Winnipeg on another occasion, interspersed with very good speakers. At the 1982 AGM celebration for NAC's tenth anniversary, Laura Sabia was reminiscing about all her old executive colleagues. 'Kay Macpherson,' she said, 'was my link between the white-gloves and the hobnailed-boots sets of NAC members.' I was flattered. At the dinner the following night, Linda Ryan Nye, with a token mink stole around her neck, sang of Laura being Pope for the day, and Wendy Lawrence's hilarious 'Feminist Update' took the theme a stage further. Toronto Alderman Joe Piccinnini was given the National Pacifier Award for the most outrageous public remarks about women ('They are all too lazy to apply for jobs at City Hall'). Some nominations had to be disallowed because nepotism was involved! The year before, Senator Harry Hays was the winner: during the Constitution hearings he had asked who was going to look after the kids when women were running around going to work. Lloyd Axworthy was only the runner-up ('Women are tedious' ... etc.), but he has since had one of Linda's songs as a memorial.

Executive member Terry Padgham 'honoured' our retiring (only in one sense) president Jean Wood in a speech stuffed with Jean's favourite sayings ('I've got a problem,' 'substantive issue,' and so on), all delivered in Terry's appalling so-called Scottish accent. By that time, Terry was living in Yellowknife; she and Madeleine Gilchrist were two of the younger and most politically astute of the many women who debated with politicians and stated our case. Both came from good, solid left-wing backgrounds, which certainly helps one analyse situations quickly and clearly. At one meeting, Terry confessed to an unlikely but heartwarming ambition. 'When I grow up,' she said, 'I want to be Kay Macpherson.'

There were some great women on the NAC executive during those first ten to fifteen years. There still are, but I don't know so many of them. Elsie Gregory MacGill was terrific. She spent hours of her time advising NAC, working on our constitution and organizing our resolutions. She had a great sense of humour and a keen eye for political timing and promotion of equal rights for women. An early officer of the Order of Canada, Elsie along with Ruth Bell, another early executive member and past president of the University Women's Clubs, was responsible for promoting more women in the Order and on every board or commission where their numbers were sparse.

On the only occasion when I missed a NAC AGM, Elsie said she'd be going to Ottawa for the weekend and travelling on her own, wheelchair and all, by bus. My friend Vi Thompson was also going, and I suggested they look out for each other. This they did and had a wonderful time together, having at one point, Vi said, an animated discussion on what it would be like to have a sex change, an unlikely topic for sixty- and seventy-year-olds. When they arrived, Elsie got the taxi driver to lift her into the taxi and then into her wheelchair at the door of the hotel. She then proceeded to attend all the sessions at the annual meeting.

Now it seems we have reached the end of an era. New brooms are busily sweeping NAC into the twenty-first century. We are becoming electronic, computerized, automated and, we hope, thoroughly efficient. I want, however, to make one very urgent plea. In my experience, the women's movement has been built on sisterhood, on understanding, on love and sympathy for others in need or in trouble, and on the support women can give each other. We are not only a strong lobby group; we are a national, even worldwide, power for equality, peace, and development. But don't let us forget what Rosemary Brown told us in 1973: 'Until all of us have made it, none of us have made it.' We depend on our members and every woman is an important part of us. We must never lose sight of the power that derives from this coming together of women, this source of strength for all of us.

This is beginning to sound like a speech in praise of the women's movement and all it has given me – and so it is!

16

Women in Politics

From its first preliminary meetings in 1966, NAC was the main focus of my energies until my last stint on the executive in 1984. Of course I kept up with VOW and ratepayers' meetings, and I was still dropping in on the Association of Women Electors at City Hall or in members' homes. I also continued as a faculty wife and managed to attend concerts, dance, and theatre, let alone giving and attending sherry (later wine and cheese) parties. Some of my friends spent most of their spare time on their volunteer work but, though many of my days seem to have been filled to the limit, I only worked around the clock on the four occasions when I was a political candidate.

For a while, there had been much talk about the need for more women to get into the political arena. This was also one of the points raised in the Royal Commission report. Early in 1972, there was only one woman in the House of Commons; after the election that fall, there were three. Based on the rate of increase in women MPs since Agnes Macphail in 1921, it was calculated that women could confidently expect to reach equal representation with men in the House of Commons after about eight hundred years. But things have improved since then. By 1990, the number of women in the House was up to 40 – just over 10 per cent. At this rate, we should reach equal numbers in a mere five hundred years.

There had been several meetings of a small group of women, including June Callwood and Barbara Frum, some of whom had been writing in Doris Anderson's *Chatelaine* about the constant cry of 'no competent women.' The need for women to be where the decisions were made was becoming more and more evident. So Moira Armour took the step that would set Women for Political Action (WPA) in motion:

she set up a time and a place for a meeting and notified everyone she could think of who might be interested.

Thus it was that, one freezing cold Saturday morning in February 1972, I was one of a small group of women who stood shivering outside the basement door of the Unitarian Church on St Clair Avenue in Toronto. Someone had forgotten to unlock the door for us and we waited, trying to keep warm, until messages had been sent and the door-opener found. We trooped down to the basement meeting room, and there we found Moira Armour engaged in a significant action. She was moving all the chairs from their staid rows one behind the other into a circle.

This was the first time I had seen someone deliberately arranging chairs in a circle, so that everyone would be equal and no one would be in a position of authority over the rest. It marked a change in my thinking, a conscious and continuing one. Again Moira was the catalyst, for which I'll always be grateful. We assigned a different woman to chair each meeting, to give everyone practice and make sure no one dominated the group. These actions exemplified, I think, what the women's movement was aiming for. We were trying to get away from the leader/led, expert/ignorant, and all those other stereotypes of our patriarchal society, to a participatory, egalitarian community.

Perhaps many of us weren't aware of the significance at the time, and there were many occasions when the conflict between this new concept and the current system was very much in evidence. In fact, one week, somewhat later, Zena Cherry ran an article about us, and when we turned up, all unsuspecting, to our meeting in the Friends' House, we wandered casually in to be faced by serried ranks of women all waiting for a formal, structured meeting. But some of them stayed with the group and learned our new ways – and worked with us when the elections came around.

At that time, I was short on the theory and politics of feminism. My devotion to getting more women into political and other careers was based on a general sense that the current situation was unfair and discriminatory and led to both the oppression of women and society's loss of women's potential contribution. Many of our members were well ahead in both theory and practice, and they provided examples and provoked thought among the rest of us. Consciousness-raising groups, too, highlighted oppressive and humiliating experiences while also increasing our openness towards each other.

It may sound strange, but WPA was the first of the groups I joined that talked about and was explicitly committed to feminism. The Royal Commission on the Status of Women, the Committee on Equality, and the National Action Committee (which was formed in 1972, the same year as WPA) all used status-of-women and equality language. Before that, it was women's liberation. WPA was clearly committed to feminism.

At that first meeting, women came in and filled up the chairs, and we started discussing how we could get more women into the political field. We chose someone to chair the meeting and went ahead full steam. We decided to call the organization Women for Political Action and, since women of all political affiliations would be welcome, to stay non- or multi-partisan. We varied from conservatives to radical feminists. Some of us had no experience but saw the need for women's presence on the political scene. Some were experienced in the political field though not necessarily as candidates. Others saw themselves as political stars. We had some conventional party members, though not too many experienced ones since they had their own commitments elsewhere. Some were simply frustrated by their dealings with politicians and were determined to show what women could do if they worked together.

Vi Thompson described her reactions to WPA – and to me:

The group met with mounting excitement every Saturday from then on. I remember following behind you, Moira, and some others as we left the Friends' House. You were planning a small meeting to discuss some aspect of WPA's goals as I trailed my way to the subway. You turned round and said 'Why don't you come?' I was surprised. I had a view of you as middle-class, married to a university professor, able to speak to crowds at City Hall square. The English class system still had me in its clutches. I did not expect to be asked to share in discussions with people like you in a (higher?) different class. It seemed that in your middle-class self-assurance you could not recognize my difficulty. I don't believe I went to that small meeting. I was very unsure.

Vi and I had both been born in England, not more than about a hundred miles apart and in the same year. Her father was a shepherd and worked in the Essex maltings to make extra money. Mine was a doctor in a small county town now part of greater London. As her father got paid more in working for the breweries, Vi was able to go to high school. So we share many school experiences: hymn-singing and Palgrave's *Golden Treasury*, a great source of half-remembered poems.

When we finally met, we had both been married for over twenty years, had three children apiece, and were both opposed to wars and concerned about women's status.

It was through WPA that I first met Madeleine Gilchrist. In fact, Mady came on the scene through her husband Kerry. He had heard of Women for Political Action and suggested that Mady, who was desperate for outside-the-home interests, go to a Saturday morning meeting in the home of one Kay Macpherson, who lived right across the ravine, on Glengowan. So Mady, on her day off from looking after their young children, followed the 'Walk In' instructions posted on the door and went down into the basement, where she was met by Moira Armour who said, 'Who are you?' and (Mady swears) offered her a beer. Mady encountered a wonderful group of women, she says, all talking politics and with all sorts of ideas buzzing about. She has never left. First lured into political action with WPA and NAC, she then concentrated her efforts in international connections for VOW.

And very valuable she has been, too. I well remember one NAC executive meeting when Mady had just come on to the executive. The workings of the executive were strange to her at that time, and she did not know the individuals. At her first meeting, a heated and confused discussion arose and continued for some time. Tempers were rising and the atmosphere deteriorating. Mady, who had been sitting quietly, spoke up in her not-yet-perfect English saying, 'The air is thick, and we need to clear the sky,' and called for a half-hour recess. There was a stunned silence. A voice of reason, in the person of our newest member, had brought us to our senses.

She became a cherished friend and colleague and we have been on many trips together, not to mention time spent in efforts to improve my French and Mady's English. It was handy for Mady who is Swiss (and for VOW!) that she could combine home visits with her peace work, and I still remember with great delight meeting her in Geneva and spending a wonderful day gossiping and sight-seeing on her home territory.

Like the Women Electors, WPA members set about becoming as well informed as possible on all aspects of the electoral process. First we had to develop our policies on women's issues and other subjects. WPA's own positions were usually, as I remember, not difficult to agree upon, and most of us had no difficulty in supporting them: choice, equal pay, day care, and so on. We obtained the policy statements of the major political parties, particularly on women's issues, if they had any. We held workshops on how to run campaigns, make speeches, and write press releases and campaign literature. We made posters and practised interviewing, being interviewed, debating policy points, and dealing with hecklers and hostile press questions. We had slogans (A Woman's Place is in the House ... of Commons) and practised canvassing and asking to speak to 'the woman of the house' about her views.

Unlike AWE, which aimed to monitor municipal government, WPA aimed to make it possible to get women elected at every level of government. As an organization, we would not back any one candidate, but members would be free to work for and support any candidate they chose. With the prospect of a federal election in 1972 quite a few women with political aspirations showed up at our meetings, often expecting to get endorsement from WPA, but this was not quite what we were aiming for, although many members did subsequently work in women's political campaigns.

Although WPA's general stance was non-partisan, when the federal election was called that October, none of the political parties was strongly in support either of women as candidates or of women's concerns, so most WPA members supported and worked for independent candidates. Aline Gregory decided to run on a feminist platform in the Rosedale riding and enlisted supporters from the New Feminists and others. I decided to run in St Paul's, where I was best known through the Women Electors and Voice of Women, and began to gather friends, neighbours, and helpers of all ages.

We collected money and rented a store on Yonge Street for our campaign office. Moira bought an old van, and we covered it with election signs, used it for canvassing, and parked it in suitably conspicuous spots. One six-year-old, Miguel Fulton, was working his head off, putting up signs and distributing leaflets. His mother, Gloria Montero, asked him, 'Why this frenzy of activity to get Kay elected?' It turned out that he'd spent a short time at Macpherson Island at Gananoque and he thought that if I were elected, I would move to Ottawa, and the Fultons could move to Gan! So much for youthful idealism.

My campaign, besides emphasizing the need for women in parliament and for attention to women's issues, also talked about peace and environmental questions, which I remember went over well in the all-candidates' meetings. We didn't have enough workers to touch all areas of the constituency, nor were we very methodical in our record-keeping. (It was not until later that I discovered just how much work goes into a formal party campaign.) But in the final count we managed

'Women and the Constitution' Conference, Ottawa: Madeleine Leblanc, Marylou McPhedran, Doris Anderson, Kay, Jill Vickers (February 14, 1981)

With Brough in Japan (1981)

Kay with Betty Peterson and Muriel Duckworth, at United Nations Rally (1982)

NAC presents its silver 'persons' medallion to Madame Justice Bertha Wilson (4th from left). With Wendy Lawrence, Rosemary Billings, Doris Anderson, and Pat Hacker (1982)

Kay receiving Order of Canada from Governor General Edward Schreyer (1982)

NAC staff and Executive members: Cathy Devlin, Betsy Carr (foreground),
Maxine Hermolin, Lee Grills, Pearl Blazer, Madeleine Gilchrist, Janet Port
(1984)

NAC 'Leaders Debate': Jean Piggott, Lorna Marsden, Grace Hartman, Kay, Laura Sabia (1984)

Sheila, Kay, Darian, and Brough (1985)

Susan Macpherson: 'Personal Collection' Dance Performance (1985)

'Panel on Feminism,' Hart House, Toronto: Nancy Jackman, Kay, Nancy Pocock, Ruth Johnson, Laura Sabia (mid-1980s)

Kay with President Harry Arthurs, receiving LL.D. from York University (June 20, 1987)

Kay and quilt-maker Ellen Adams with 'C.B. Macpherson Memorial Quilt' (1988)

Edmonton: Dave Mardiros, Louise Swift, Betty Mardiros, Kay, Hilary Brown, Tony Benn (1988)

Margarita Papandreou lunch with VOW members: Madeleine Gilchrist, Ursula Frankin, Margarita, Anna Lou Paul (Little), Kay (1988)

Nancy Jackman displaying Kay's T-Shirt Collection at Kay's birthday party (1990)

Grandson Darian Chase (1990)

With Miriam May and Vi Thompson, Gananoque (1990)

to gather some 3000 votes, quite a good number. We felt we had learned a good deal and pushed the idea of women in politics a bit further along the road.

After the election, I was faced with some choices. I spent two months in a state of indecision – not unusual, as my friends know. 'I'm not going to help you decide; this is your decision,' said Judy Lawrence firmly. 'Do you want to carry on outside the party system? Do you, or do you not, want to join a party and run for election?' Did I want to have another try at being elected? Yes, I did. As an independent? Very few independent candidates succeed in winning a seat, and independent members cannot draw on the resources, research, and facilities available to party members. It's a lonely and probably expensive life.

The only party that appeared a practical choice was the New Democratic Party, although in the past I had considered myself too left and had been too critical of the NDP to consider joining. Also I believed, especially on the municipal level, that, in many of the areas in which I was interested, one could be more effective outside the political parties. However, as I said to myself when I first joined the Women Electors, I could 'bore from within' and try to change party policy where I felt the need. So, on January 1, 1973, I paid my first membership fee to the NDP, and promptly left the country. I was on my way to Australia to join Brough in Canberra, where he was being a visiting professor at the Australian National University.

On the way, I went to Mexico to meet Ella Manuel, and I have a vivid memory of us waiting for ten hours somewhere on Mexico's west coast until one bus for Tijuana finally had two square inches for the two of us. But that trip also had such delicious moments as Ella and I sitting up in our twin beds in some seaside hotel in Mazatlan madly trying to finish the two-volume paperback of *Jenny*, about Churchill's mother, which we were both finding tedious but were bound and determined we would finish and leave behind for others, meantime helping our reading with cups of Ella's bedside-made coffee and frequent nips of kahlua.

In Australia, I met some of the Women's Electoral Lobby (which included Elizabeth Reed, who worked on women's rights in Iran before the days of Khomeini and company) and found that they thought Canada far ahead in women's liberation because we had had a Royal Commission. Brough was giving a lecture in Melbourne, so I had a chance to spend twenty-four hours with Jean McLean, whom I'd met at the Paris women's conference on Vietnam in 1968. I spoke to the peace group in Melbourne and enjoyed a wonderful night in Jean's house on the beach, with a view of the enormous bay.

I arrived back from Australia in time for WPA's Women in Politics conference. Since I had been in Australia while it was being organized, I had the fun without the hard work. The conference brought elected women together with aspiring candidates, and both party and non-party women came to discuss the political process. It was memorable for a number of happenings, and particularly for the electrifying speech of an unknown (to me) MLA from BC, Rosemary Brown, who was the first black woman to be elected to a provincial legislature. Women all over Canada are still quoting from her speech at that meeting: 'Until all of us have made it, none of us have made it' and 'Silence can be golden, but sometimes it's just plain yellow.'

Vi Thompson and I were in a workshop on feminism together with Nellie Peterson, a farmer from Alberta. We spent most of the time trying to *define* feminism. Later, on a panel at the Board of Education, I remember Lorna Marsden, Jean Pigott, and me being asked for a definition of feminism. Three definitions were promptly supplied, and they varied markedly, though I don't think we actually contradicted each other. My own definition varied daily. None of us can remember exactly what we said, but Lorna later worked out an all-purpose response, and I think we would all agree with it. It is: When power is being divided, a feminist thinks of women first.

One or two notes from the 1973 conference provide a bit of colour. During the evening plenary some disruptive male elements invaded the registration area and overturned the book-display tables. Whatever happened, one of the organizers dealt with it all, and no one inside the hall knew about it until afterwards.

On another evening, there was a party at my house. Both Muriel Duckworth and my physio friend, Valerie Johnston, were staying with me. Where my family was I have no idea. Brough may have still been in Australia or may have hidden away in his study. Some of the more youthful elements were raiding the wine cupboard and getting noisy. I conferred with Muriel and Val. Muriel immediately announced in a loud voice, 'Sorry, but Voice of Women is going to have a meeting right now. We must ask you all to leave!' And surprisingly (to Muriel too) they left.

It wasn't the end though. The 'radicals' repaired to someone's apartment and became belligerent. They made objection to one woman's gorgeous long red hair. 'A really liberated woman doesn't have long hair,' they said and proceeded to find some scissors to start cutting it off. WPA member Jan Barnsley got her thumb jabbed in the scuffle to defend her friend, and blood flowed! The first we knew about all this was when a phone call came, asking Muriel to go on 'Metro Morning' instead of Jan, who was said to be wounded and thus hors de combat.

This was in the period when there were many stories about the militants going round beating up the husbands of feminists, and also more fun times with spray cans and billboards, invasion of TV studios during beauty contests, and so on. But my favourite anecdote comes from that same Women in Politics conference. Doris Anderson, who had chaired the panel on political women, asked some of us to go back to her house for a drink with one of the panelists, Liberal MP Albanie Morin, who was staying with her. I went along with Muriel, Moira, Judy, Terry Padgham, Nellie Peterson, and Betty Mardiros. Terry was complaining, furiously and eloquently, because she could no longer buy her boys' skates from CCM, the bicycle firm, who had stopped making skates because they'd got a contract to make weapons for the military. Finally Albanie said, 'But we have to have the weapons to defend us from the Russians.' She was promptly given a detailed lesson on the horrors of war, alternative means of settling disputes, the benefits of manufacturing for peaceful purposes, etc., etc. The poor woman was quite unprepared for this onslaught. It turned out that every one of those present was a member of the Voice of Women. Doris' only comment, in her gravelly voice, was, 'I thought Voice of Women was dead.' She had just received evidence to the contrary.

At about this time, Moira Armour, who was always alert for ways to further my political career, suggested that it would help my reputation, or image, or whatever, if I joined the CCLA (Canadian Civil Liberties Association). And since I supported and worked for civil rights and liberties, I did join, and eventually served on the CCLA board for several years. I made some good friends amongst the predominantly male legal members of the association and sat through many confusing discussions on various legal niceties. I always intensely admired June Callwood's ability to grasp and understand so many of these points that left me floundering and befogged.

In 1973, WPA co-sponsored a meeting with Berit Ås, the dynamic Norwegian feminist, psychologist, and member of parliament. I had met Berit years before in Paris when we had been opposing a NATO nuclear force, and we had written a press release jointly as women coming from the less-powerful member countries of NATO. We have been friends ever since, and she has visited and lectured in Canada several times. Later in the 1980s, when Brough was attending a conference in Sweden, I slipped into Norway and spent a wonderful twenty-four hours with Berit and her family.

It seemed to WPA members at that time that one of the parts of getting women into the political process was getting them a higher profile in the media. We joined with the OCSW in presenting a brief to the Canadian Radio-television and Telecommunications Commission (CRTC) hearings on the licensing of the CBC and other broadcasters. Our brief on sexism in CBC television involved dozens of women spending many hours monitoring programs. I remember being bored to death having to watch a popular comedy called 'Gilligan's Island.' We documented the numbers of males and females in leading roles, and generated a host of other statistics, which then became a detailed and extensive brief, and we hied ourselves up to Ottawa to present it to the CRTC. The CRTC did not produce any specific recommendations, but the government eventually took some action. The CBC set up its own task force and more women have since been appointed to high-profile or decision-making positions. The group Media Watch took on the monitoring of programs, but efforts to decrease the violence on television, even in cartoons and dramas, have been singularly unsuccessful.

WPA continued to run workshops and meetings for women candidates. The political parties began to develop policies on women's issues and, led by the NDP, began encouraging greater participation of women as candidates and in high-profile positions. Women were usually relegated to running in ridings where their party had little hope of winning, but slowly we gained more experience and confidence. Alexa McDonough became leader of the NDP in Nova Scotia. Eventually, Rosemary Brown, Flora MacDonald, and Sheila Copps all tried for federal party leadership, and finally Audrey McLaughlin won it. WPA meantime went on with its efforts to educate and increase women's expertise in the political field, celebrating with an annual dinner on Persons Day, October 18th.

My first federal NDP convention was in 1973. Since then I don't think I have missed any federal convention and only one or two provincial ones. The 1973 convention was planned for the July long weekend in Vancouver, which of course was an added incentive, and I planned to meet the Mardiros family and other friends there. This first convention shocked me. Although there was general friendliness amongst the delegates, male chauvinism was rampant. The macho union hordes disappeared during the long business sessions (to the Vancouver beer parlours, it was said), returning only when needed on a crucial vote, and then, we assumed, they voted in a block as directed. Very few women came to the microphone, and they were not heeded when they did. There were a few, competent, token women who usually spoke for the establishment, but most women were silent – in public anyway.

The one bright light at the convention was the women's caucus, which generated a real feeling of power and expectation. The BC women played a prominent role. They were not afraid to speak up and to risk opposition when they did. Having a recently elected NDP government did a great deal for BC women's morale, and cheered up and encouraged the rest of us. Nevertheless, we felt isolated from the party mainstream. On one occasion, at 9:00 a.m. on a Sunday, when most delegates were slowly beginning the day's activities, an executive member introduced a motion to abolish the Participation of Women Committee. The women rallied and, thanks to BC NDPer Hilda Thomas and a few other stalwarts, the committee was saved, to do sterling work in later years.

Many women attended left caucus meetings as well as the women's meetings if they could be fitted in, and more often than not we found ourselves voting against the mainstream, on some women's issues, on energy and conservation issues and nuclear power, on jobs versus the environment, and on Quebec. 'Self determination for Quebec' was always watered down to something less than definite. In recent years policy statements on Meech Lake and NATO have received the same treatment to the disgust of a growing number of delegates.

I had attended NDP riding and women's committee meetings, and tried for a nomination in a by-election, the Broadview-Greenwood nomination which was won by Bob Rae. 'May the best man win,' said retiring MP John Gilbert benevolently, when blessing Bob, John Harney, and me at the nomination meeting.

In 1974, and with greater success than before, I sought the NDP nomination in York East for the federal election. At one NDP meeting I came under some suspicion for having subscribed to the Waffle group's printed material. The Waffle débâcle had taken place when we were on sabbatical in England and I wasn't a member of the NDP or the Waffle, although I had attended some of the Waffle's meetings and read their publications. To me, from outside the party, the Waffle had seemed to present an inspired new hope for renewed socialism in the party: equality for women and a general progressive attitude. But obviously my feelings were not shared, and it still mattered to some party members five years later! Anyway, I passed whatever test I was supposed to be facing and was considered all right to run in York East. It was a great and satisfying experience. The stalwart York East NDP members supported me as their candidate in three federal elections, and I hope they enjoyed the experience as much as I did.

Vi Thompson worked with me on this campaign. She and I now shared a new source of continuous education and delight: the creative-writing group run by journalist Isobel Warren, which Vi joined the year after I started. Vi's memory is phenomenal, and the stories she wrote about her childhood in the Essex countryside were enchanting. I hope one day she'll put them into a book. We looked forward to hearing the next instalments of long stories and were sometimes amazed or shocked by our colleagues' experiences or imaginations. Isobel encouraged us all, criticizing as we progressed, and the group became a consciousness-raising one as well.

Consciousness-raising had not been one of my strong points, but somehow we found it was easy to talk as we discussed each other's efforts and heard Isobel's friendly comments. A Japanese woman wrote the story of finding that her youngest child, a charming three-year-old girl, had fallen from the window of their tenth-floor apartment. She described looking out of the window to see the child's body on the street below. She could only read part of the story, and Isobel read the rest for her. The woman later told us that it was the closeness of the group which had given her the strength to put the whole story on paper.

Vi remembers me at that time as being a mixture of uncertainty and confidence:

I think our visit to the East York women's committee was before your nomination. We had had an invitation to one of their meetings. However, when we eventually found Dorothy Johnson's house, we stood on the sidewalk and asked, 'Did they really invite us? We're late.' We decided to knock at the door anyway, so as not to insult the hostess. Of course they welcomed us as VIPs. I had not expected to find you so hesitant and unsure on the sidewalk.

And, more flatteringly:

You were a fine candidate, following directions from your committee, not try-ing to run the campaign, active, busy, thoughtful. But you so often knocked at the doors and omitted to say who you were. And I remember [publicity direc-tor] Meg Sears' criticism, when during the question period at an all-candidates meeting, you responded to a question with, 'But I've already told you that.' The point was, it was up to you to get across to your audience, not for them to hear everything. I liked your response to her: no embarrassment, but a real grati-tude for an insight that a friend had given you, a nice humility.

As a candidate, one must work solidly all the time to try to reach every possible voter in the constituency. One needs a huge amount of energy, and a car, and fortunately I had both, though often enough the car was a source of frustration. I remember one day which began with the leftovers from the two previous days: two parking tickets in one week. Then a series of those telephone calls which lead to at least five other follow-up calls and more things for me to do. Then Mrs P, our weekly, so-welcome, miracle-working cleaner, found that the vacuum cleaner didn't work. So I had to go up to Oakwood Avenue and from there to Lawrence and Dufferin. It was cold, way below zero, but at least the car was plugged in and startable. I finally succeeded in buying a new part, and thank goodness they still had one for our 1940s vac-uum cleaner. The bad thing was a ticket for speeding – of course on a perfectly clear upper Avenue Road, because the Forest Hill residents complain. 'People on poor streets where the kids play don't get such service,' I said. Then on to the office, as usual later than I expected, and just when I wanted to get away early for canvassing in East York. It was 4:30 when I went to start the car. Dead battery ... Eventually I gave up on the evening's canvassing and went home to dinner, delicious and welcome, but otherwise definitely not my day.

I enjoyed being a candidate; it was more fun than skivvying away at all the other campaign jobs. As amateurs, our WPA gang had done a pretty good job in getting the number of votes we'd obtained in 1972. Canvassing with one or more people is more encouraging and morale-building than working alone, and of course working with committed feminists and peace activists was a delight. But being part of an NDP election campaign made me realize what a difference a party organiza-tion can make.

After the attempt, at the 1973 convention, to disband the women's committee, both the committee and the women's caucus became more active. A women's conference was held. About that time David

Lewis announced his retirement as leader, and a CBC interviewer asked a woman NDP executive member almost jokingly, 'Do you think a woman will run for the leadership?' 'Oh no,' she replied, 'I don't think so!' From that moment the NDP women started lobbying for a candidate, and the federal leadership campaign of 1975, International Women's Year, was a landmark in Canadian politics.

After much consultation and soul-searching, Rosemary Brown agreed to try for the leadership. A wonderful demonstration of a new type of campaigning, a women's campaign involving the support of women members from coast to coast, was mounted for the 1975 federal convention in Winnipeg. The campaign was remarkable in that most of the party establishment and unions were opposed to Rosemary, and still she took Ed Broadbent to four ballots with no bargaining, no deals, and complete participation of her supporters in all decision-making. There was a wonderful, dynamic sense of cooperation and friendship amongst the Brown supporters, and all of us felt that progress had been made in advancing women's status in the party.

I was increasingly occupied with NAC executive work, but my stint as president ended in 1979 and when the next federal election was called that spring, I again ran as an NDP candidate in York East, and this time was beaten by a Conservative. I enjoyed the '79 campaign very much. It was spring – easy for canvassing – and we developed a special campaign folder for women, which had helpful hints and notes as well as information on policies. We gave them useful local telephone numbers, asked them questions, and obtained their opinions about issues and policies. At that time, no party had established funds or official support for women candidates. Ours was one of the first to emphasize the need for and importance of having women represented in the legislatures of the country.

Joe Clark's government lasted only until the late fall and, at the beginning of 1980, I once again was an unsuccessful candidate. It was during one of these campaigns that I told the press that I wasn't too likely to win. This horrified and infuriated my committee. This was NOT what a candidate was supposed to admit. Also, the press blazoned my age in the headline. How many men get that treatment? 'Kay Macpherson, 66.' Which provoked one of my NAC executive friends to say, 'Gee, Kay, I didn't know you were *that* old!' Fortunately, in this, as in all of my NDP campaigns, we collected more than the required percentage of votes, so that we could claim the financial rebate for campaign expenses.

The 1980 election was called early in January, right on the day I got back from Belgium, where I had spent a week in Brussels as VOW representative at the December 1979 NATO anti-nuclear meetings. So I plunged back into campaigning, but that didn't mean everything else stopped. 'When in doubt, do both.' It was never just one thing or one organization at a time. I have a two-part letter I wrote to all my friends in 1980 (did I ever send it?). Started in January, as an apology for not responding to Christmas cards and letters, it was finished in March with more excuses. I felt that I was a poor organizer and commented, 'A time/motion study needs to be done on me, but then I'd probably ignore it.' In March, I added:

So much for good intentions. Having done with the election, I set about helping with the NAC annual meeting. Just before it, I was in the hospital having my bladder looked at and cleaned up. (What an unromantic thing – just like Noël Coward and his sordid piles, as he said.) Anyway, having mentally had my own lovely memorial service (terrific music and dance), I thought I'd better clear up the chaos known as my study. Well, it's improved, but there's still about two tons of paper to dispose of.

I'm at this moment supposed to be writing an article dealing with a travel fund for an NDP women's conference, putting NAC's *MEMO* together, and adding some additional snippets to NAC's brief on medicare. We also seem to be set for weekend visitors every weekend in April. Never a dull moment.

Towards the end of the 1970s, many women were expressing their dissatisfaction with the slow pace of the political parties in moving towards greater equality for women within the parties and their programs. Discussions amongst academic, activist, and politically minded women were going on about the possibility of trying to form a women's political party in Canada. The group held its first meeting in 1978. Hours of debate and organizing culminated in an open meeting, in June 1979, and this was the official launching of the Feminist Party of Canada. The meeting was held at OISE, the Ontario Institute for Studies in Education, the place which had held so many women's and social-justice and peace gatherings. The 'feminist' in the title of the party allowed for the support of feminist-minded men. OISE professor Mary O'Brien was one of the most articulate and profound theorists in the group, which set to work to develop policies and structure for the party. Regular and special meetings were held and an office was established, large enough for discussions and meetings. The group finally aimed to try for a political foothold in one province rather than on a national basis, but failed to gain sufficient members to make this legally possible. Eventually money and woman-power ran out, and the Feminist Party remains an interesting part of women's history.

Among the political parties, the NDP has led the way in emphasizing sexual parity on their federal and provincial committees and in giving financial support for women candidates. Rosemary's feminist, grass-roots campaign, with consensus decisions and many innovative techniques, raised party and public awareness of the needs of women and paved the way for the other parties to follow suit and, fourteen years later, for the eventual leadership of Audrey McLaughlin.

Audrey McLaughlin's election as leader in 1989 came after Ed Broadbent had made progress in building the party and in establishing greater equality for women in the party itself and in its policies. Her election gave a tremendous boost to women of the party and in the country as a whole. It seemed a reward for all our education and work. Audrey brought to party activities new attitudes and new methods of working, which include both listening and nonconfrontational ways of negotiating policies. The contrast with Dave Barrett's bombast led the press and many party people at the convention to dub her weak, uncertain, not forceful enough; they feared excessive compromise and lack of definite policies. But hopes have risen for a new process and a new way of running things, as well as for solving problems, from local to international ones.

In 1990, the astonishing NDP victory in Ontario raised hopes that perhaps, just perhaps, in spite of daunting economic and social conditions, a new era of honest and open government might begin and that we might see more humane ways of running governments and developing policies for people. Eleven women cabinet ministers is a sign of hope even with recession, unemployment, and wars clouding our horizons. Yet, although the changes in attitudes and structures within the NDP during the past twenty years have been basic and significant, there is still a long way to go to reach a satisfactory state of feminism and socialism.

17

Greece, Part One

For me, the 'Greek connection' started after a 1964 women's meeting in Paris when some of my American friends went on to attend the annual peace demonstration in Athens. Then, in 1967, we heard of the coup by the Colonels and the jailing of Andreas Papandreou. This was the year Hélène Kazanzakis gave the keynote speech at VOW's international conference in Montreal, and she filled us in on the situation.

Andreas Papandreou, the son of a former Greek prime minister, was married to Margaret, a tall, blonde, and beautiful American journalist, whom he had met while teaching in the United States. After Andreas was jailed by the Junta, Margaret was left looking after their four young children and working desperately to secure Andreas' release. Later that year, he was released but exiled. He was invited to teach at York University, and the family moved to Toronto where they stayed for nearly seven years. Andreas set about organizing PASOK, the Panhellenic Socialist Movement he later headed as prime minister. Margaret, while teaching, raising her children, and writing a book, *Nightmare in Athens*, also began her work of organizing Greek women to obtain better conditions for themselves and their children. Both Margaret and Andreas worked tirelessly with Greek people here in Canada and elsewhere for the restoration of democracy in Greece.

It was through our friends the Buttricks, that Moira Armour and I first met Margaret (Margarita to the Greeks, and Maggie to her close friends). We had lunch in a small College Street café and talked of women, peace, film-making, teaching, and how to get press coverage for whatever scheme we were hatching at the time. I was immediately captivated by the friendliness and charm of this woman who had so recently come through the most terrifying experience at the hands of the Greek Junta. She became my friend and role model from that day.

In fact, my next federal election campaign, in 1974, was to benefit considerably from the help of Margaret and her Greek friends. I ran in York East, which has a large Greek population, and they buckled down and spent hours combing the voters' lists for Greek names and followed up with canvassing. I recall with delight an outdoor picnic party held some time after that at the Papandreous' home in King Township with their children, lots of Greeks, music, wine, and above all food.

That year, the Papandreous returned to Greece, and Margaret immersed herself in her work with the Union of Greek Women, which she helped found. We met again in Cyprus in 1975. Cyprus was populated by both Greek and Turkish people and, when the Turks had invaded the island in 1974, they had driven the Greek Cypriots from their homes. The women were now organizing a series of meetings culminating in a walk home – back through the Turkish lines. Famagusta was chosen as the destination, because it was one of the completely evacuated towns, previously popular with tourists and visitors and now empty, guarded by the Turks.

UN resolution 3212, section 5, passed unanimously by the general assembly the previous November, stated that all refugees should be allowed to return to their homes in safety and called upon 'the parties concerned to undertake urgent measures to that end.' The women intended to give a petition to the commander of the Turkish force, demanding the implementation of this resolution. On Sunday, April 20th, twenty thousand Greek Cypriot women met together to try to walk back to their homes.

They were joined and supported by women from many foreign countries. I was surprised and honoured to be one of the two women invited to represent Canada during the walk. We landed near the coast, since the main airport was in Turkish hands, and were welcomed by Greek Cypriot women in Nicosia. We were going part of the way to Famagusta by bus, making great headway along the narrow and bumpy roads, when suddenly there was a tremendous lurch, and the bus came to an abrupt halt. Amid a torrent of furious Greek, everyone strained to see what had happened. Some crazy driver had tried to cut in and our bus driver had avoided calamity by jamming on his brakes. The furious voice was that of famous actor and singer Melina Mercouri, saying, when the sentiments had been translated (and the language cleaned up a little, I suspect), 'I am prepared to die for my country, but *not* for some inept bastard like that!' Everyone relaxed, and the journey continued.

Thousands of women arrived in cars and buses (500 cars and 266 buses), with thousands more on foot, and were organized by teams of Greek Cypriot women. A huge crowd prepared to walk the remaining two miles to the barrier created by the UN peacekeeping force (among whom were included a number of Canadian servicemen). Before the walk started, additional UN troops were assigned to the area to prevent any incidents, and helicopters flew back and forth. The Turks, for their part, brought up reinforcements and barricaded the road. They also issued a series of statements that included 'We're waiting to rape them' and 'Anyone crossing the border will be shot.'

When the women reached the village of Derynia, they were greeted by hundreds of men and children (most of the women were on the walk) with great enthusiasm; they threw rose petals and smiled support. One old woman came to walk with Melina Mercouri and Lady Amalia Fleming (Greek widow of the discoverer of penicillin), and young girls flung their arms around them. Others offered drinks of water. The verandas and roofs of every house held welcoming people, cheering and clapping.

The huge crowd of women, watched by press from all over the world, rallied outside Derynia. Speeches were made with loudspeakers from a makeshift podium in a field. We heard from foreign women (the African bloc, France, Canada, Greece, and Britain), from leading Greek Cypriot women, from Lady Amalia Fleming, and from Melina Mercouri. All were inspired by this non-violent and peaceful event. The women then lined up behind more than a hundred flags of the countries of the women who supported them, and Women Walk Home moved off down the remaining two miles of country road. I helped carry the Canadian flag, and we walked until we arrived at the UN barrier, where the women stopped and sat down on the road. There were guards, UN and Greek Cypriots, then a no-man's-land before the UN guards connected with the Turkish troops. Procedure was discussed with the UN commander.

Two Greek Cypriot women went forward with a message of friendship for the Turkish Cypriot women. After some time they returned. The Turkish women had refused the message and had proffered one of their own. One phrase in it, 'We will give back your homes when you give back our dead,' and the general tone of the rest was thought to reflect Ankara's view rather than that of the women. Next, two women asked the UN officials to let them through to present to the Turkish commander the petition for the refugees' return. The UN official refused to allow this, because he thought the danger of shooting was too great, but he offered to try to deliver the message to the Turkish authorities himself. To highlight this refusal, three separate pairs of foreign women repeated the request and were also refused. (I was one of the women in this action.) Finally, the last group handed the petition to the UN commander and returned to the seated women. The next day we learned that he twice attempted to deliver the message and was rejected both times.

As if to symbolize the failure, the rain poured down. The flags of all the participating countries were placed sadly on the ground at the UN barrier, to signify our failure, and there on the cold wet road a group of women started a day-and-night vigil which they resolved to maintain until their petition was received. But although the immediate objective of the walk was not achieved, we hoped that the united and non-violent action of so many women would lead to other initiatives.

In the meantime, 200,000 Greek Cypriots were now refugees, homeless and living in tents without work or the necessities of life. A third of Cyprus' total population had been driven from their homes. The huge citrus-fruit industry was abandoned, farm animals and crops died from neglect, and the tourist industry had come to a halt. Cyprus depended on all these. It was the aim of Cypriot officials to set up rehabilitation and building programs so that the majority of the refugees could eventually become self-supporting. But a solution to Cyprus' problems is not possible without a unified policy for the whole island.

Three years later, in 1978, I went with an international group on the Greece Through New Eyes tour, and this is how it came about. One day in the winter of 1977, I was given a bright orange and blue brochure which read, 'Greece Through New Eyes: A Unique Tour Organized by the Women's Union of Greece' – a different perspective on Greece's culture and historic monuments. So enticing was the idea of a feminist tour of Greece that six months later I found myself in Athens.

My friends and I were part of a group of forty-five, six men and the rest women. On that first beautiful August evening we gathered together to contemplate the spectacular view of the Acropolis from the roof of our hotel. The group was very varied. A number of us were from women's organizations and were intensely interested in the progress Greek women were making. Four women friends from the University Club in Vancouver seemed never to have met a feminist or a socialist before, but they survived the experience. Other women included a nuclear physicist from England, a New Zealander who was organizing a women's film festival in Tokyo, and a young Norwegian socialist who was a single parent with three children and a member of the Oslo City Council. Most of the men were travelling with their wives, though there was one man we couldn't figure out. We dubbed him variously a CIA agent or a playboy who had entertained mistaken thoughts about the nature of a women's tour. He only lasted a few days.

There were eight Californian women whose consuming interest was Greek dancing. The high point of the tour for them came when they danced on the mountain top where, the story goes, besieged Greek women, rather than be captured by the Turkish invaders in 1821, hurled their children off the precipice and danced over the edge themselves. Two baby girls survived that ordeal, we were told, and one of them became a nun.

Margaret Papandreou, our long-time friend, was one of the organizers of the tour. The Colonels' régime had ended in 1974, and in 1976 Margaret's work had resulted in the founding of the Union of Greek Women. Union members were generally sympathetic to PASOK, and Melina Mercouri, Lady Amalia Fleming, and other women Members of Parliament were part of the Union. Membership in the Union stood at about five hundred and represented many parts of the country, with new branches being formed wherever possible. Because many Greek women, the rural women particularly, were not accustomed to uniting for political action, Margaret and her colleagues regularly visited the rural areas to get to know the women and to hear about the problems there. We learned how difficult it was for them to find time in their hard-working lives or encouragement from their menfolk to meet and organize with other women.

Nevertheless, it was these women, though mainly those based in Athens, who had planned this very ambitious tour. Now that their visitors had actually materialized, they were understandably nervous. They need not have worried. The Greeks are past masters at organizing tourists. The two-week visit included a week's tour in northern Greece, so, after a couple of days in Athens and having done all the right tourist things on the nearby islands, we set off in a luxury Mercedes bus in the company of a delightful and efficient tour guide called Helena, on a trip to Delphi, Corinth, Yannena, and many of the fabulously scenic mountain villages around Monodendri.

Away from Athens, the air was clean and clear, like the sea. The canal near Corinth which joins the Ionian and Aegean seas connects two dazzling blue bays and is a deep cut in the yellow rock. I bought a fertility symbol, made from woven wheat sheaves, from an old woman selling them beside the bridge over the canal. We crossed on a ferry, admiring the skill of the bus and truck drivers who parked their enormous vehicles on the boat with literally six inches between them.

In Yannena, we met women who had been active in the Resistance thirty years before and heard how they had carried great loads of ammunition and supplies up treacherous mountain paths to the men hidden high above. We talked to village women who began their day before dawn, when they helped their husbands herd the sheep or goats to pasture. The church and big landowners control much of the land around villages so, rather than pay rent to graze their animals, many villagers take their animals long distances to free feeding grounds in the hills. The women return at daybreak to get the children to school, work on the vegetable crops, weave, sew, and see to all the chores. Their day ends when they fall into bed about ten at night.

From Yannena we made a special trip to a village where we met the entire population, headed by the mayor, and proceeded to discuss conditions in the village and, of course, the government. The villagers spoke of the difficulties they faced in getting education for their children. High schools were situated in the towns, so rural children had to board or the whole family had to move for the children to continue their education. This partly explains why only 44 per cent of Greek women completed elementary school and most others were illiterate. Fewer than 2 per cent of women were university graduates. We heard that there were only three universities in all of Greece, so competition for places was fierce. Families would spend all their available money on fees and special coaching for their children. One woman we met in Yannena was selling the exquisite lace she had made herself to help finance her son's schooling. The town was filled with the families of students there to compete in the gruelling examinations for places at the university.

We talked to some of the young unmarried women still living in the village. To continue their education or find work they were going to have to leave their homes. There was a terrible lack of jobs for young people altogether, which was the reason so many crowded into the cities or emigrated. Fewer than 30 per cent of Greek women worked outside the home, and 97 per cent of them were characterized as 'unqualified,' which excluded them from benefits and security. Legislation allowed girls of fourteen to work in factories. Women were not considered equal with men, and still had prime responsibility for the children. Day-care centres were very few in number and very costly, and of course women were being paid less than men and working chiefly in the service and 'nurturing' jobs.

Health and social services, even when they existed, were too expensive for people with low incomes. A doctor told us that she could be prosecuted for advocating an abortion and that she was forced to lie about her patient's condition to perform one. Church, society, and government were opposed to sex education, contraception, and abortion. Some women who married would face a hard life as the wife of a shepherd or farmer. All the women aimed to give their children a better life than the one they themselves were leading, but the prospects were not bright.

Greek women had few property rights or rights within the marriage. In one village, we watched a procession with pipe and drummer bearing all the objects of a bride's dower to the house of the prospective husband. We thought this custom of dowries out of date and reflective of the concept of women as property. But then the North American custom of shower-giving isn't so very different.

As we drove on through spectacular mountain scenery with monasteries perching on pinnacles and accessible only by rope- or rock-climbing, our guide, Helena, told us about the history and geography of the country, the crops and occupations in the different areas, the temples and theatres, Mounts Olympus and Parnassus, and so on. At times, it was difficult to distinguish myth from ancient or even modern history and to separate stories of the two world wars from the recent dictatorship of the Colonels and the happenings in Cyprus. One got a very strong impression of the intense nationalism and fierce independence of the Greek people. The women played active and militant roles in the defence of their country, in the distant as well as the recent past.

We also used the bus microphone to take turns telling each other something about our own work and interests, and discussed the politics of the women's movement and of Greece itself. Finally, we drove back through the smog of Athens and Piraeus to reach our hotel by the sea for the final three days of our holiday and the memorable dinner prepared for us by the members of the Women's Union for our farewell party.

The party was held at the Papandreous' house (also used by Andreas as his office). The women had prepared a sumptuous feast with dozens of special dishes, as well as ouzo, wine, and punch. Greek food is most delicious and the Greeks take it very seriously. We had had many delightful fish dinners during our stay in Greece, but nothing touched the food prepared for us that night. At one point during the evening, I noticed Lady Fleming and some of the other women engaged in an intense discussion. 'What's going on?' I asked, 'A political crisis?' 'No, a very important matter,' Amalia Fleming told me, 'Food.'

Among the women present that evening were Andreas Papandreou's mother, then in her eighties, the first woman lawyer in Greece. Melina Mercouri was there too, tall, statuesque, and dynamic in a scarlet dress. She had just returned from the opening of her Medea film in New York to continue her work as an MP. She delighted us all, dancing and singing with young Andy Papandreou, and later she danced a fantastic 'macho' impersonation with an American woman as her partner. Dancing and singing in the house and in the dimly lit, tree-lined garden, brought us all closer together. We made speeches and hugged, with warm feelings of friendship and admiration for these women who had welcomed us to their country.

I didn't see Margaret Papandreou again for quite some time. But in 1981 she was touring the United States, speaking at universities and the United Nations. She was hoping to enlist support in setting up an institute for studying the situation of women in the Mediterranean region.

We spoke briefly on the telephone, and she told me about the conference of Mediterranean women held in October 1980, in Athens. Women came from all but a few of the countries bordering the Mediterranean to talk about the problems facing women in this area. The rights of Palestinian women and building a bridge between feminism and socialism were amongst the subjects considered. This marked a whole new era for these women, since government relations are often strained, so international cooperation between women's organizations is not always easy.

The United States wanted to be able to mount military operations around the oil-producing nations and was therefore seeking to extend the jurisdiction of NATO through bases in Turkey. This move was seen by many as escalating the arms race and threatening war in the Middle East. This dangerous situation was obviously much closer to the lives of women in the Mediterranean area than to us in Canada. Margaret remarked that the conference was covered by about seventy press representatives, none of them Canadian. What we tended then (and still tend now) to forget is that any future involvement of the United States may very well put Canadians, civilians in particular, in the front line of a nuclear exchange.

18

Greece, Part Two

The next stage of this Greek epic takes place in 1983. One day in February, I was waiting for my plane in the Ottawa airport when a short, dark man came up and said, 'You won't remember me, but I know you. I worked with you in your election campaign, along with my brother, Perry Economides.' He told me that the Papandreous would be coming to Canada in March on an official visit.

We talked it over at NAC and decided to send a cable inviting Margaret to speak at our annual meeting in Ottawa on March 26th. For several days there was silence. Time was passing and our meeting agenda was gradually filling up. Then I had a telephone call from Athens one morning. Mrs P regretted that she would not arrive in time for our dinner, but would be very happy to meet with progressive women on the afternoon of March 30th in Toronto.

We had about ten days to make plans, hampered somewhat by no one knowing where the Ps would be at any given time in their visit. By dint of telephoning the Greek Embassy, the Greek community in Toronto, and our friends at York University, where Andreas was to be presented with an honorary degree, we finally narrowed down the time when Margaret might be free. With about a week to go, we organized a meeting. The feminists at OISE rallied round, and we managed to book the auditorium there. We commandeered the willing NAC staff's abilities for making up an announcement, including a brief biographical note about Margaret, which mentioned last of all that she was the wife of the Greek prime minister, 'just for identification purposes.' Then we leapt to the telephone, delivered notices to the Greek community, contacted media people, and crossed our fingers.

We then dashed to Ottawa for the NAC annual meeting, and, during the lobby of the three party caucuses, Margaret Papandreou found a free second to come in and hear some of our questions. I was glad to have a chance to greet her and to check with her about the Toronto meeting. She was as charming and beautiful as ever, and I was very pleased that Brough and I had received an invitation to the Greek ambassador's reception and would be able to meet her again in Toronto.

Suddenly, on the day of our Toronto meeting, the press was interested in Margaret. Everyone wanted an interview, preferably half an hour or more, and we didn't even know whether she would be with us for one hour or three. When she arrived, however, she had already arranged to see the reporters back at her hotel, so we were able to settle down to our meeting.

She spoke to us of the condition of Greek women before the reforms that the PASOK government was putting into effect, and the changes those reforms were making in women's lives. Before 1983, a Greek husband made every decision about his wife's property, the children and their education, and where the family would live; he also had charge of his wife's dowry. The dowry was so entrenched in tradition that it could not be abolished; the new legislation meant that it would at least remain under the wife's control. The new laws also provided for joint decisions. Women could now use their own names and make their own decisions about residence and employment. Divorce could be granted by common consent or after four years' separation; alimony and support would depend on economic means.

Margaret told us of the enthusiasm and initiative of the Greek women and of her work with them in the small rural communities that make up so much of Greece. Her work is really revolutionary, and she pointed out that she had warned the Prime Minister that she reserves the right to demonstrate in front of Parliament for women's rights. After Margaret had spoken, there were questions and comments, then people crowded around, asking for information, sending messages to friends, and expressing their delight at seeing her again, until our time ran out. I saw Margaret again briefly that evening at the Greek ambassador's reception, a truly Greek occasion marked with wonderful food and drink for about 1500 people. The Papandreous 'mingled with the crowd,' as Margaret laughingly called battling their way through the surging mob. Later, we saw brief television reports of the Papandreous' visit, but the CBC steadfastly focused its reporting on Andreas and preferred to cover three Canadian women at the Trudeau dinner rather than giving us a glimpse of our distinguished visitor.

After this visit, many more of us wanted to visit Greece to see and hear more about the progress of the Greek women's movement, and I was lucky enough to be able to go to Greece at the end of that year. It came about in this way.

One day towards the end of October, I had a telephone call from the Greek Embassy informing me that the ambassador, on behalf of the new Greek government under Prime Minister Papandreou, was extending an invitation to me to go to Athens, all expenses paid (this punch line came later in the conversation). PASOK was celebrating the tenth anniversary of the end of the Colonels' régime, and a number of Canadians who had helped exiled and imprisoned Greeks during the régime were being invited to join the Greek people in celebrating.

I found it difficult to figure out why I had been selected for this honour. Contacts I had with Greeks during that period seemed to be ones in which *they* had helped *me*. They had worked in my 1974 election campaign and had given me the opportunity to go on the walk home to Famagusta in 1975. But I received a letter of confirmation a few days later with the welcome news that my friends John and Ann Buttrick and Milly Ryerson were also in the group of eight or nine Canadians invited to Greece.

I was worried about whether I could leave my sick husband for nearly a week, but my stalwart daughters and friends reassured me. Then I thought, 'Olympic Airways goes from New York, and the States would probably refuse me entrance' (I had been stopped at the border in 1982), but I explained it to the embassy and they graciously re-routed me and Milly through Amsterdam by KLM from Montreal. And so I set out, armed with messages of greetings from NAC and VOW for the Women's Union of Greece, and gifts and buttons supplied by Milly. We arrived in Athens airport on the afternoon of November 1st and were met with a bustling welcome by Perry Economides, who was in charge of us and the thirty or forty other guests arriving at the same time.

Milly and I were sharing a room in the King George Hotel on Constitution Square, right beside the Parliament buildings in the centre of Athens. It was a splendid, old building with tapestry and silken wall coverings. The balcony of the roof restaurant had a wonderful view of the Acropolis, provided the smog wasn't too thick. We just had time for a bath and a nap before the welcoming reception and dinner, where Prime Minister Papandreou gave an address and we met Margaret and Melina Mercouri (now Minister of Culture). After an excellent meal –

Greek fish and desserts are particularly tempting – we fell into bed to catch up on our sleep. We noted that, at this dinner and every other occasion, women were outnumbered by men by about ten to one, and that in Europe, with the exception of the Scandinavian countries, the equality of women had not visibly progressed in any dramatic way.

The next day, Tuesday, we joined the group of official guests and travelled in two buses to the university, which proved to be within easy walking distance. There we filed into a large hall, where we were addressed by Mr Xenophon Peloponnisios, president of the Society of the Imprisoned and Exiled, and were ceremoniously presented with honorary diplomas quoting from the 410 BC decree of Demofantos: 'the capital penalty to traitors of the country to be extended also upon those who hold an office during the period of subversion, and more so without standing trial, and those who killed them not to be punished, but to be honoured as heroes.'

This seemed a bit bloodthirsty, but then we hadn't suffered as many of those present had done. The first to receive the diplomas were cited as receiving it for the father or relative who was killed in front of the US Embassy or in similar circumstances. My embarrassment grew with the realization that everyone was to receive this honour. Fortunately I was given the chance to say something on the radio immediately after the ceremony, which gave me an opportunity very briefly to express my feelings about some of those heroic Greek people.

We went on to the Polytechnic Institute, the site of the student uprising on November 15th, 1973, where the Junta had brought in tanks and many students had been killed. This day, which marked the beginning of the end of the dictatorship in Greece, has been marked annually as a day of mourning and dedication. The wreaths placed in memory of the students increased all week until they must have numbered in the thousands.

Then we took the opportunity to visit the nearby museum with its magnificent monuments and wander around the narrow streets window-shopping until it was time to get ready for the reception at the Grande Bretagne Hotel. While we were thus peacefully occupied, Rauf Denktash, leader of the Turkish Cypriots, was making a unilateral proclamation of the independence of the part of Cyprus that the Turks had occupied by force in 1974. Considerable political and media activity resulted. Condemnation by governments was almost universal, and only Turkey and possibly Bangladesh had recognized the illegal action. Of course we Canadians wanted to know the stand of our own government, so we contacted the Canadian Embassy. Canada deeply regretted that the action had 'recognized only one state of Cyprus' and expressed firm support for the position of the Greek government.

After the reception, a few Canadian friends and I had been invited to Margaret Papandreou's home in Kifissia, a suburb of Athens. We drove off in official cars through the crowds of demonstrators and spent an enchanting evening beginning, in true Greek fashion, at about 10:30. We sat at two tables among what Ann Buttrick jokingly called the Papandreou dynasty and discussed many things, including the speech their eldest son George was to make in Parliament the next day.

Margaret told me that the Greek Women's Union membership now numbered about fifteen thousand women and described the trips she and her committee members made all over the country. She said, modestly, that it was useful for her to go along, because then, instead of a small meeting of just the women, the entire village would pack the hall. The women were delighted for the men to hear how women saw their very hard lives and responsibilities. Margaret laughingly told us that any idea she might have of her importance was dispelled by the frequent question: 'And when is Andreas coming to see us?' On one occasion, the men (consulting very seriously with each other) asked whether she would take their kisses to Andreas. She smilingly refused. She would keep them for herself, she said, and not pass them on to her husband. Consternation and no further action until, at the end of the meeting, one very shy (and gorgeous-looking) young man was pushed forward to give Margaret a very hasty and embarrassed peck on the cheek, before retiring in confusion.

That Wednesday, by way of a break from the ceremonies, we had been offered a tour to Corinth, Mycenae, and Epidaurus, the fabulous outdoor theatre that I had missed seeing before. It was well worth the visit. The size of the theatre and its incredible acoustics make one marvel at the technical ability of the designers and builders of such a perfect edifice, constructed so long ago.

That evening, Margaret took us over to the parliament buildings to hear young George Papandreou speak. We entered the building as guests of the Prime Minister's wife, with guards and executive assistants (all male) saluting and bowing, until we arrived in the anteroom to the Prime Minister's office, where Andreas was closeted with advisors discussing the Cyprus situation. We then went into the House, which contained only a sprinkling of the three hundred members (thirteen of whom were women, only a little less than Canada's percentage). The assembly was being addressed by a Conservative member extolling the benefits of private enterprise. Then George rose to give the history of the country-wide consultations leading to PASOK's new five-year plan. By this time, it was well past midnight, so we soon left and reached our hotel exhausted.

Thursday was the day of the Polytechnic demonstration and march. Few of us had any idea of the organization and size of a big European demonstration. Mr Gombay, the political advisor from the Canadian embassy, had suggested that we not go near the demonstration in case there was violence. Naturally we ignored this advice, and there was no violence of any kind. These marches have taken place every year since the end of the dictatorship, but this year there were added concerns. 'US bases out of Greece,' 'Greece out of NATO,' and condemnation of the Turkish action in Cyprus all featured among the slogans. We learned that an agreement had been reached to remove the US bases within five years, but this was not fast enough for some.

We climbed up the marble steps of the Polytechnic Institute and stood on the stone balcony-like platform to hear speeches from students, the mayor, and other leaders. When we were escorted down by Perry, we and the whole crowd stood during the playing of what must be the Greek equivalent of the Last Post. It was played on what sounded like an amplified mouth-organ.

I chickened out from the three-mile march and watched it go by from the steps of our hotel from 5:45 until 9:15, which was about an hour and a half before the march ended. The banners were often ten to twenty feet high, and the marchers stretched across the street twelve to twenty abreast. Everyone shouted slogans, but the contingent from the Women's Union, led by Margaret Papandreou, sang. According to some estimates well over a million people took part, yet few newspapers mentioned it the next day.

Some of us had relieved the weight on our feet by repairing to the bar for a couple of drinks during the final stages of the march past. After the others came back, it was time for the final reception and dinner. Another wonderful meal, then the farewells had been said, and we went upstairs to pack. Next morning, it was pouring with rain, but our efficient escorts got us all sorted out and finally put us on our planes bound for the four corners of the earth.

Arriving in Amsterdam with only an hour or so to change planes, I dashed around getting edible gifts and changing my money. Finally, on the upper deck of the KLM plane, I settled down to enjoy the extra amenities of 'business class' before I decided to write up the trip, which took me most of the way to Mirabel and thence to Toronto. I sailed through Customs, collected a taxi, and was home to a wonderful welcome and a birthday party for Brough by the time it was about 2:00 a.m. in Athens.

The Greek connection continues. In 1985, I returned for a second women's tour with Pat Boulding, my BC VOW friend. And then, after the Nairobi congress for the end of the Decade of Women in 1985, VOW was active in promoting the Forward-Looking Strategies and VOW members worked with Margaret Papandreou in Women for Mutual Security to have women present at summit meetings. As 1990 closed, a group of women, led by Margaret Papandreou, was setting off for Baghdad to try to avert the war in the Gulf.

19

The Constitution

Until 1981, Canada's most significant human-rights legislation, enacted in 1960, was the Bill of Rights, but this had not proved a great asset to women. In 1973, for example, Jeanette Corbière Lavell (who was held to have forfeited her Indian status when she married a white man) challenged the Indian Act, but the Bill of Rights did not forbid 'inequality within a group or class by itself, by reason of sex,' and so it proved useless.

Now Trudeau and his Liberal government were planning to bring Canada's Constitution back to Canada, and women were anxious to find out whether their rights would be protected this time. NAC, the Ontario Committee on the Status of Women, and Women for Political Action joined to organize a conference, which was held in Toronto's City Hall on October 18th, 1980 – Persons Day. About two hundred women attended and, with the help of expert legal women such as Mary Eberts and others, they absorbed a great many facts and came away disturbed by the prospects for women as seen in the proposed Charter of Rights and Freedoms.

Lloyd Axworthy, the Minister Responsible for the Status of Women, was speaking that evening at a dinner organized by WPA to celebrate Persons Day. Addressing about two hundred well-informed feminists, he made a patronizing speech in which he in essence told the women not to worry their little heads, Big Daddy would look after them. During a noisy question period, lawyer Marilou McPhedran, looking rather like an innocent teenager, reminded Mr Axworthy that she had once been a student of his in Winnipeg, and then told him exactly what the women thought of his arrogant speech. He retired from the dinner in disarray, but apparently learned no lesson from the experience.

In Ottawa meanwhile, Doris Anderson, now president of the Canadian Advisory Council on the Status of Women (CACSW), had been organizing research on the whole question of women's equality and the Constitution. She was convinced that the Charter posed serious problems for women and had written to the government to say so, but had met with no response. CACSW therefore had begun to plan a Constitution conference for women that fall, but it was postponed. Mr Axworthy, the minister responsible for CACSW, believed that such a conference might 'embarrass' the government. This difference of opinion led to a full scale blow-up. The Council, to their shame, did not back Doris' stand and, in January 1981, she resigned. Several of the staff and research team resigned with her.

The news spread fast, and women were furious. Questions were raised in the House of Commons. What was to be done in the face of this government arrogance?

Here is what I wrote for the January 1981 *Broadside*: '"Hi! Would you be able to come to a meeting at lunch time tomorrow?" I was asked over the phone. "We're so mad about that women's constitutional conference being called off that we want to do something about it. It's at the Cow Café on John Street. Upstairs at 12:30. See you!"'

A noisy meeting was in progress when I arrived. Many of the women were experienced members of the women's movement: Moira Armour, Laura Sabia, WPA member Linda Ryan Nye. Nancy Jackman was there, too. She had only recently come into contact with NAC in Toronto, but she became very involved with the conference and constitutional issues. She was to act as the continuity person for this ad hoc committee and was later largely responsible for laying the groundwork for, and then promoting, the Women's Legal Education and Action Fund (LEAF). She listened eagerly to the talk about the Constitution.

'It's shocking,' said Laura Sabia, 'We get pushed around all the time.' 'Well,' said Linda, 'some of us think we should have a conference anyway.' 'Terrific,' chorused the rest of us as we reflected on our resources and potential allies. MPs Flora MacDonald and Pauline Jewett came to mind. 'D'you think Flora and Pauline would help us get the same room in the House that the Advisory Council had booked?' 'Great idea. Let's ask them. Let's ask Doris what she thinks.'

So telephoners were dispatched while the rest continued eating and plotting, gloating over what the Opposition had been saying in Parliament and lamenting about Lloyd Axworthy and the easily swayed executive of the Advisory Council. The telephoners returned. 'Flora thinks it's a terrific idea and she's going to talk to Pauline to see what they can do. Now let's try Doris.' 'Why not?' came Doris' distinctive gravelly voice over the phone. 'Sounds like a great idea to me.'

So we went on with the planning. We must tell the press. We must raise money. We must get out a flyer. We need a committee to raise funds. We need people to work on an agenda. We need women in Ottawa. Everyone volunteered for various tasks and started to work on organizing a major women's conference in Ottawa, without any visible funds or support and with three weeks to go. The conference had to be held on the date planned by the Council 'so that women won't be disappointed, and to show the government that women can do a few things without their help.'

One stalwart woman called from Ottawa with the message, 'Pat says she'll do everything she can on the spot.' Pat Hacker proceeded to call together a committee for organizing accommodation, billets, translation, media, and support from everyone ranging from Joe Clark's wife Maureen McTeer, who offered Stornaway (the house of the leader of the Opposition) for a reception, to Ottawa Mayor Marion Dewar, who provided us with the City Hall for one day. Saturday, we had agreed, was to be devoted to serious consideration of all aspects of the Constitution that might affect women. It was not to be 'government-bashing' but constructive consideration of the needs of women, what the government had proposed, what we would recommend and what action we would take. As soon as we had facilities for the Sunday also, we decided that the meeting could be extended so that we could talk about the Advisory Council and make suggestions for improving it, if in fact its existence was valid.

Dawn MacDonald, editor of *City Woman* in Toronto, launched the Butterfly Campaign. 'Wear a butterfly on Valentine's Day, the day women are going to Ottawa to hold their own constitution conference. Phone ten friends and tell them to do the same. Sell butterfly buttons to raise money.' The YWCA took on the job of distributing and selling buttons. Air Canada flight attendants were asked if they could wear butterflies on the Day. Registrations started to pour in.

At one of the Cow Café meetings, two men were sitting at a nearby table. It was impossible for them not to hear what was going on. One finally came over to us as they finished eating. 'I heard what you were saying, especially about media coverage,' one of them said. 'I happen to be a reporter from CTV, and we've got our equipment right here. Could we shoot you and do an interview?' Could they! Seldom do such opportunities fall into one's lap.

Publicity proceeded apace. The media took it up in a big way: interviews and reports were scattered through the press and on television. Michele Landsberg wrote columns; so did Sabia. Linda was interviewed. Laura made pronouncements. NAC just happened to be having a party, so 150 women heard all about the plans and started spreading the word. Several women's organizations had mailings going out and included the flyer with their newsletters. Our own monster mailing was accomplished by an efficient and raucous team of lickers and stickers who kept getting more brilliant ideas as the evening wore on. In the middle of it, we (all four of us) listened to CBC's 'Fifth Estate' over the telephone, chortling over the discomfiture of Axworthy when confronted with his talk of embarrassing the government.

By this time, friend Lloyd had announced that he was inviting 'major women's national organizations' to meet with him to discuss how to improve the Advisory Council, and he planned this for the day after the weekend of the conference he had called off. OK, we'd give him some ideas too. His offer was even helpful to us, since it provided travel money for some of the women, who could thus come to our conference before going on to advise the Minister.

The single phone in the Women's Credit Union was ringing constantly as Illa Drever, our 'paid' worker (minimal wage all right for her nine-hour-day devotion to duty), piled up registrations and forwarded requests. 'We're chartering a bus,' she announced. 'In fact, we may even need two buses.' Another woman offered to type the cards for registration and organize the bus travellers. Meantime in Ottawa, plans were in hand for billets, day care, meals, and transportation. Documents and fact sheets were being produced and maps prepared to guide out-of-towners around Ottawa.

The organizing committee prepared to meet before the day. Linda spent two full days discussing all the minute details with Pat and her Ottawa committees, thereby missing three planes (or, at least, the third missed her by having some mechanical difficulty and sending the passengers back into the airport). Moira had an offer to make a film and started negotiations with the National Film Board, and women photographers offered their services. One woman offered to match individual contributions up to $1000, and in no time had to reach for her cheque book. The chairpersons of the New Brunswick, Saskatchewan, and Newfoundland Advisory Councils immediately offered to come and to help. Others followed as the news got around. Women called from all over Canada to say they were coming. The profits of Ma Bell and the other phone companies must have soared from the urgent business transacted by long distance. There was little time for mail after the first notice had been sent.

We tried to get support from all three political parties. The two opposition parties offered us food, coffee, reception, and use of offices in the House. Only individual Liberals helped, not the Liberal Party, which was a pity. We didn't want to be partisan. The object was to discuss Canada's Constitution, not what the different party points of view were, but what women wanted regardless of party. Native women had special needs. They were to have their say. Quebec women, with their particular perspective, must be heard.

As of Wednesday, C-Day minus three, the press coverage coming up was the answer to our prayers: 'Canada AM' on Friday, Betty Kennedy, 'Morningside,' 'As It Happens' with Elizabeth Gray, CFTO women covering the conference from Toronto, and so on. As Doris said, 'If we'd held the conference as the council planned, probably no one would have taken any notice. Now they've got the whole press covering the thing.' Full glare of publicity? Who's going to be embarrassed this time?

Both before and at the conference, everyone wanted to help, and anyone who turned up was immediately given a job. Women dealt with officials or the press, went on television at a moment's notice, made instantly decisions that would have taken a formal committee weeks to decide, and trusted one another to come through with whatever they'd undertaken. Officials and reporters had difficulty coping with the idea that there was no proper coordinator or organizer. 'Who's in charge?' was met with 'I guess I am, for the moment,' or 'Oh, speak to Pat, or Linda, or anyone will help you.' No requisitions. No orders. No paper work except for telephone numbers scribbled on pieces of paper. It would boggle the mind of any bureaucrat. And it did.

During the weekend we began to get a sense of the power women can generate when they unite. We realized that those 'feminists' and 'libbers' were concerned about the same things as the 'ordinary' housewives, business women, students, and grandmothers. We came home understanding more clearly why a Charter of Rights and Freedoms must define the rights of a person, male or female, and pinpoint each kind of discrimination. Some of us remembered when married women were barred from holding jobs, while others had lost jobs or homes or had been jailed for political beliefs or sexual orientation. We wanted marital status, sexual orientation, and political belief added to the specified categories, which include sex, race, and so forth. Women have suffered because the jurisdictions of federal and provincial governments are not clearly set out. Medical and social services, child support, housing, education, and training may be denied as governments pass the buck. We understood more about these issues as facts emerged and were discussed in our small groups.

The women's instant do-it-yourself constitutional conference made a place for itself in history. The response of women from every province and territory astounded not only the organizers. They had first thought two hundred an optimistic estimate of attendance. Yet, without government support and with less than three weeks' planning, over 1300 women registered to discuss Canada's Constitution. Women really wanted a say in the constitutional debate.

What sparked this remarkable response? Anger! Anger at being pushed around. Anger at being thought too dumb to be interested in the Constitution. Anger that Doris Anderson who, as editor of *Chatelaine*, had pinpointed serious women's issues long before they became fashionable, had been made scapegoat for government's high-handed treatment of women. We were told that all sorts of things were impossible: meeting rooms, translation services, travel, day care. But we had seen our male decision-makers ignore women's needs in the discussions on the Constitution until we took matters into our own hands. The ad hoc committee was very determined. The impossible, as they say, just took a little longer, and 'longer' was measured in minutes, not days.

My recollections of that historic period come in flashes, and I am thankful that I recorded some of my impressions on the spot, as I realize now how little my memory retains. Penney Kome's book, *The Taking of 28*, gave me forgotten names and incidents, and many women have their own special memories of what went on. How did we travel to Ottawa? Where did everyone stay? I remember how one hotel bedroom with two double-beds and a cot provided cheap accommodation for five enthusiastic women. I was recently reminded of how two tins kept frozen on the window-sill provided our breakfast orange juice. I remember the final planning in the Chelsea Club on the night before the conference. I remember the hundreds of women squeezing into the overflow rooms with the monitors and how no one attended the reception because everyone was still deeply engaged in working out the final recommendations and statements.

With the end of that February weekend, the ad hoc committee was to discover that the struggle for women's equality in the Constitution was only just beginning. None of the women who came to that conference expected miracles, but they were determined that their demands be heard. Every Member of Parliament was to be visited and advised of the conference resolutions. Women used their networking techniques to keep up the pressure. MPs, after all, would go home to their constituencies, and women have votes that can be crucial.

But on Monday, February 16th, the morning after, our first task was to make sure that every Member of Parliament and every bureaucrat involved in the constitutional process was informed of the conference resolutions and was then lobbied for their inclusion. It meant hours and hours of discussions with legal and political women and men, the drafting of statements, letters, and press releases, endless journeys between Ottawa and Toronto. It meant women trying to catch up with their non-constitutional family and work lives, let alone their studies, finances, and other daily living. But the pressure was kept up on the government, and finally the equality clause was included.

At last the summer came, and Brough and I went for a month to Japan for his lecture tour, exhausting for him but fascinating for both of us. We had Setsuko Thurlow, VOW member and Hiroshima survivor, to thank for our stay in the International House in Tokyo. Brough lectured and was showered with presents and honours, as he was well known in Japanese academic circles. Meanwhile, I was taken to both the Kabuki theatre and the magnificent puppet theatre.

Brough and I spent some days in Hiroshima, where we visited the Peace Park and Museum, which brought home again the horrors of the war. The total devastation of the centre of Hiroshima has been documented, both on film and in pictures painted by survivors. The film at the time could only show black and white, but many of the paintings are vividly coloured, increasing the impact of the appalling scenes. Everything burned. An orange-red light lit up the city, and many people perished after the blast as buildings collapsed. One of Hiroshima's seven rivers, part of the estuary of the main river, was at the epicentre of the blast and disappeared completely. The Peace Park and other memorials contain the unidentified remains of thousands who died.

I met poet and activist Sadako Kurihara, who brought me some of her poems and some articles that had been written about her. Although she had herself missed a newspaper interview by coming, she smiled and allowed me to finish an interview about the women's movement in Canada. Sadako is a tiny woman with a smiling face and eyes that seem almost closed to shield them from the light. The strong sunlight bothers her, one of the symptoms remaining from that morning in August 1945. She is a hibakusha, a survivor of the A-bomb. She has devoted her talents and energy to trying to prevent a repetition of that hell on earth which killed 300,000 men, women, and children in Hiroshima and Nagasaki.

When the A-bomb exploded in Hiroshima, Sadako was only five kilometres away. She saw a flash and felt the blast that blew out all windows in the neighbourhood. Luckily, her two children were at school further away from the centre, but the confusion and panic affected everyone. She found the two little girls on their way home. She put them on her bicycle, which had a little trolley attached, and rode all night to get away from the burning city and leave the children with relatives in the country. The next day, she bicycled back to the city to help a neighbour find her little girl's body in the school where she had died. They brought her home to be buried. The child's handkerchief was stuck to her burned face so that her mother could not pull it off to look at her face for the last time. Sadako Kurihara's husband had been drafted to help clean the city. His clothes were covered with spots from the black rain which fell and he was later hospitalized for a month, but he recovered from the effects of the radiation.

We talked a little about the opposition to nuclear bombs and the desire for peace which dominate the life and work of many Hiroshima survivors. Sadako Kurihara's poems reflect this passion. She is considered a radical by many and has not always been popular with a government planning to increase its 'self-defence' forces and sell arms to the United States. We talked about education in our two countries and about the increasing violence among students. There have been instances in Japan of young people, apparently quiet and cooperative, suddenly attacking their parents and going wild without any particular provocation. We agreed that one factor might well be that young people today cannot be sure that they will have a chance to grow up at all. They don't know whether they will live very long, so what is the point of preparing for the future? It's as if they were saying, 'Eat, drink, for tomorrow we die.'

When the Pope visited Hiroshima earlier that year he said, 'To remember the past is to commit oneself to the future.' It is this conviction which motivates the present citizens of Hiroshima. They remember those who died and how they died, and realize how future war can only lead us all to a similar fate. This is why the children of Japan are taught in their school classes about the bombing of Hiroshima and why Sadako Kurihara and her colleagues spend their energy on promoting peace and disarmament.

This, too, is why I agreed with a woman professor whom I met at Kyoto University, who said that women must now take responsibility for making the decisions about war and peace that so far have been made only by men. If we don't do it soon, we may well be too late. This is where we must speak up and take actions, not only on Hiroshima Day, but whenever and wherever we can. When Sadako Kurihara visited Toronto in 1981, I was glad to have the chance to write in *Broadside* about her experiences and her struggles – all our struggles – for peace.

When we came back from Japan, the ad hoc committee on the Constitution was meeting on a gloriously hot summer day in Nancy Jackman's garden, swimming to keep cool, writing the final report, and sorting out the finances. The telephone network had been used extensively in the spring, and women's continuing anger and frustration kept them sending in financial contributions whenever they could. The whole operation had been made possible by donations in kind and, of course, hours and weeks of volunteer time from women. Women MPs from all parties, their staffs and the House of Commons staff, as well as Marion Dewar and her civic staff, all made huge contributions.

When those of us who had been away came back from our summer holidays, another crisis hit the ad hoc committee. The hard-won equality clause, section 28, was threatened by the 'notwithstanding' clause, which might invalidate women's equality rights. This clause would have allowed the provinces, for a period of five years, to pass legislation overriding the Charter. Each provincial premier would have to be convinced that section 28 should not come under the 'notwithstanding' clause. The whole business of networking, lobbying, meetings, and press releases started over again. This time, however, the federal government was helpful. And so, in November 1981, the last provincial premier was persuaded, the 'notwithstanding clause' overcome, and women at last felt they could celebrate.

After the celebration and the homecoming of Canada's Constitution, there was the three-year wait for the equality provisions of the Charter to come into effect and for legislation to be changed to comply with the Charter's provisions. Women lawyers were monitoring the laws in preparation for the cases that would come before the courts in the future. During this period, and thanks to a few persistent women, the Charter of Rights was not forgotten. The seeds of the Legal Education and Action Fund were firmly planted, thanks to the far-sightedness of some of the legal women and the stolidly persistent efforts of Nancy Jackman, who set about raising money and establishing an organization to assist in the costs and litigation of women whose cases might be significant in developing the law resulting from the Charter of Rights and Freedoms.

In 1985, the Constitution came into effect and women across Canada celebrated their equality rights. In 1988, the Supreme Court brought down its decision to remove abortion from section 251 of the Criminal Code, and we rejoiced with Dr Henry Morgentaler and prepared for whatever course the government might take next.

20

Early 1982

If I were much given to praising 'God from whom all blessings flow,' then I would have been kept very busy during 1982. All in all, it was a pretty good year for Kay Macpherson. It was the year I spoke at the UNSSOD rally in New York, after being initially rejected at the US border. It was the year in which, to my incredulous surprise, I got the Order of Canada. I'd been to San Francisco, Mexico, Edmonton, and Lethbridge by the end of February. It was a singularly exciting, challenging, and satisfying year for me, filled with wonderful expressions of fondness, love, and even admiration, which is puzzling but certainly gratifying to an attention-getter like me.

But later, when I tried to remember it all properly, laziness and poor work habits got in the way. First, I found that I was getting it mixed up with other years, sometimes only one year away, but sometimes two or three. So I went back to my little blue pocket diary for 1982. It is both sketchy and illegible. What am I supposed to make of '12 Ursula B of E,' or '8 St John P St George'? I wish I hadn't been quite so cryptic.

Nineteen eighty-two really began for me on Christmas Eve of 1981, when a choice assortment of family and friends came for dinner. It was a lovely party. Besides daughter Susan and her partner John, son Stephen was there, as well as Herbert Whittaker, Nancy Jackman, and others. All our waifs and strays came laden with presents, which left us with almost, but not quite, an embarrassment of riches.

On Christmas Day, we had no obligations, just breakfast in bed with books and music and beginning to write my Christmas cards and letters. Susan and John left to join Danny Grossman and Germain Pierce in San Francisco, where Brough and I were to meet them later in the week. Susan had first met Danny when they were dancing in New York, and later Danny and Germain became friends with all the Macphersons. It took years for us to realize that Danny was the son of Hazel Grossman, whom I had met during various peace actions with Women Strike for Peace. I also discovered that Danny, in his teens, had visited the Soviet Union with his mother and my good friend Mary Clarke of Los Angeles WSP.

Danny and Germain house-sat for us one spring when Brough was off on one of his visiting-professor sessions in Israel or Denmark. And Brough and I, together with some of our friends, were members of Danny's first board of directors for the Danny Grossman Dance Company. When I was being a candidate in a federal election, I would sometimes crawl wearily home and find Danny and Germain had cooked and were about to serve up a delicious dinner. We have celebrated all kinds of occasions together, so we were looking forward to spending New Year's Eve with the Grossman family in San Francisco.

Nancy nobly drove us to the airport, whence we travelled to Los Angeles for Brough's political-science convention. The American Poly Scis (Political Scientists) were meeting there to read papers about Brough at him and each other. Los Angeles is an enormous place. I think our hotel dazzled us the most. The outside was black glass, with elevators that went up and down outside our windows and an outdoor swimming pool (no fun in that cold, wet weather), and shopping plazas with all kinds of food stores where we stocked up so we could eat in our room.

Brough spent all the next morning rewriting whatever he was going to say, and I was picked up by Mary Clarke and driven out to her house. It had a gorgeous view as far as the sea, when there was no smog, and was filled with fascinating mementos of all her gadding around the world working for peace. Mary had bad bouts of arthritis, which meant no typing and even having special fixtures attached to the phone, but she was better now and nothing ever stopped her actively planning all the next moves for the peaceniks and activists.

The next day, after a little light shopping (mainly bras for Nancy, the search for which took Brough and me to assorted lingerie departments), we partook of a liquid lunch and set off, fortunately by taxi, in good time for the LA airport. World Airways turned out to be a one-man show almost, owned by the guy who brought the boat people over from Vietnam. We hadn't bargained for the very crowded flight, originating in Italy and making assorted stops on the way to Oakland. It was late when we arrived, but we were collected by peace activist Madeline

Duckles, who put us up and gave us a wonderful gourmet dinner (caviar spread over creamy cheese is superb) and some good conversation, as friends of hers were just back from Poland and had many stories to tell. The next day we settled in to our special old Beresford Arms Hotel, small and old-fashioned, with its mirrors, white paint, and lovely red carpets. There was no restaurant, but we had a little kitchen and were able to stock up on groceries across the street.

Later we were picked up by Danny, and out we went in the rain to the Grossman house. Daughter Sheila had driven down with some friends in a truck from Hornby and it was wonderful to see them all. Danny and Germain had been with Aubrey and Hazel for a few days, and everyone was busy getting dinner ready. There was a general reunion and celebration, and a superb ham and salad and dessert and wine, and wine, and dancing, and general merriment, and talk, and talk, and phoning Dale on Hornby and Herbert and Nancy in Toronto. All very jolly, and we even got home to bed before New Year's Day, everyone being exhausted and having celebrated it on Eastern Standard Time.

The next day we tried to see the film *Reds*, but so did everyone else in San Francisco, so, rather than queue forever, we switched over and got into the queue for *Ragtime*, which was much better than we had expected, gloomy but well done. We were ready, after a little nip, to be picked up and taken out to dinner at the Rendezvous, courtesy of Aubrey and Brough. Only Germain stayed home, exhausted. We all had a very good time. Hazel and I are twins, we discovered, even to the day I believe, but she can outdance Danny at that cossacks' knee-bending dance, and my leg muscles will only just get me upstairs. Oh well.

The weather cleared the next morning and it was beautifully sunny for our ferry trip to Sausalito. This was great, and we met Susan and John for lunch. Susan gave me a lovely necklace, and we bought a baby hippo (stuffed toy) for Nancy. We returned on the ferry, having said goodbye to the Hornby trio, then took a taxi to our cosy nook, where we cooked our supper and went to bed.

The weather was at it again next morning: all kinds of floods and mud-slides made us wonder whether the planes would be able to take off. We caught the minibus in pouring rain and wind, were delayed until 2:00 p.m., but arrived in Toronto to be met by Noble Nancy at 10:30. That gave us one day to get caught up on washing and such, before Nancy's fortieth birthday party. It was fun, a wonderful mixture of feminists and family, friend and foe all mixed together very congenially. I think Nancy enjoyed it, and I stayed to help clean up. It's a wonderful house for a big party, provided the heat is on.

January was well on its way by now, and on the weekend of the 9th, the Science for Peace people organized a symposium at Massey College, with a couple of Soviet scientists, a man from Suffield (Alberta), and various other government and official types, all discussing chemical and biological warfare. I finally met Margaret Fulton, Muriel's friend from Mount St Vincent, and what a powerhouse she is. In no time we'd got a women's caucus going and put together a statement of how we felt about things. It was a good day, with a lot of facts about how Canada's forces (not civilians of course) are protected against CBW (chemical and biological warfare), should they be attacked. It certainly would be a very unpleasant way to have to manoeuvre, clad in some of these protective garments.

A man from Finland was helpful about getting over the verification problem, ascertaining the truth of countries' protestations that they are not manufacturing or storing any means of CBW. This has been a major obstacle holding up talks so far. It's something Canada could contribute to, since Suffield already has the techniques and equipment for finding minute quantities of chemical/biological substances, and they are not too costly; only it had never occurred to the Canadians that they might do something positive with such a technique. Oh, they might just give the material to NATO, they thought!

I ended up that day by having Nancy to dinner, then going to the Dan Heaps' party, which had good talk about foreign policy, etc., and then to Herbert's (can't remember what the occasion was). The diary for the rest of that week has little notes about VOW, NAC, IWD (the International Women's Day Committee was already meeting to plan the March 8 events), DGDC (the Danny Grossman Dance Company), and *Broadside* meetings, and I haven't a clue about the content of any of them. I really will have to be more explicit in my jottings.

Then Brough had another conference, so on Monday the 18th, after a NAC weekend meeting, we, escorted by Nancy Jackman, set off for Mexico City. We stayed in the Grand Hotel, which was handy for meetings since it was just around the corner from the Zoccolo where the other professors were staying. Each room in the Grand Hotel had a laid-on fridge/bar – not on the house, as we later discovered after drinking champagne and liqueurs.

While Brough was off being academic, Nancy and I explored. On the first day, we happened on the city hall, where everything looked very jolly, with a band practising and dancers joining in. It turned out that the King and Queen of Sweden were visiting, so we hung around and saw them and all the city officials on parade. We saw some of the Rivera murals in the palace, looked at dozens of gold and jewellery shops, went to the Folklorico and even a bullfight school, though not by design.

Nancy wanted to go to a bullfight, so I said I'd go too, although it isn't exactly what I would pick. But there were no bullfights scheduled, so the tour man took us off to the suburbs where the student matadors were practising. There weren't too many people there, but the whole routine was strictly adhered to, and there were even one or two exciting moments when a matador got himself into trouble. When the bull was finally finished off, what should appear amongst all the venerable trappings of the historic bullfight but a little Volkswagen bug to tow him off. However, bullfights, seal hunts, fox hunts, and all the rest ... I suppose someone can always say they depend on it for a living. But at least a seal hunt isn't done for sport or in front of a cheering audience. Oh well, I'm not going into moral and ethical questions at the moment.

One of the best afternoons Nancy and I had was walking all over the place looking for a glass factory. We finally found it, and it was just the kind of place I figured a glass factory should be, dusty and scruffy, with glass that was imperfect but just what I like, and cheap. The man demonstrated making incredible lilies and spoons, which he 'gave' us for a consideration and which we later gave to a friend who said she was enchanted by them, though we'll never know what she really thought.

Brough having decided that a bus trip and walking up and down hills in San Miguel were not for him, Nancy and I set off one morning on our own to visit our old New Brunswick friends, Ros and Ted Campbell, the artists who used to be joint curators of the museum art section in Saint John. Now they lived in San Miguel except for infrequent bus trips to Canada. No one has perfected the art of travel by bus to the extent that the Campbells had. Organizing food and drink, getting the best seats – they'd got it down to a T and consequently enjoyed themselves immensely.

Our bus journey to San Miguel took four hours or so, and this precipitated a slight crisis. Even when the bus stopped, I was too scared of missing it to go looking for a washroom. Consequently, when we finally arrived at the hot, dusty bus station in San Miguel, we were pretty desperate. There didn't seem to be any washroom for miles, so, casting desperately around, I found a suitable wall hiding a yard full of tumbledown brick and junk, and there, hidden from the milling crowds on the street, we proceeded to relieve ourselves. What joy, and what a sense of relief. We gathered up our bags and laboured in the hot sun up to the hotel where we were to meet Ros. She guided us down cobbled streets and narrow alleys to their little house, which was quite charming. Ros kept painting all the time, and Ted did the shopping and puttering around, including taking us to see the sights.

Shortly after this side-trip, Nancy, Brough, and I shipped ourselves back to Toronto, laden with pictures and glass and heaven knows what else as well. The first thing we attended after getting back was the Danny Grossman Dance Company recital and reception in the studio. Danny's new work-in-production was aired to a rather bewildered audience. This was the dance that required a lot of jumping over sofas, rolling up in rugs and mattresses, and a good deal of what Brough called a Freudian romp. However, whatever people thought of that, everyone enjoyed the party afterwards. Then came Dan Heap's Chinese banquet, a Tafelmusik and a New Chamber concert. On reflection, this seems a standard selection, and my diaries confirm that I went to the same events several years running.

I was hoping to be a delegate to the upcoming Ontario NDP convention, so I attended a meeting of the St George riding NDP, but no supporters of anyone but Bob Rae got to be delegates. The same process was repeated at the St Andrew–St Patrick meeting. I finally got to be a delegate from Nickel Belt, of all places. The NDP convention was the usual mixture of fury, some victories, and incredulous disbelief at the perfidy of the party brass (including manipulation of the nominations by way of messages to a babysitter). I even felt some degree of fellow-feeling with Lynn McDonald, who was new to all the goings on and found them hard to believe. Only dear old Alice Heap broke the slate. Bob Rae and Richard Johnston were evenly matched contenders for the leadership, but Bob Rae got to be the new leader and everything appeared to be oh-so-spontaneous.

The next week we were off to the west. Brough left for Winnipeg on the Wednesday and made his way to the Mardiros' in Edmonton by Saturday. I gave a noon-hour talk at the Board of Education, had a birthday party for Dorothy Smieciuch, then national-office coordinator for VOW, and got myself off to Edmonton for a wonderful welcome and lunch (largely liquid) with Brough and Tony and Betty, and then we all slept until it was time for dinner and an inundation of friends. Yatter, yatter, until the small hours.

Brough and I eventually both arrived in Lethbridge (can't remember in which order), and we had a nice room looking across the wide ravine to the university, which resembles a concrete railway station. The hotel had a nice swimming-pool/bar, where Doris Anderson and I had the longest and best talk we'd ever had (over several drinks). Apart from the women's group inviting me to take part in a day-long conference, the university guys had cooked up a job for me chairing a debate on the women's movement between Doris and Barbara Amiel. I knew nothing about Barbara Amiel except that she wasn't a Good Thing by my standards, so I figured I'd better read her autobiography. Oh dear. It was terrifying. She is bright, clever, and astute, with all the right left-wing origins (if that makes sense), and is totally reactionary and opposed to almost everything I'm in favour of and vice versa. Not a pleasant prospect. Actually, when the time arrived, Barbara Amiel confessed that she had had a miscarriage the day before and was feeling awful. She bore up well enough (being quite fiery for the students, I'm told), but by evening she'd run out of steam and wasn't at her best/worst. So Doris could do a good job. But the whole affair was DULL, and of course we had to feel rather sorry for her (maddening!).

On the way through Edmonton, on our way home, we had a very good supper and meeting at Terry Padgham's, and the Voices there seemed to be bestirring themselves again, which was good news, especially since the cruise missile was about to be tested on their doorsteps.

The rest of February seems evenly distributed between various peace-ish meetings, talking to schools, and having friends to stay. Hilda Thomas of the BC NDP was in town for a meeting, and we had a long talk all about NAC and POW (the Participation of Women Committee of the NDP). I also went to dance performances like the National Ballet and Mummenschanz. Mummenschanz is an extraordinarily talented company of three which combines mime with all kinds of almost contortion-like movements and the acting out of stories and situations. This continued right through the intermission when they appeared amongst the audience. I made the mistake of sitting upstairs and therefore missed some of the close-up effects and gestures, but they were remarkable even from a distance.

In March there was an International Women's Day march and fair. At one time, Vi Thompson and I used to attend all the IWD planning meetings as well as going to the events. I remember one March 8th march, trudging along Harbord Street in the snow. IWD took different themes each year, and there were some particularly fierce discussions on racism. Along with many other groups, VOW always had a display table at the fair, and often ran a workshop or discussion. VOW always used to receive cards from the Soviet Women's Committee and other organizations in the socialist countries, although IWD did not become a regular celebration of the Canadian women's movement until the mid-1970s. Before that, only the old left-wing women's organizations such as the Congress of Canadian Women and some union women had been aware of the day.

Over the years, we have selected a number of special days, marked for activities of all kinds: Hiroshima Day, United Nations Day, Persons Day, and now, after the Montreal massacre, December 6. And Take Back the Night marches and supportive rallies outside abortion clinics – all these events bring women together and increase communication. Many women, too, have taken to non-violent resistance such as joining picket lines and forming peace blockades. These are a far cry from the ladies with baby carriages on VOW's first polite walk to the Metropolitan Church, but all contribute to making peace and women's issues part of Canadian life.

More Toronto meetings, then I was off to Moncton, where I'd been invited to attend a meeting. Its purpose seemed unclear at the time but turned out (as Madeleine Leblanc, chair of the NB Advisory Council, had hoped) to be forming a status-of-women coalition of groups to take some of the burden off Madeleine and her Council.

The meeting was on a Saturday, however, and there was no way of getting to Moncton early on Saturday morning from Toronto. So I got hold of dear brother Richard who lived near Dorval airport in Montreal, and he was enchanted to meet me, give me a bed for the night, and drop me at the airport next morning. His wife Sheila was away, so he really liked having something to do. Richard and I got into the scotch and reminiscing, which went on until 1:30 a.m., and very pleasant it was too. We hadn't had a decent chat for years. We had a great time remembering how we'd argued over my Girl Guide signalling flag until I broke the stick over his head, trying to figure out which year we had been to the east coast for our holidays, finding out which of our old school chums he still saw when he went back to England, and talking about how our home town had changed.

And whom should I find in Moncton, besides Madeleine, but Norah Toole from Fredericton with a young VOW member, which made the meeting a very good one. We all met around a table and discussed ways and means of solving the French-English problem, which seemed to be the main stumbling-block to communication between women's groups. French women speak both languages, mostly, but the English? Not a hope. We saw a slide-show by Shirley Bear about native women in New Brunswick, after which there was a good party, and, since there was lots of wine left over and we couldn't possibly manage to drink it all up there and then, we took some up to bed with us.

On the next morning, after the final session, we walked around the little town where the meeting had been held. We lunched at a restaurant which had lobster rolls, a speciality of the place, then went home with Madeleine for a short visit and to meet her daughter, who is a dancer. Madeleine told me horror stories of trying to catch planes in the middle of blizzards and ploughing her way through the drifts to get to Council meetings. You certainly have to be tough to be an activist in a New Brunswick winter.

And so we continue the saga of 1982. It reminds me of one of those stories on the BBC radio game, 'My Word,' where the panellists are asked to make up the derivation of a well-known saying. On one occasion, Frank Muir or Denis Nordern (I can never distinguish them) was given 'charity begins at home.' There was this family called Biggins – father, mother, and the girls whose names were Faith, Hope, and Charity. And it turned out that Charity was writing the story of her life. It was a long, long history, and when it was finished, there was the question of a title. *The Biggins Family Saga*? But it was mostly about Charity. *Charity's Autobiography*? But it was so long. Finally they hit upon the ideal title (and Frank Muir on the winning fantasy): *Charity Biggins: A Tome.*

For the next few weeks, I seem to have spent quite a bit of time talking to high-school classes, where we usually had good discussions about disarmament or about feminism and sexism. There was a panel at Seneca College, where the staff people were more interesting and interested than the students.

Then there was once-a-week Sprucecourt School and grade-one cooking and all kinds of handicrafts that most of the kids managed better than I could. I had begun my career as a school volunteer with my old friend Mary Hecht at Kensington Community School in the same year the school started. When Mary left, she passed me along to Tanis Sigurjonsson, and when Tanis moved to Sprucecourt, I went with her. It all started in the usual way. A heartfelt plea came my way, 'Could you possibly come in and help?' So I went. Each year after that I would get a cheerful and hopeful phone call towards the end of the holidays, saying, 'You will come back this term, won't you?' So I did. Here are some extracts from the piece I wrote for the teachers' journal, *Roll Call*.

When I was first inveigled into helping out, my own children were almost ten years out of the school system, and I had nearly forgotten what six- and seven-year-olds were like. But at one time, I was volunteering four mornings each week, so I got to know the children really well. It was in the days of the open-plan, three-classes-in-one-big-space program. Although with 75 kids and three or more adults in one room it may have seemed chaotic to an outsider, thanks to the meticulous planning and cooperation between our teachers it was one of the most rewarding and inspiring periods in my volunteer life.

There were times when my feelings about Joey, or Orlando, or even that charming, sweetly dumb Walter, were less than kindly. But not Tanis. She would hug them instead of screaming at them, which I sometimes did. There were certainly times when Robert was sent off by himself to calm down, or Veronica was denied some special treat, but most of the problems were sorted out quickly. It always helped when I could be told that José was sleepy or distracted because of what was happening at home or had some problem that I knew nothing about. I was asked to help with Albert, a newcomer from Jamaica who had what I was told was a 'perceptual problem.' I never quite figured out what that was, but Albert alternated between driving us all nuts and being quite enchanting and hilarious and bumbling and noisy and violent and bullying and lovable in turn.

I remember the whole class being occupied with making a wonderful model of the school and the surrounding streets, all constructed from milk cartons, tins, corrugated paper, and dozens of other recycled scraps. Another highlight of that year was a bus trip to the farm owned by one of the teachers. I think it was springtime, and fields and lanes were soggy and dripping. It poured with rain. Somebody, probably Albert, fell into the stream, but everyone had a wonderful time jumping into the hay in the barn and swinging on the truck tire strung on a rope from the roof. By the time we got home most of us had dried out in the bus. For me, watching city children experiencing the delights and surprises of the countryside or youngsters coping with a tool or a machine for the first time was fascinating. I found I recalled experiences from my school-days – in the parks, on camping trips, and on country walks in England – which helped me explain things to today's children.

One tends to remember the highlights, the special afternoons for all the kids together, divided into groups each with an adult to help and advise. There were experiments with magic (a professor of chemistry can be a wonderful volunteer), building a robot with flashing lights for eyes and a tape-recorder voice.

We cooked everything from spinach pie to gingerbread houses, with side trips to buy the ingredients to (where else?) Kensington Market. Five whole books were made in consecutive years – written, illustrated, and translated. One day a teacher, well-known to the children, came in and offered to show them how his artificial arm with the hook for a hand worked. Everyone gathered around, and Menno stripped off his sweater and gave an absolutely fascinating demonstration and explanation of how the pulleys and elastics worked and how his shoulder muscles could make things work further down his arm. The kids, and the adults too, sat spellbound, and then the questions tumbled out: 'How do you pick up a pencil?' 'What does it feel like?,' and so on.

Swimming was a highlight. Contrary to some teachers' routines, Tanis and I always went into the pool with the children. Why miss the opportunity to swim and splash? And watching a small, dripping, terrified character, scared silly of the water, turn after a few weeks into an underwater expert, is something I won't easily forget.

One day, in the playground, we noticed that the girls all took skipping ropes and the boys grabbed the basketballs. So we got them to change over, and most of the kids found it quite difficult to grapple with the new games. After a while the boys got the hang of skipping, and the girls began to tackle the balls with more confidence. We weren't sure whether we were counteracting unconscious sex stereotyping, but the children had learned new skills anyway.

We also liberated the class photograph. The photographer started his usual routine of sitting the girls on the bench with the boys standing behind or sitting on the floor. 'Why do they have to be separated?' we asked. 'No reason. Just a habit,' he said. So henceforth the photographs were taken with girls and boys mixed up together.

Kensington had a second playground on the roof. I wonder how many of our children will one day tell their children how they watched the helicopter, back in the old days, lowering the top-most steel beams on the CN Tower.

When Kensington Community School was officially opened, there was a tremendous parade all around the Kensington Market area. Preparations went on for weeks. Everyone made costumes, including all the teachers. Our class made a dragon, a fabulous monster constructed of wire and papier maché, painted and decorated and pulled along on wheels. He was a masterpiece. The principal of the school, wearing a big fire helmet and sitting on the fire engine from the next-door fire hall, led the procession, and all the parents and shopkeepers of Kensington came out to watch. It was a great occasion, but only one of the many that make life as a volunteer, particularly with the teachers I have known, a very, very rewarding experience.

21

Mid-1982, UNSSOD

In mid-March of that year came a trip to Ottawa for the NAC annual meeting, a particularly stormy one, but to my delight the one at which NAC's Survival of the Planet Committee was begun. I followed that up, at the beginning of April, by acting as a resource person for one of the Introducing the World sessions. These day-long sessions for high-school students from around Metro Toronto were organized by a Toronto couple, using volunteer resource people. I always enjoy talking and discussing things about peace and war, foreign affairs, and so on, and the high-school students were bright and lively, so we had a good time. The workshops came out with some good suggestions, though the organizers seemed less than happy with an excellent and unanimous resolution for the government on the subject of disarmament and were somewhat reluctant to send it up to Ottawa. The head of CIDA spoke at one of the sessions and seemed to be saying that Canada's aid programs were impeccable, with no hitches and barriers to the provision of food and help. Too many people in the audience knew better and resented an External Affairs apologist appearing as an unbiased expert. Interestingly enough, I heard at a concert soon after (it's surprising how much information one can pick up at concerts and parties) that Introducing the World had gone out of business.

Easter was early that year, and the Cruise Missile protesters held a service at Bloor Street United Church and then a big demonstration out at the Litton factory in Rexdale. The church was crammed, with a few pro-war types getting press for a very small (though noisy) demonstration across the street. The peace demonstration at Litton was impressive, peaceful, and friendly, but of course not nearly as exciting for the media as a riot or any other kind of violence. We need to invent some action that is rivettingly exciting for the press without being at odds with non-violent principles. Quite a problem.

With all this uplifting demonstrating I must have felt the need for diversion, since I notice from my diary that we managed to take in two films, a new dance-in-progress by Danny Grossman, and an opera, before I plunged back into almost daily meetings. The next weekend was a two-day NAC executive meeting. Twenty or so women from across the country came together. I had most of them to dinner on the Saturday night, and a couple or three staying with me. On Sunday, Brough came back from a few days in London, Ontario, and three Montreal friends had dinner with us. Monday was spent in talking with a Survival Committee member and in putting together the NAC *MEMO*, which comes out after each executive meeting.

After craft afternoon at Sprucecourt on Tuesday, there was a pre-UNSSOD (UN Special Session on Disarmament) press conference and panel discussion at the 'town hall,' which I chaired (easier than making a 'presentation,' I think). The next day I talked French for an hour with Mady, had another friend to dinner, and went with her to see Twyla Tharp's dance company in the evening.

On Thursday, I dashed off at dawn to catch the Montreal train which, as it happened, sat in the station for an hour after I rushed onto it. Arriving late, I continued to dash, this time to queue up to see Judy Chicago's *Dinner Party*, since we thought it wouldn't be coming to Toronto. I ran into lots of friends, including my daughter Susan, who all said it took them three hours in the queue but it was worth it, and actually my wait wasn't so long. I had the book with me and listened to the taped description and, since progress was slow, I managed to juggle book, headphones, and tape recorder, purse, clothes, and other oddments quite adroitly. It amazed me to be confronted by the patience and persistence that went into the assembly of all the various parts of the work, the new techniques of pottery, needlework, tile-making, and painting, let alone the design and imagination that was lavished on its production. After a quick look at the rest of the gallery, I was picked up and whisked back to dinner with my friends the Ryersons who were also going to see Susan dance with the Danny Grossman Dance Company that evening at the Centaur Theatre. It was a good evening, and we had a brief chance to chat with Susan and the company before it was time to leave.

I caught the train back to Toronto the next morning, went to a fiftieth anniversary party at the York Club (not somewhere I go very often), and ended the evening by seeing the Judy Chicago film at OISE. That was a money-raiser for CARAL (the Canadian Abortion Rights Action League), whose AGM I attended the next day at Hart House. I had to leave at noon to dash down to College and Bathurst where I was speaking at the send-off for the people starting their peace march to New York for UNSSOD. I was due to join them in New York in June. It was a good crowd, very cheerful, and the walkers got off to a good start. I returned to the meeting in time to hear about the court case brought by Joe Borowski (ex-Manitoba provincial MP) in an attempt to make abortion illegal throughout Canada.

Somewhere at the beginning of May, I got away for a weekend in Newfoundland to visit my old friend Ella Manuel. It had been one of the worst Newfoundland winters, with Ella having to be dug out of her front door on a couple of occasions. Now it was spring and, though there were still enormous, old snowdrifts along the roadside, Ella's car had to be left at her gate as the grass was so soggy. The sun was lovely, and Ella's living-room has picture windows on three sides (the men who helped build the house thought she was crazy) so that wherever one looked there was the sea and the mountains. We drove from Woody Point to Trout River, where we finally found a fisherman who had some lobsters which we devoured for our second gourmet dinner. I had cods' tongues the first time. We visited the Bonne Bay Craft shop (run by two physiotherapists!) and saw some lovely woven things, then went over on the ferry to Norris Point and gazed at Gros Morne and the changing cloud and sea patterns above and below the mountains of the National Park, for which Ella had campaigned so hard, and which was finally established after incredible wrangling during the last days of the Joey Smallwood régime.

The next week I went up to Ottawa on the bus to join some of Halifax VOW who were presenting peace petitions to women MPs and Senators. One day soon after, I came home at noon, picked up the mail inside the front door, and found a brown envelope with a red crown on it. The postman had added a scribbled note which said, 'I signed this for you to save you having to come round to the Post Office.' That was kind, since it's an awful nuisance to have to go over to Spadina for a registered letter.

The envelope was stuffed. I opened it in my usual way, which starts off by trying to save the envelope intact by unsticking the sticky part. It invariably ends with an untidy jagged edge of torn paper instead of a tidy slit with a knife (the procedure neatly adopted by my husband).

There were booklets, and a letter headed 'Order of Canada, Rideau Hall, Ottawa,' which came from Roger de C. Nantel, Director of the Chancellery of Canadian Orders and Decorations. I thought at first it was for Brough, but looked again and read my name, so I opened it. It said: 'I am pleased to inform you, in confidence, that the Governor General has received a recommendation for your appointment as a Member of the Order of Canada.'

Then, please let them know if I was prepared to accept this appointment and, if so, send a photo and biographical notes. I recognized the glossy pamphlet from having seen it on Brough's desk when he received a similar package. It was the list of companions, officers, and members of the Order of Canada. It has a beautiful colour reproduction of the Order insignia on the cover and contains the names of all the people appointed to the Order since it was created in 1967. Next came a shiny black pamphlet, with another coloured cover decoration and 'The Order of Canada' printed on the front. This was a description of what it is all about: 'The Granting of Honours,' 'Insignia,' 'The Queen of Canada is the Sovereign of the Order,' and 'The Constitution of the Order.' Then came a lovely picture of the medals and miniatures given to the three levels of members and the Seal of the Order.

My first reaction was disbelief. Then astonishment. Why pick me, who have none of those great accomplishments, degrees, books, good ·works, successes in the arts, or anything that reflects 'outstanding achievement' or 'service to Canada'? My next thought was to begin a long list of people (mostly women) who deserved this honour more than I did. The thought after that was, 'I must have an awful lot of devoted and conscientious friends who take the time to make this kind of effort for their friends.' (You have to write letters and collect curricula vitae and all those things that to me are a bother.) And then, lastly, came guilt – that I hadn't made those recommendations or got others to do likewise for all the people I think deserved the Order long before they picked on me.

After all those emotions and reactions, I started reading the fine print, the who, what, and how, then the list of names, 'the exact form in which you would like your name to appear.' Oh dear. What was I to call myself? Kay? Kathleen? Or both, one bracketed after the other? Ms, Mrs, or nothing? Eventually, we scoured Brough's old lists to see what everyone else did. And, I thought, they'd better spell Macpherson correctly. (That always reminds me of the time Brough made the Oxford University Press tear all the covers off the new paperback edition of one of his books because they'd spelled his name with a capital P.) And also, if my name had been 'recommended' to the Governor-General, did this mean he was still thinking about it? If I wrote something inappropriate in the brief biographical sketch they asked for, would the recommendation be rescinded?

I thought I might write something like this: 'I question whether my actions have reflected much in the way of service and achievement, since I have nearly always been criticising or condemning the government of Canada for various sins and omissions. I have consistently been opposed to sections of our foreign policy and said so.'

One of my most cherished moments was being swept into a paddy wagon by the Paris police in the company of various dedicated women, including Thérèse Casgrain, later to be a Senator and Companion of the Order of Canada – but then she had already got the vote for women in Quebec and done a whole lot of other good things. And what about being very critical of and nasty to our Prime Minister? And talking about peace when it was definitely thought subversive? And consorting with all kinds of leftists and militants and feminists, and even people who had been to jail?

I left the whole package on the kitchen table and went out. When I came in Brough met me with a radiant look on his face and a delighted greeting. 'But, but, but,' I said. He didn't have any hesitations. 'Never mind that,' was his reply. 'Isn't that lovely!' And he proceeded to tell me what I must do, and how wonderful it all was, and he reminded me of the very good meal recipients get after the ceremony (which I certainly remembered from the time I went up to Government House with him).

So then I had to think about writing a non-scurrilous reply, conning our heroic office staff into doing a decent typing job on the brief biographical notes, digging out a photo taken seven or eight years before. ('It looks just like you,' said my noble spouse.) I'd already decided to get the Human Rights Commission onto the discriminatory aspects of the medals (no nice little lapel buttons for the 'ladies'), especially considering Laura Sabia, June Callwood, Elsie Gregory MacGill, and Ursula Franklin were amongst the gang. As Brough said, 'They'll be sorry they ever gave you the Order.'

I was sworn to secrecy for about six weeks, and these weeks included the dramatic occasion of my being refused entry to our great neighbour to the south, the United States. The irony of this was exquisite.

Early in June, I set out for the UNSSOD rally. The hopes of millions of people round the world were pinned on the United Nations Special Session on Disarmament, held in New York in June and July 1982. The first special session in 1978 had worked out the priorities and laid a good base for a start to disarmament; its final document was adopted by consensus of all UN countries. VOW had attended the 1978 session as an accredited observer, and we had felt that something had really been accomplished. Four years later, we could see that nothing had been done to implement the plan. In 1982, people wanted concrete action. They hoped in vain. The 1982 session ended with little changed, in spite of the millions of petitions, the huge demonstrations, marches, and delegations, even the media attention, all of which prefaced the session by demands for action.

But nothing can detract from the impact of that June 12th rally on everyone who was lucky enough to be part of it. A new, powerful, friendly, and peaceful spirit was instilled in all those who were there, together with the onlookers and the millions linked around the world by the media coverage and by supporting vigils, demonstrations, and gatherings.

In Canada, there were hundreds of groups and coalitions working across the country before the session. Aided by the women in the national office, Nova Scotia VOW members organized the women's petition. Ann Gertler in Montreal was vital in getting us the necessary information and, in particular, the status of an NGO (non-government organization) observer group, which enabled us to participate officially at the UN. Ann was also the chief mover in getting VOW's statement on disarmament prepared for our own government and a similar statement for the delegations at the session.

On June 2nd, Muriel Duckworth and I met in the Montreal bus station, looking forward to a twelve-hour journey of talk and planning, relaxing and sleeping our way to New York. All went well until we arrived at Champlain, on the border. The US immigration officers turned everyone off the bus, an unusual procedure. We were all questioned and our names checked on their computer. Muriel was without blemish (naturally), but I got stuck. I was asked to step aside to be asked certain questions, the nature of which the officer could not disclose. My baggage was searched. They gave me a section of the Act under which I was being detained, five pages of what I later learned was the McCarran-Walter Act, but did not specify which section I had transgressed. Anarchist? Communist? Planning to overthrow the government by force or violence?

Muriel decided to miss the bus and stay with me while we telephoned Alan Borovoy of CCLA for advice. At his suggestion, since I could complete formalities in Ottawa if I was denied entry, I refused to answer the questions I had not been asked. So Muriel continued her journey to New York and I went to Ottawa to find husband, friends, and the US embassy. I found Brough at the Royal Society's one hundredth anniversary dinner. I had not planned to attend the dinner in my 'You can't beat Nellie's' T-shirt, but it was a good conversation piece and many of the dinner guests learned about the disarmament session in the course of the evening. Nor had I intended to put my case to Jean Chrétien, at any rate not quite so soon. At last I consulted Doris Anderson by telephone, made plans for the following day, and went to bed.

The next day, June 3rd, with the inestimable help of my long-suffering hostess and fellow NAC member Pat Hacker, we enlisted help from all three political parties (it was good to be a unifying factor!) and anyone else we could implicate. Pauline Jewett of the NDP, who had started the ball rolling with her contact at External Affairs, agreed with Liberal David Collenette that he would ask a question in the House of Commons that afternoon, and later in the evening Conservative Flora MacDonald, having heard me on the radio, offered to telephone her US Embassy friends to speed up their response.

Meanwhile, since I was still in Ottawa, I joined the NAC executive and Doris Anderson in their celebratory lunch with Madame Justice Bertha Wilson to present her with the Persons Medallion, saved by NAC since 1979 for the first woman to be appointed to the Supreme Court of Canada. Our guest was delighted to hear that I was an 'undesirable person' and told us that she too had been rejected by the US immigration officers. In her delightful Scottish lilt, she described how she was once stopped at the border because, they said, she had a Russian accent! So the rejects were photographed together on this memorable occasion. Then I left to keep a date with Elizabeth Gray on the CBC's 'As It Happens,' heard, as I later learned, from Dawson City and Hornby Island to Labrador. In this interview, I told the anecdote about the old lady asked by the border guards whether she was plotting 'to overthrow the state by force or violence.' She thought for a moment and replied, 'Violence, I think.'

The women with whom I had been at the one-day conference in Lethbridge earlier in the year must have heard me on 'As It Happens,' too, and they sent me a lovely telegram saying: 'Dear Grandma, the circle of women in Lethbridge supports you in your choice of violence over force in your mission to promote peace and disarmament. Strongly condemn the McCarran-Walter Act but applaud your reading of same. Could this be an item for future conferences? Write soon. In sisterhood: Janet, Lorraine, Lisa, Amanda, Kris, Liz, Susan, Elise, Carol, Femke, Janis and Debra.'

We had discovered from a *New York Times* reporter that several hundred individuals, including many Japanese Hiroshima survivors, had been denied visas under a re-invocation of the McCarran-Walter Act, which originally had been passed in the McCarthy era. Two other Canadians had been refused entry, and Setsuko Thurlow (VOW member and Hiroshima survivor) was hassled at the airport on her way to make a speech in Chicago. The rally committee in New York had brought a suit against the US immigration department for preventing Americans from having the right to communicate with other nationals and for violating the right of free passage to the UN for official NGO delegates. Muriel and many others had been protesting the US government action, and the Canadian press had got wind of it.

Pressure was applied, and we tried unsuccessfully to hurry up the process of getting me a 'waiver' for entry into the States. In the end I went back to Toronto and wasn't called by the Embassy until June 7th to complete the formalities of the waiver. So the next three days were spent in giving one or two more interviews and planning our strategy for the group including VOW members from Edmonton, Vancouver, and Victoria which was going to New York on the VOW bus. Much of our discussion focused on the question of the border: if we were stopped, what questions should we answer? if only some were stopped, would the others continue on their way? We were followed to the border by a CBC French TV network reporter, which made us feel good, and I had been asked to report back to CBC Radio.

At the border, I was asked for my name, destination, length of stay, purpose of visit, and whether I knew why I had previously been stopped. I said I did not, and after he had stamped my passport 'C2' and given me a paper threatening dire consequences and deportation if I overstayed my seven-day limit or went more than twenty-five miles from the UN Building, I was through. I rejoined the others to find them in a state of shock. Everyone was through, with no questions asked. We then settled down to enjoy our trip, introducing ourselves on the bus's speaker, telling stories, reciting poems, and making more plans.

On arriving in New York, we headed for the reception held by the

Canadian ambassador to the UN, Gérard Pelletier, and were received with open arms even though our whole bus load had not actually been invited and we were nearly an hour late. Then we proceeded to our sparse and unattractive accommodation at Barnard College. Fortunately, we had brought snacks with us, and we made do with no sheets or blankets.

The next morning we set off for the auditorium under the Dag Hammarskjold Library at the UN to present to the Canadian Ambassador the 100,000 signatures on the Canadian Women's Petition, which had been initiated and collected by the Halifax Voice of Women. Betty Peterson of the Halifax Voices had made an eloquent speech as she presented it to the Secretary-General of the United Nations the day before when the millions of signatures from all over the world were formally presented. Almost two hundred Canadians attended this smaller meeting with the Canadian Ambassador. Muriel Duckworth chaired the meeting, and Betty Peterson presented the petition, reading out the very moving wording.

Ambassador Pelletier responded. He said we must remember that Canada was a small and not very powerful country, and that we would look ridiculous if we tried to take action for disarmament on our own or to push the great powers. (Someone in the audience said, 'I'd rather look ridiculous than be bombed.') Disarmament Ambassador Menzies expressed the usual cautious External Affairs line: we must negotiate from strength; we cannot take unilateral action. We talked about the cruise missile, and Terry Padgham spoke for the people in Alberta. The meeting expressed considerable dissatisfaction with the official responses.

After a busy day full of workshops, receptions, vigils, and visits, I got down to serious work. I had been invited to be a speaker at the big rally. When all the missed messages and phone calls were sorted out, this meant I was to give a one-minute (*no more*) speech and to be in the speakers' enclosure in Central Park at noon on June 12th. It was now about 8:00 p.m. on Friday the 11th. A speech-making committee of more than a dozen women volunteered to help me compose this one-minute all-inclusive speech: for Canada, for women, bilingual, mention the cruise testing, talk about the Candu, the freeze, nuclear fuel to Argentina, everything. I took all the pieces and fled back to Barnard, where everyone was recovering from an exhausting day with a noisy nightcap in someone's room and was only too delighted to get into the speech-making business.

Finally Vi Thompson and I got back to our room, where we promptly started re-writing again. It was 3:00 a.m., and Vi was falling asleep when we were finally satisfied with the speech. I wrote it out legibly and got into our bunk bed. Sleep? Not a hope. Did I have to miss the first part of the rally at the UN? Oh, I couldn't miss that. Well, then, how was I going to get from the rally to Central Park? Susan (my daughter, who was here to march with the artists and dancers) said the Lexington subway went near the entrance to the park. Would the crowds be too dense to get through in time? Worry, worry.

All too soon it was time to get up, and we went to gather with the other Canadians at 47th Street and 2nd Avenue, fortunately just under the windows of the Vanderbilt YWCA, where Muriel was staying. We then joined the main rally, set up the VOW banner, and watched the other international delegations. Holland, Japan, and Australia were nearby. Gertler sons and a Duckworth came by. Ann Gertler and son Alfred took pity on me and offered to escort me to Central Park, which was a great relief. We found our way to the speakers' enclosure, and Ann and Alfred talked their way in with me, which was a bonus as we had a couple of hours to wait. We wasted no time in contacting radio-network commentators and giving interviews. I joined the other speakers and danced with Bella Abzug and WILPF's Edith Ballantyne to the music from the platform. The whole program, with music and speakers, took over four hours. We left the park before it ended, well after 6:00 p.m.

Here is what my speech-writing committee of twenty-nine had come up with:

I am happy to be here. The United States Immigration Department did their best to keep me out.
Thousands of Canadians are here to say:
NO to cruise missiles made in Toronto, tested in Alberta, or anywhere else;
YES to making Canada a nuclear-free zone;
NO to Canada exporting nuclear reactors and fuel;
YES to disarmament now.
Today we have started to turn the tide of arms buildup.
We, the people, must lead our government to disarmament. We, the women and men, have the power to give the world a future.
Thousands of Canadians say, in the words of our Women's Petition for Peace:
We say: NO TO WAR – NON À LA GUERRE.
We say: YES TO LIFE – OUI À LA VIE.

The speakers had been assembling in an enclosure behind a high fence. When I went up on the platform, I saw the crowds for the first time. What a sight! Thousands and thousands of people wherever you looked. Banners and flags too small to read, and the crowds stretching so far that there was no way the sound from the huge amplifiers could reach them clearly. Many people listened on transistors; one station broadcast the whole program. But it was that huge crowd – a million people coming together for disarmament and peace – that inspired everyone more than any speech or song.

Afterwards, everyone had stories about the rally. They talked about the friendliness and support people showed each other, in the park, on the streets, in the subway. They spoke of care and kindness to old people and children, the volunteers who spent all day on their feet helping, guiding, and encouraging the crowds. Everything was cleaned up by evening. The street and park cleaning crews were stunned because the crowds had picked up their own garbage. There were no incidents with the police, no bad feeling or opposition. The police were cheerful and smiling; they looked after lost children and people suffering from exhaustion. Strangers spoke and became friends. Crowds stayed on singing and dancing in the park after the mikes had been turned off and the music stopped. No one wanted to leave. People crowded into the subways and exchanged news and buttons and papers.

There was excellent PBS television coverage that evening. Nancy Pocock and I watched it at Ann Gertler's suite at the Plaza 50 (provided courtesy of the Canadian government since she was an official delegate), but most of the others sitting around were exhausted and had fallen asleep. I did one last radio interview and took a taxi back to Barnard. I had to be woken by the driver when we arrived. That was some great day, as the Newfoundlanders would say.

It was raining when we left New York on Sunday morning, and we realized how lucky we had been the day before. Not too hot and no rain. A rainy drive home bothered no one. Everyone had a chance to talk about their experiences, and to say what the day had meant to them. Some women said that it had been the most moving experience of their lives, and several joined VOW on the spot. Some of the young women expressed their surprise and delight at getting to know the 'wonderful older women' they had met, and a few of the older women were near tears with delight at the way the young ones were getting into the action.

After we had been singing and story-telling for a while on the bus I asked if we could sing the song that had been running in my head all day. Terry Padgham knew all the words, and I scribbled them down, 'Last night I had the strangest dream I'd ever had before. I dreamed the world had all agreed to put an end to war.' There is a great deal to be done before that dream comes true. For the present, we must get on with taking the next steps towards that goal.

The UNSSOD rally led to one of my moments of revelation. Just after we arrived home, while our living-room was crowded and everyone still talking about the rally, Susan phoned from New York and described how she had heard me speak. She and her dancer friends had been so long in the march that when they reached Central Park they thought they had missed the speeches, so they were just sitting on the grass when suddenly they heard an announcement about women. 'And there I sat,' she said, 'with tears streaming down my face, so proud. That's MY mother, speaking to all those thousands of people. What a wonderful thing.'

I think that was the highlight of the rally for me. I'd never really thought about what it might mean to my kids, or friends, or how lucky I was to have had such an opportunity, on such a day! I don't know how to describe my feelings: warmth, love, thankfulness, overwhelming gratitude for all the blessings I've been showered with – family, friends, and the incredible good fortune to be able to enjoy, to be active, and to take part in all that goes to make up the human experience.

22

Late 1982, Happy Valley, Awards

At the beginning of August, Ella Manuel and I were invited to visit Happy Valley, Labrador. We were to show an anti-nuclear-war film, lead discussions, give interviews, and meet the women of Happy Valley and other nearby communities. Happy Valley is the dormitory town for the big Goose Bay airbase, about four miles away, and came into existence around 1941. This date is way back in history and pioneer times to most of the people who live there now.

The first thing we learned was that our visit coincided with Armed Forces Day. Perfect timing for peaceniks! So, on that gorgeous hot afternoon, in between inspecting B52s and helicopters and watching parachutists make pinpoint landings in front of the spectators, we distributed pamphlets warning against nuclear war, yet not deploring force and violence so much that no one would listen. Some of the local women were told we should go do our leafleting in Moscow, but most people were quite friendly.

We also learned that Governor-General Schreyer was to visit Happy Valley the next day. Our friends, none of whom had been invited to any of the planned functions, were very sceptical about the visit. It was said that the Mayor and his wife wanted to keep Ed and Lily Schreyer to themselves and their friends. And the Mayor, it appeared, chose friends only from his own political party and ignored the university people, which cut down the invitation list. His wife was the editor of the local weekly paper and refused to put a report in the paper about the activities of the women's centre or committee. So no Brownies and Scouts waving flags, no parades or crowds for the Governor-General.

All this led to great doom and gloom amongst the younger set in the family where I was staying. Willow, the nine-year-old daughter, had been all over Government House when they visited Ottawa the previous month, but the Schreyers had been away. Now she was again to be deprived of catching a glimpse of them. This situation must be rectified, felt her mother. On Saturday morning Mr Schreyer was scheduled to open the new Municipal Depot (snow plough and truck garage to most of us) so we all trooped over there. Willow got out the special WELCOME SCHREYERS poster she had made, and we scuffed around on the sandy waste ground where the building stood.

Soon, two limousines rolled up, and out stepped the Schreyers with their seven-year-old, Tobin, and their old friend Farley Mowat (*not* the favourite author either of Ella or my hosts Laurie and Laura, who gave instant derogatory assessments of his literary inaccuracies and writing habits). The Mayor and his wife (the latter in harem pants) joined the group, which included a Mountie or two resplendent in gold braid and scarlet. Willow was almost too overcome to display her poster, so her mother helped her, and the rest of the children divided two or three paper Union Jacks amongst them.

The Mayor made a brief speech and invited the GG to cut the red ribbon which was being held stretched across one of the garage doors by two local Works Department officials. Ed stepped forward – and made scissor-snipping motions with his fingers. They'd forgotten the snippers. Someone found a knife or something, the garage door rolled up on schedule, and the great ceremony was accomplished. The vice-regal party moved inside. 'What on earth can they say?' asked one of us. 'Isn't it large! What lovely grey paint!'

After due time for inspection, the party moved into the other half of the building for a refreshing snack. Tobin wandered back, followed by his mother, and started talking to our kids. 'At my school I'm in grades two, three, and four,' he said. 'Wow!' said the kids. This was something new and very impressive. Not wanting to be outdone, Ella and I introduced ourselves to Lily.

Ella and Lily had in fact met the year before in Ottawa when Ella received the Persons Award. She had made a point then of asking whether there were any Newfoundlanders at Government House, and had been introduced to the one Newfoundlander on duty. Now she went up to one of the gold-braided policemen escorting the Governor-General and started to ask whether Arly Dancey was still around. 'I'm Arly,' the man replied, and their enthusiastic reunion was a sight to behold.

After a while, it was suggested that Tobin have his picture taken with the children, then Lily joined in and called, 'Come on, Ed.' And, to our delight and no doubt the chagrin of the Mayor's wife, this shot of the whole group, with welcome poster but devoid of any sign of Mayor or wife, was the one that got on the CBC news.

When the official group left, we took a look at the delicious repast furnished for them. I kid you not: there was a small urn filled with hot water, a pot of instant coffee with a spoon in it, and a packet of tea bags. An opened tin of Carnation milk, with styrofoam cups and plastic spoons, completed the array. The doughnuts, tastefully arranged on paper plates, were now being demolished by the remaining Mounties.

All in all, we had a good time with enough laughs to keep us going for the rest of the day. By breakfast next morning, Laura had put the whole saga into verse and set it to music. This must be how those Newfoundland songs get put together.

In October, Brough and I set off for Ottawa for me to receive the Order of Canada. The autumn-tinted trees looked beautiful as we came in to land at the Ottawa airport. In the general chaos at home, I had lost my detailed instruction sheet from Rideau Hall. I had phoned to ask if I might pick up another one (how could anyone be so careless on such an occasion!), so the taxi driver took us up to the main entrance, where we were directed to the administration entrance and a kind lady gave me an envelope containing a replacement. Now I would know how many paces to take, when to bow to the left or right, and where to sit.

As usual, we and the taxi driver got lost in Rockcliffe, but we were rescued by a charming young man who turned out to be headed for lunch with our friends Irene and Graham Spry and family too. We were plied with sherry, roast chicken, and wine, and after a very pleasant time discussing Ottawa politics, we were driven to our hotel. We checked in and went up to our room, where we unlocked the door only to find a very surprised occupant comfortably stretched out on the bed. After apologies all round, we were given the correct key, inspected the adjoining 'parlour' where we intended to entertain our friends later, and admired the gorgeous flowers we had been sent.

We then changed into full evening dress at four in the afternoon. (The only other time we had done that was going to the opera at Glyndebourne, except that then we changed in a quiet English country lane). We proceeded to the lobby, where we found a crowd of rather nervous-looking men and women being politely herded into a bus for the trip to Rideau Hall. Of course, there was one life-of-the-party retired colonel, from Brandon, Manitoba, who welcomed us all and stirred up a little jollity, but there was a general feeling of solemnity, which made us all look rather like tourists visiting a stately home or a cathedral.

At the entrance to Government House, the sheep were separated from the goats. While the guests were shepherded into the ballroom, the Recipients were given final instructions, and a small metal bracket was pinned on the left breast of all the women ready to receive the medals. The Orders of all the men were hung on ribbons round their necks – rank discrimination. Perhaps it is thought in government circles that the Governor-General shouldn't have to put his arms round women's necks to pin on their decorations.

Eventually we were escorted to our seats in the ballroom to await the beginning of the ceremony. I found myself (alphabetically) next to Cliff Lumsden, one-time coach of the swimmer Marilyn Bell. On my other side was a charming woman from Calgary who said that the last time she had been at Rideau Hall she was up above the ballroom ceiling examining the architectural features of the roof.

Some of the men looked nervous and uncomfortable, fingering their collars and sweating. The women seemed more interested in discussing where they could deposit their purses and programs while they walked up to the front. I was surprised when I counted the names on the program to find that a third of those invested were women; there seemed to be many more men in their black suits. Two women were made Companions.

There was a fanfare, we all stood up, and the Governor-General and the Chief Justice, followed by church, state, and aides-de-camp walked up the aisle and took their places. The vice-regal salute (half the national anthem) followed, and a prayer. Then the business of the Investiture began. Sixty-six men and women were invested by the Governor-General. Our names were announced and up we marched one by one, then the citation, the affixing of the medal, a smile and a word, handshake, bows, and a walk to sign the register, then back to one's seat as the next in line took his or her turn. When I went up to receive my medal, the Governor-General asked me, 'And what have you been up to lately?' 'Revolution,' I replied. He smiled, and we shook hands. When everyone had returned to their seat, 'O Canada' was played, and the vice-regal party left.

Afterwards, we were given drinks and met some of the other people present, including the Prime Minister. When I expressed my pleasure that there was now a woman on the Supreme Court, Chief Justice Bora

Laskin was quick to assure me that it was merit, not sex, that had counted in the appointment. He even said, 'The trouble is that there are so few qualified women.' (Unfortunately, I could think of no suitable instant response, such as, 'It must be equally difficult to find competent men.') He did go on to say that the Minister of Justice had been insistent that a woman be appointed. So at least all our letters and telegrams to Jean Chrétien had had an effect. When my husband and I were both formally introduced to Mr Schreyer, I gave him the photograph of him I had taken in Happy Valley that summer by the municipal garage. He remembered the occasion!

The dinner was a superb buffet. We sat at round tables for ten in the big dining hall, walls draped with red-and-white-striped awning like a great tent. Abby Hoffman joined us. I went up after the first course with her mother Dorothy Medhurst to help ourselves to dessert. Government House's chefs had outdone themselves: Order of Canada Cake, pecan pie, raspberry cheesecake, fruit, cheeses, tarts, chocolates. We sighed in unison when our eyes lit on the specially made plates which we were rapidly loading. They too were designed for the Order of Canada. With the Order's emblem in the centre, a broad red band in the middle, and gold edging, they were very handsome indeed. Our only regret was that our purses or pockets were too small to slip one in as a souvenir. After coffee had been served and very smelly cigars handed out, we made our way (courtesy of the waiting buses) in the rain back to the hotel.

At the door of our sitting room, we were greeted with cheers and raised glasses. A lively party was in progress. Friends from Montreal and Ottawa had been getting to know each other, helped by my brother's adept dispensing of refreshment. Toasts were drunk, photographs taken, kisses exchanged, and the French version of the Proclamation of the Order read with due ceremony by one of our legal friends, the inimitable Fraser Macorquodale in fact. Even in this strange mixture of ages and occupations, everyone managed to find lots to talk about, and I was amused to see the three lawyers in the company, aged approximately twenty, forty, and seventy, gravitate towards each other. Perhaps they have a secret salute, like Freemasons or Girl Guides.

The Montrealers, who didn't have to go to work the next morning, and who had the greatest staying power, were eventually swept off to their rooms, and we were free to go to bed ourselves. It certainly had been a great day, and a very happy one for us all to remember.

Perhaps the last great day of the year was November 10th, when we went back to Ottawa again to be part of the celebration for Sarah Binns when she received the Persons Award. Sarah had been campaign manager for Agnes Macphail, Canada's first woman MP. (A male member of the campaign committee had objected to her being hired, on the grounds of her being in a wheelchair. 'I hired her for her head, not her legs,' snapped Macphail.)

The Persons Awards are presented annually to five Canadian women who have worked to promote equality and improvement of the status of women in Canada. Muriel Duckworth was one of the first to serve on the selection committee for these awards, and I followed her. Given how many marvellous feminists there are across Canada, the choice was always a hard one. The award was established in 1979 on the fiftieth anniversary of the UK Privy Council judgment (overruling Canada's Supreme Court decision) that women were in fact 'persons' and therefore eligible for appointment as judges or Senators. The award celebrates the five Alberta women – Emily Murphy, Nellie McClung, Louise McKinney, Irene Parlby, and Henrietta Muir Edwards – who had won this ruling.

Sarah had up days and down days. Sometimes, owing to weakness and the pain in her joints caused by every movement, it seemed almost impossible to expect her to survive the trip to Ottawa. But survive she did, with a glowing tenacity and her ever-present courage and humour. Linda Ryan Nye and Pat Hacker, her bodyguards and loving companions, were responsible for every tiny detail: the cushions and padding for the wheelchair, the flowers and wine, buying the new dress given to Sarah by her friends, and discussing all the plans and excitement so that Sarah could enjoy every minute of the preparations and the anticipation of receiving the award.

In spite of all the planning, it was touch and go as to whether they would make the plane at Toronto airport. Time rushed by and shoes wouldn't fit, moving around took longer than expected, the traffic lights always seemed to be red. But the cavalcade arrived. The airline staff were kind and solicitous to a degree. Sarah sat in the front seat of the plane, almost holding court as Grace Hartman and other friends greeted her and were warmed by her happy smile. Cookies and juice were in abundance, and we discovered that those little stirring sticks are also drinking straws, just what Sarah needed.

At the Ottawa airport, Sarah was met by a film crew, who kindly used their big station wagon to drive us all in to the Château Laurier, where Sarah finally had a chance to lie down and relax for a few minutes. A little shot of brandy at the right moment, always on hand from Nurse Hacker 'for medicinal purposes,' also did wonders.

All the planning paid off. Mary Lou Levitsky of Status of Women Canada had been measuring all the official doorways for the wheelchair, and Linda and Pat's timing for the whole operation was impeccable. The Binn's Progress made its way past Confederation Square to Parliament Hill, enjoying a brisk, bright day with everything sparkling in the sunlight. The cracked pavement and bumpy curbs provided their problems, but Sarah smiled bravely at every jarring bump, and Pat and Linda were the most careful of attendants.

We went to the House of Commons for the Persons' Lunch given by Judy Erola, Minister Responsible for the Status of Women. Four of the five Persons were present for the occasion, and each spoke briefly about her life and activities. Then Sarah was whisked along the corridors for a historic meeting with long-time MP Stanley Knowles, whom we found waiting at his desk all spruced up with poppy in buttonhole. Sarah was almost, but not quite, speechless on meeting Stanley, which was one of her great ambitions, and Stanley was filled with admiration for Sarah, and they also shared memories of the origins of the CCF. All too soon the house bells had stopped ringing for the beginning of question period, and off we went back down to the Château and, in no time at all, Sarah was thankfully in bed.

After a short nap and some tea came the preparations for Government House, the changing of stockings, the dress, the corsage, and all the trimmings – mink stole, pearls, you name it, Sarah had it. I was off buying a tinkle-bell for summoning assistance in the night and some wine to tide us over. Eventually we swept out of the Château and along Sussex Drive to Rideau Hall.

There had been some discussion about who should be asked to push the Royal Wheelchair when Sarah's award was presented to her. An aide-de-camp with gold braid? A Senator? There were at least two in attendance. 'I'm not going to be pushed around by a Senator,' said Sarah firmly. So I was the lucky Person Pusher, who got to sit amongst the Persons' relatives and steer the Chair around, to the deafening applause of the assembled guests, after Sarah's long and remarkable citation had been read by Senator Florence Bird and the medal presented by the Governor-General. It was a great moment, and Sarah looked dazzlingly happy.

After the vice-regal party left, everyone crowded around, and radio and television reporters and friends took up all Sarah's attention. Then

Sarah decided that home to the Château was better. (I was lost, chattering with Margaret Fulton, also on the selection committee, and therefore missing all the food. We had plenty to drink though.)

The evening developed into one of those wonderful Women's Old Home Week or Old Girls Networking sessions. Greetings, committee meetings, dates for later, contacts, and 'I've always wanted to meet you' were heard everywhere. Sarah, fortified with pills and brandy, held court from her bed, and we all managed to settle down with sustenance, drinks, and talk, every so often tiptoeing in to find Sarah waiting to see herself a star of television, or greeting an old friend or a new one.

Finally she was tucked up for a well-earned rest. Gradually the other guests and Persons went off to their beds and billets. It had been a miraculous, historic, and joyous day. Sarah was given just a small part of the thanks and celebration which her active and dedicated life deserves.

Who would have expected to start the next day with Sarah's first champagne breakfast? But that's what we did, toasting 'Heroines, Past, Present, and Future.' Later we were off, through wind and rain, to the Arts Centre for a wonderful performance of that sexist romp *The Mikado*, followed by a midnight supper party. After a trip that would exhaust most stalwart youngsters, Sarah headed back to Toronto, just in time to celebrate her birthday.

23

Looking Back and Looking Ahead

Nowadays, as my eyesight gets worse, I read less and less and find myself listening more to the CBC. Recently, I heard a program about people in an old people's home being given a chance to talk about their lives. They get into groups and pick a subject, say birthday parties or sad occasions, or they just reminisce. Actually, we worked in almost the same way when we were doing creative writing with Isobel Warren, and I can certainly recommend it as a good way of digging up memories and also of getting support for who you are or what you've done, or sharing pleasure, or getting sympathy when it's needed.

My friends Anna Lou Paul and Sue Findlay don't think I have enough of what Anna Lou calls 'feelings expressed' in whatever I write, so I thought I'd follow the suggestion on the radio and talk about – well, I suppose I could talk about the times one would have considered sad, depressing occasions or something like that. Just a nice, cheerful subject.

By now, many of my friends have survived loss. Usually the husbands died before their wives, as the statistics say, but these survivors are wonderful women who go on to greater activities and contributions. Take Frank and Norah Toole in Fredericton, for example, whom we'd known since Brough and I first met. When Frank died, Norah went valiantly on being the queen-pin of the NB Voice of Women. When Jack Duckworth died, Muriel carried on their joint determination to work for peace and justice. On Hornby Island, when HB died, Hilary Brown continued with the co-op and the old people's program, and went on to become chair of the Gulf Islands Trust. Nancy Pocock keeps up her peace and refugee work, and Betty Mardiros, too, pulled it all together again and goes on putting on conferences as she would have done if Tony was still alive and helping. My two-doors-away neighbour, Kay Graham, started a new and successful career after her husband died, and is now a well-known painter. Another good painter and friend, of course, is Erma Sutcliffe, who is still having her own shows. Her husband, Ingham, died soon after Brough died.

Which brings me to Brough and Stephen, and the years when the men in our family departed this life. Brough went gradually downhill with his emphysema, surviving a couple of crises and recuperating successfully. Then we went with Sheila on a wonderful trip to England in 1986, which he must have found terribly wearing. We saw all our old friends, except for the Medawars, which I regret because Sir Peter died just after Brough died. We had Herbert Whittaker along for part of the trip and we had Sheila to drive us, so we had a good time and Brough managed to enjoy parts of it in spite of feeling dreadful at various times.

I suppose most wives feel guilty and wonder what more they could have done. I certainly do. Brough had finally said he preferred to spend his summers at Gananoque and so, on two or three occasions through the 1980s, we had split up for anything from two to six weeks in the summer when I went to Hornby and visited friends and daughter Sheila and so on. Probably I shouldn't have done this, because I suspect when Brough was on his own, which was generally a bit of the time and a good deal of the time on Gananoque, he probably didn't eat as much as he should have, and did drink and smoke more than he should have, and didn't do his emphysema any good at all.

Perhaps it's not guilt so much as sadness that so many opportunities were missed. There was so much I didn't know. Since Brough died, I've learned more about his writings and his activities than I knew when he was alive. People wrote me letters recounting all sorts of small and large incidents he had been involved in and contributions he had made that I seldom knew about.

I think I could have given Brough a more open and loving life. Perhaps married couples can talk together the way women can talk to each other, but it doesn't seem to happen as much, and I think I was a more closed-up male type of personality in those days. I see all this now, since I have learned a great deal more in the past years, often from my women friends and my children, about what is missing, what was missing, in me. I just wasn't the kind of person that anyone could confide in. I can confide in other women – on second thoughts, perhaps I can't. Other women can confide in me on occasion, but I still find it very difficult to open up to anybody, with one or two exceptions.

So the children opened up to Brough far more than to me, which is another regret I have. Stephen talked more easily with Brough and with his sisters; his communication with me was rudimentary and mostly monosyllabic, at least on his part. On one occasion, at Gananoque, I was shouting from the kitchen, probably for help with the dishes. Stephen was in the boat-house twenty or thirty yards away, and Fred Poland, the messenger, climbing the pathway up from the boat-house, carried the message, 'He said, "What?"' This laconic phrase was often quoted by the family thereafter.

In the spring of 1984 or 1985, when Sheila came east, Stephen would come in to see Brough from time to time, but not very often for me. He had been very much put off me in particular. But neither of us saw very much of him; he just kept his own counsel and went his own way. Anyway, he was having therapy at the time, because he seemed to be pretty miserable and depressed, and it was agreed that the whole family would have a meeting with the two therapists and talk about our difficulties – a very interesting session.

Both Stephen and Susan, with Sheila coming in here and there, told me how I had affected them in one way or another during their childhood, and about the difficulties they had now with being able to express love or affection to people because they had had very little overt, if that's the word, affection expressed to them. Stephen talked about how I cared for his physical needs but none of his emotional ones. And I heard some horrendous stories of what they remembered about being small, with graphic descriptions of times when Sheila, on occasion, would cry herself to sleep because there was no one to tuck her in. (Still, I can't really believe that Brough wasn't around, if I had deserted the family. We certainly never left them on their own, though by the time we were in London Susan was old enough to keep an eye on everything.) So we went through this description of the miseries everybody had been feeling.

I don't know whether Brough really grasped what all this was about. I think it was outside his frame of reference somehow, because at one point we were agonizing about how Stephen might be able to make more contact with us, and it ended by Stephen inviting us to dinner, which was a great occasion, but Brough said something in the middle of that to the effect that, well, if one knows what is wanted and everybody is interested in doing it, why don't we just do it? Maybe that's a reflection on how he did do things.

Anyway, things improved then, and we saw more of Stephen and got into a somewhat happier relationship. Stephen had so many mechanical, mathematical, and musical talents, let alone mimicry abilities, which I envied and admired. He was loaded with the handicap of a bossy and undemonstrative mother, and I loved him for all his efforts to overcome this legacy.

I guess it was in 1986 that Stephen teamed up with his Susan (whom we called little Susan, as opposed to our daughter, big Susan). She moved in with Stephen, and eventually they announced they wanted to get married, which was not usually the thing done among the Macphersons. They went to City Hall, which is required, and then we had a garden wedding with Nancy Jackman officiating in the ceremony they planned, with costumes devised by the bride and groom and big Susan as Person of Honour. A good time was had, except that there were one or two people who weren't on the wedding list because little Susan didn't want them, which was the beginning of the alienation of Stephen from his friends.

Nevertheless, big Susan was a constant visitor to their house, and on one occasion we all got together with all our friends and relatives. This was in 1987, when I got the honorary LLD degree from York University, which happened, coincidentally, on my birthday. Mady Gilchrist was tremendous in making all the arrangements, special parking and so on, for Brough to come in a wheelchair. The ceremony took place outside in the glorious sunshine, then Brough went home to lie down and relax, and the rest of us went on to my birthday party, held in Nancy Jackman's garden. Susan danced to a tape Germain had made, including Janet Baker singing some of my favourite music. Everything was just beautiful, we raised money to get the Voice of Women a computer, and almost forgot the birthday cake. It was a grand occasion.

Almost exactly the night after this celebration with everybody around us, Brough began to go slowly downhill. He spent more time in bed and on oxygen, but managed to read a bit and listen to music. We had a nurse to check on him, as well as constant advice and help from Mady and others. Then on the morning of July 20th, he just couldn't get up and dear Mady came quickly and helped call the ambulance, and organized everything to get him down to the hospital. They set up various support things, but we decided there was no point in going to extreme measures because he was pretty low and his feet were swelling. He did talk to us, said hello, and was conscious until the evening. When we went down early the next day, he was still breathing on his oxygen. Stephen and his Susan were there, and then daughter Susan and I took over that afternoon and were sitting by him when he just stopped breathing.

After that, we were grateful for the people at the Toronto Memorial Society, who were extraordinarily helpful and unobtrusive, taking care of everything. Little Susan phoned; big Susan did the press notices and phoned Sheila, who was ready to come as fast as she could. I phoned Nancy Jackman at her cottage and asked if she would not exactly conduct a service (since Brough would certainly not have required one), but organize a gathering of people at the chapel in the Mount Pleasant Cemetery. And Nancy immediately drove down to Toronto to help us plan the ceremony.

We gathered at the chapel on Mount Pleasant, where Susan had made an absolutely beautiful arrangement of flowers and leaves for the coffin. Peace activist Jean Smith started us off with some beautiful Bach on the little harmonium organ and Germain had put together more music on the recording apparatus down in the basement of the chapel. Nancy acted as sort of a chairperson in her ecclesiastical robe, and encouraged everybody to talk about Brough. First she gave a couple of reminiscences of her own, which cheered everyone up a bit: she described the times she had come to visit over the years. Of course she was not quite in the same political stream as Brough, and when they discussed matters of right and left politics, Nancy kept wiggling maybe slightly to the left. During the course of these discussions at dinner, she squirmed so much that she broke a couple of our dining-room chairs. She described how she had fallen heir to some of the little Order of Canada emblems that her father had worn. Knowing how both Brough and Herbert Whittaker loved wearing their Orders, Nancy gave them each a tiny button, to wear on their pyjamas if they wished.

This lightened the atmosphere a little, so then we just talked to each other, and after that everybody came up and held hands around the coffin with its flowers. We ended with our favourite music, and Nancy officiated over the final necessary rites of the coffin going down somewhere. Then we chatted and reminisced on the steps, and eventually everyone came back to our house, where we spilled over into the sunlit garden for food and drink and more memories. It was a good experience, I think, for most of us.

After that, I went out to Hornby for a couple of weeks, then came back to help the Department of Political Science organize a memorial for Brough. I had many consultations with the recently appointed chair, Marcia Chandler, and the secretary, Vera Melnyk, the indomitable Vera. The memorial ended by being just about exactly what I would want and, I hope, just what Brough would have wanted too. It was held at the University of Toronto, in Convocation Hall, on September 30th. Brough's U of T colleagues John Polanyi, Northrop Frye, Ursula Franklin, Peter Russell, Alkis Kontos, and U of T president George Connell all spoke at the memorial (all immediately accepted when I asked them). Music was provided by the Orford Quartet, who were the U of T's quartet-in-residence at the time, and by John Tuttle, the university organist. We ended the memorial with Brough's voice on tape reading the final words of 'The Real World of Democracy,' his 1965 Massey Lectures. Then John Tuttle played us out of the building with the Bach 'Gigue Fugue,' that joyful music which had been our wedding march. Altogether, it was a very moving experience, and I have it on tape. Then followed a magnificent reception at Hart House.

Soon after the memorial, Erindale College put on a show of Barker Fairley's paintings of his academic colleagues, and Brough's portrait was included. It was also on the cover of the catalogue, which was nice.

I have a great many press clippings and obits and several folders of inspiring and illuminating letters from colleagues and friends, one of whom sent this quotation from Pericles about the young men killed in the Peloponnesian war: 'They receive, each for his own memory, praise that will never die and with it the grandest of all sepulchres, not that in which their mortal bones are laid, but a home in the minds of men, where their glory remains fresh and stirs to speech and action as the occasion comes by. For the whole earth is the sepulchre of famous men, and their story is not graven only on stone over their native earth but lives on far away without visible symbol, woven into the stuff of other men's lives.'

Then I had to sort out Brough's papers and books. Mary Rous, our old neighbour from Wilberton, came in and was tremendously useful because she knew so much about university affairs. Betty Fairbank came from the west coast and stayed for five months, helping me sort out my life. What miracles she wrought in helping me tidy up, organize, and repair the house! She and Nancy Jackman formed my escort to Ottawa that October when I went to receive the Persons Award. Betty, who is originally from the US, was most excited to be seeing Canada's capital for the first time.

That year, 1987, the award ceremony was moved to the Senate, and the awards were presented by the Speaker of the Senate rather than the Governor-General. I thought the Senate Chamber was a good place for the presentation. Later, the five award winners and their friends attended a reception with Prime Minister Brian Mulroney in the West Block, where the constitutional hearings and the women's ad hoc conference had been held. Here there was a one-night show of women's paintings, and the Prime Minister spent his time posing with the artists in front of the artwork. The next day, we had lunch with Barbara McDougall, then Minister Responsible for the Status of Women, the Speaker, Senators, and MPs.

Afterwards, we stayed on in Ottawa, and Muriel Duckworth and I went to an Operation Dismantle conference where we met the secretary of the New Zealand peace organization and congratulated him and his country on their refusal to offer entry to ships of the US nuclear fleet. VOW members were happy to encourage trade in NZ goods (we called this a girlcott, a positive term, and the opposite of a boycott).

The following June, I went to the Learned Societies' meetings in Windsor, where a whole session was devoted to Brough's thoughts and so on, which was wonderful. Historian Christopher Hill came over from Oxford, and though he had little time to spare, it was great to see him. He and Charles Taylor, a political scientist from McGill, gave the major papers; with no prior consultation, they fitted together beautifully. Muriel came with me to be my seeing-eye dog, as we said, and we spent a very pleasant night in Windsor.

Then farther on, in the fall of 1989, the Political Science Department of the U of T put on a two-day session, 'The Intellectual Legacy of C.B. Macpherson,' which was doubly oversubscribed and had to be moved to Victoria University. I attended some of these lectures, most of which were over my head to say the least, but I found a soulmate in student peace activist Seth Klein, who sat with me at one of the sessions. At the reception, we displayed the C.B. Macpherson Memorial Quilt made by Ellen Adams out of the hoods from the honorary degrees that Brough had acquired, as well as the non-honorary, fully earned one from London University. The colourful quilt was a great addition to the eating and drinking and talking that was going on at the time.

After Brough died, it took a long time for all of us to accept the fact that Stephen too was dying. Treatment for his cancer – chemotherapy, operations, everything from group therapy to meditation – raised and dashed hopes. Stephen himself finally came to face the situation, and one morning he phoned me. I can't imagine what he had gone through to come to this point; we were almost completely cut off by this time. Eventually our friend Germain was the only go-between who seemed to be acceptable. Although, when we were told, 'Stephen doesn't want to see you,' or 'Stephen doesn't want anyone to visit,' or whatever, we couldn't tell whether it was Stephen or his wife who had decided. We could only guess. Perhaps Susan felt threatened by us, but it was impossible to figure out why she would feel that we were so threatening.

Anyway, Stephen told me straight out that he was going to die. Daughter Susan said later that he was saying goodbye to me then, and that may have been so. What did I do? What did I say? I don't know. I talked on, and finally he interrupted, 'I tell you I'm dying, and all you can do is to talk about trivial happenings.' I was saying something about life going on, I think, but we said a few more words and the call ended. I saw him once for a few minutes on the morning before he died. Perhaps *that* was his farewell.

When Brough and then Stephen died, Vi Thompson provided matter-of-fact, comforting words of understanding. Vi's son Richard had died, too, perhaps a victim of the unrest and storms following the sixties. The plight of the world's people and the political turmoil worried and depressed him. She told me once he had spent hours telling her why he must end it all and, after several tries and bouts in the hospital, he succeeded. It was a dreadful time for Vi and her husband. All I felt I could do was to go to their small silent house and put some flowers on her doorstep.

Vi and I have shared a great deal. We have been to innumerable meetings and conferences together. At one (I think it was the NDP women's conference), we shared a room and labelled it the geriatric ward. At another, we ran a speech-making workshop, cheering on the 'nervous Nellies' as they shook with fright before the microphone, just as we had done in our time. We wrote letters to each other on 'growing old' and they were published in the spring 1984 issue of *Canadian Woman Studies*. When she won the Agnes Macphail Award, given by the NDP to a woman who has been outstanding in working for the NDP and women, Vi said, 'But I'm just an ordinary person. I can't win something like that.' But she did, and we couldn't do much better than to copy the example of Vi, the 'ordinary person.'

Unfortunately, the women's groups have suffered their losses too. Some of the Women Electors died, and it was very sad to see them go after all the ground-breaking work they did. I think of Theresa Falkner and Margaret Walker in particular. When Elsie Gregory MacGill died, Vi was so sad and said, 'Just when I found a wonderful new friend, she had to die'; but I'm sure she'll never forget the time that she did meet and know Elsie. The Voice of Women lost some fine women over time. I'm thinking especially of Ella Manuel, that wonderful woman from Newfoundland who had a great influence on all of us, but also of Thérèse Casgrain and Ghislaine Laurendeau from Quebec, Diana Wright from Saskatoon, and Beatrice Brigden from Winnipeg with her bowler hat and her curls.

But we must never forget the work they did and the inspiration they provided for us all. And one film at least will help us keep the past alive. The idea for making a film about the Voice of Women came to Margo Pineau and Cathy Reeves, two young film-makers, after talking to Lea Roback, a stalwart eighty-year-old Montreal Voice. Then Raymonde Bowen, a Quebec executive member who had been with VOW at the beginning, suggested a series of 'conversations' amongst older VOW members. So in June of 1990, we Voice of Women oldtimers found our-selves at Raymonde's lovely farmhouse, near Cornwall, where we spent the weekend filming *Voice of Women: The First Thirty Years*. (And we were happy to note, among the assorted technical crew, one Martin Duckworth, well-known film-maker and son of VOW's fourth presi-dent.) Then after the filming, naturally, we had to add a party, so we celebrated VOW's thirtieth anniversary with other Quebec Voices over a potluck Sunday lunch.

The VOW national celebration, including a biennial national general meeting, took place in Ottawa, followed by a lobbying session. One of the highlights of the weekend was provided by Brigid Grant's report (she called it a 'portrait') from Fredericton, New Brunswick. The fifty or so women present were so touched by her words that they burst into spontaneous applause. She had mentioned her mother, Norah Toole, who had died a few months previously, and we felt that Brigid herself was carrying on splendidly in her mother's footsteps.

The board meeting started with an ultimatum from the BC women that unless communication and cooperation improved, BC would operate autonomously. The problems of communication and organi-zation of a relatively small group with members in every part of Can-ada have always been formidable, and they grow worse when the national economy is depressed. It is hard to keep in touch when our scattered members are faced with financial problems, lack of time, and too much to do. But women from all parts of the country came to that meeting and, by the end of the weekend, when many old friends had come together and new friendships had been made, there was a revived feeling of hope and determination to make things work, to trust one another, and to try new ways of communicating.

Working for change is as important as ever, and radical ideas thrive in many places. Later in 1990, I attended one of the Elder Hostel group's winter sessions at Lake Couchiching, where they had asked me and Nancy Pocock to talk. We called our talk, 'So you want to change the world ...' Some fifty people were there, and we got everyone discussing today's problems, interspersed with our and their experiences, and including a CBC film of Nancy at work with her refugees. Then people divided into small groups and came up with ideas for action, local to global. We noticed that they carried over their discussion to free time and at meals.

Nancy and I spent four days with this friendly and enthusiastic group of strangers. We talked about change, learned about Emily Carr, saw Eskimo art and artifacts, became acquainted with Tai Chi, and still found time for walking in the early snow.

We were sorry to leave, but Nancy had to get back to work and I had to catch a plane for Charlottetown to attend the CRIAW conference on women and disability. Muriel Duckworth and I had a date with film-maker Bonnie Klein (who made *Not a Love Story* and *Speaking Our Peace*). Bonnie was recovering from a devastating stroke which still restricted her activities, but she went from strength to strength and the workshop she chaired developed into the most moving, self-exposing, consciousness-raising, mutual support that many of us experienced during the whole weekend. Add to this wheelchair-dancing, poets Nicole Brossard and Maxine Tynes (Maxine was also a winner of the Muriel Duckworth award), and it was a very good weekend. Never, I suspect, have so many wheelchairs been seen in the Charlottetown hotel. Their owners were a wonderful group.

24

Hornby

I first visited Hornby Island in 1966, when Hilary Brown brought me to see Heron Rocks, her home since 1938. Hornby seemed to me to combine all my nostalgic memories of England's countryside and beaches with a perfect climate and exotic additions such as eagles, oysters, and snow-capped mountains. It is quite a small island, about eight by seven miles, and in those days it still had unpaved roads and only a small number of year-round residents.

My enchantment with Hornby continued and, until we bought our cabin there, I and my family exploited our BC friends unmercifully. It was mostly me, since the others were only out a couple of times and I went west on every occasion I could manage. When Judy Lawrence decided to build a cabin on the cliff at Downes Point with all the sweep of the Georgia Strait below her, I went out with her to help and to share in the excitement. She had been mentally arranging and adding to that 'panabode' (a prefabricated, half-log house) for most of the year back in Toronto, and in the ensuing years she made it a beautiful home. She did a lot of the work herself, including the building, gardening, and plumbing. Moira Armour, by contrast, bought an almost finished house facing Little Tribune Bay. At low tide, we were able to pick oysters off the rocks there. She, too, added to her house, and I stayed with her, sometimes inside and sometimes in my tent.

Pat Boulding, my BC VOW friend, is the daughter of the man who was Hornby Island's first postman, and she still owns the little cabin which was, in a different location, the old post office (she calls it the OPO). Her cabin, just by a beautiful sandy bay called Whaling Station, is surrounded by huge cedar trees, and you can sleep out in the rain with very few drops of water falling on your bed. I've probably spent more nights sleeping under the stars and cedars with Pat than any-where else on Hornby, though of course I also slept in Hilary's guest house, and on her verandah, and in a tent in the garden.

Sleeping out on Hornby is marvellous. The night sky really is spec-tacular. You see shooting stars, the odd high-flying plane (probably one of those round-the-clock American bombers – oh well), the occa-sional night bird flying and calling. Just before dawn, it is very quiet and dark. The stars are still bright overhead and the moon has dropped behind the barrier of tall cedars and pines. It is chilly cold, and a heavy dew covers the grass and the groundsheet over the sleeping bags. The stars overhead seem close by.

Gradually there is a change in the feeling of the darkness. There is the beginning of a vague greyness in the north-east. Slowly the outline of trees and branches can be sensed. One or two birds wake up, but usually they decide they've made a mistake and silence reigns again for a while. In summer, that's soon after four o'clock, quite a while before that gradual glow in the eastern sky that tells you where the sun will be rising. Slowly, outlines become clearer. Far off, almost outside the range of hearing, a cock crows. There is a sound of wings as a bird flies almost noiselessly over the trees. An owl? A hoarse croak identifies it as an early-rising crow. Only the very brightest of the stars can still be seen in the greying light.

Suddenly there is the sound of a door banging, then the whirring discord of a car starting shatters the stillness. It seems so penetrating that one wonders how the neighbours can sleep on. The gears scrape, the car moves off along the lane, and the early-morning fisherman is on his way. After the sound of the engine dies away, the silence is not so profound as before. Notice has been given that the day is dawning, and many small rustlings, chirpings, and scrapings can be heard. A dog barks, a robin tunes up, then a heron croaks its slow flapping way over towards the seashore and its first fishing foray of the day. There is an orange glow in the east, and the warmth of the rising sun takes some of the chill from the air. A child's voice calls down the road. A truck goes by. Now it is light enough to see the time on one's watch, to think about putting more than one's nose outside the snug sleeping bag.

We turn on the little transistor and listen to music and then the news. The weather and marine forecast take up some time – the weather is much more important on an island off the west coast than in an eastern city. It is great to hear, during July and August, those cheering words, 'Today will again be sunny and warm, with no break in the weather for at least the next few days.' That kind of report can be repeated sometimes for a month. Of course, at another time of year it can be 'The rain and wind will continue' for weeks on end. The islanders know that heaven doesn't last forever, but for those visitors lucky enough to see the islands at their summer best, it's hard to believe that winter ever comes.

More people have moved to Hornby, of course, and there are houses going up now in the field where Pat and I counted thirteen deer grazing one evening. But despite the influx, there is still plenty of space on the huge beaches for families to play volleyball, run their dogs or horses, swim, sunbathe, launch their boats which slide easily over the smooth, flat, sandy beach, and go fishing.

Round the point that marks the end of Whaling Station Bay, one can look due east to the mountains of the BC mainland, with the bulk of Texada Island rising in the foreground. Here the beach is all stones and rocks. If you follow it southward you come to Helliwell Provincial Park, which stretches past Flower Island, a tiny spit of land separated from Hornby by a narrow channel. The cliffs are high, the gulls and cormorants wheel and call, and the view of the whole sweep of water over to Lasqueti Island, twenty miles away, is magnificent. The lighthouse on the white rocks stands out and the flashing light can be seen even in daylight. The ship bound for Prince Rupert passes far away on the mainland side of the channel and dozens of boats dot the water when the fishing is good. One hot day at Helliwell, gazing out over the sea, we saw a mirage. It looked like a long, low island with palm trees on it, but we knew there was no island there. So we tried to take pictures of it, but nothing came out when we had the film developed.

One day in August 1975, when I was out with Pat Boulding, we saw an ad on the co-op store notice board: Cabin for Sale. Tempted and curious, we went to see. It turned out to be about five hundred yards from Sandpiper Beach – an enchanting cabin built for himself by an old Hornby Islander. (Sheila later described it as 'an A-frame turned sideways.') It had a rain-water storage system and pump, a small wood stove, and a propane-fuelled cooking stove salvaged from a trailer. The half-acre lot had paths and a vegetable garden as well as a wood shed and workspace. To me, it was sheer delight. I went home to Toronto dreaming about that cabin. Then, luckily, Brough had a conference in BC, so we were able to go and look at it together, and start the negotiations. With Sheila's support and Pat's knowledge and help, arrangements were made to buy the cabin, and there we were.

The cabin was rented to various winter tenants before Sheila moved in, and again later after she moved over to the Shire with Dale, her partner, mate, spouse, or whatever the correct word is these days. Dale had come up to Canada during the Vietnam War as a draft-resister. His father was an army man and must have found it difficult to face the fact that both his sons opposed the war. Dale is a 'doer.' He works for the Parks Department and is an expert tree surgeon, arborist (forest manager), fisherman, carpenter, and builder. He isn't very talkative, not to me anyway, but he works with his hands and puts his whole effort into the job of the moment. Sheila added another room to the cabin and all sorts of amenities, but when she moved out I spent less time there and eventually sold it in the mid-1980s, since there were always people needing housing on the island.

In 1981, Nancy Jackman spent several weeks on Hornby Island staying in the cabin with me. Nancy was something new to Hornby, and she found the island and its people a fresh experience. Nancy is enormously enthusiastic, and insisted on supplying all kinds of equipment for my cabin, which I had been quite content to camp in. Poor little city girl, she mistook the white oyster shells lying about the beach for styrofoam cups!

That was the year Nancy first went to the Hornby Island Fair. I still have a couple of Hornby Island Fair T-shirts, one green and one yellow. I had to get two, because I couldn't decide between them, and, when in doubt ... The fair grew out of a 'happening' organized by a group of Hornby's craftspeople: potters, knitters, weavers, sheepshearers, and so on. They wanted to show off their wares and their skills and, at the same time, provide fun and games for the kids and anyone else who wanted to enjoy themselves. Puppet-maker Judy was there and she helped the children make special puppets out of driftwood, seaweed, and shells. Over the years the food has become steadily more imaginative, delicious, and of course healthy. (One of my favourites was an 'ice-cream' cone, made with frozen fruit.) Nancy was studying clowning that year and, with a parasol and an enormous hat, was a colourful addition to the parade that launched the fair.

That same summer, 1981, Sheila's son Darian was about eighteen months old, and Sheila had two of Jim Lawson's grandchildren staying with her, as well as hosting a family reunion of something like twenty additional relatives of Dale's. There was a children's horse show, and the Lawson kids and others made and sold cookies and lemonade. Stephen came, driving out by himself in his Porsche, visiting a few friends on his way. He stayed with Sheila, but wouldn't come near me. It was an acutely unhappy time for both of us. I didn't know how to communicate with him, and he seemed so lonely and depressed. Nancy was able to persuade him to go and see my cabin, which in any other circumstance he would have loved, only when I was safely away from it. During the horse show, I went over to stand by him and watch the show. We exchanged a few brief words, and then just stood there, side by side, both of us completely miserable – at least he looked it and I felt it. He left soon after and drove his solitary way back to Toronto to work.

In August of 1989, I was back on Hornby for the Hornby Island Festival, a music event. And while I was there, the following incident occurred. Soon after sunrise one summer morning, curator and art critic Doris Shadbolt was taking her regular morning walk before starting a long day at her desk. As the spry, grey-haired woman started up the steep hill with its glorious view of the Gulf Islands and the sea, she caught sight of a slight figure hurrying out of the woods, stumbling under the heavy burden of suitcase, bag, and musical instrument. Catching up, Doris found that the fleeing figure was a young Chinese woman in a state of extreme anxiety. Unable to speak more than a word or two of English, she was clearly appealing for help and refuge.

Doris took the young musician home and phoned Hilary Brown, who knew the Chinese community well and had helped organize the visit of the Shanxi Folk Artists, the troupe with which, it turned out, this young woman had come to Hornby. 'I have never done anything like this in my life before,' said Doris, 'but if that is what she wants, then I want to help this woman evade the authorities.' Hilary immediately summoned a local woman who spoke both Cantonese and Mandarin, and arrangements were then made to hide the young woman. Soon, the Chinese Consulate had been apprised of the defection and was directing a search for the errant musician.

This all happened soon after the Tiananmen Square massacre, when almost everyone in Canada had agreed that the Chinese government's treatment of the students and their supporters was despicable. Some people supported the government simply because it was the government in power, but more have come to question the kinds of governments which come to power and the methods they use to stay in power. The Canadian government had righteously condemned the Chinese government, which they felt free to do as long as it didn't interfere too much with trade.

But now the situation had been brought close to home, and many Hornby Islanders faced a moral dilemma they had never experienced before: Should they help an individual to escape danger even if her actions might threaten others in her group? Should they cooperate when the Chinese Consulate asked about her whereabouts? One older woman who had lived through the Hitler era had no qualms at all, and concern for an individual up against the power of a repressive state was clearly expressed by most of the island people. This particular defector joined the thousands who cannot safely return to their own country, and whose fears for friends and relatives grow greater with the passing days. For us, the incident demonstrated that human feelings can still bring ordinary people together to aid their sisters from a foreign land.

I had been fortunate enough to visit China in 1984 with Nancy and members of a women's group organized by Hilary Brown. There were some twenty-four women on that trip, including my old friends Betty Fairbank from the Gulf Islands and Betty Peterson of Halifax, MLAs Rosemary Brown and Barbara Wallace, and ex-MLA Lois Haggen, who climbed the Great Wall on her eighty-fifth birthday and was the proud recipient of a T-shirt proclaiming, 'I climbed the Great Wall.'

We had meetings with members of the Chinese Federation of Women and visited schools, hospitals, and other institutions, including some in South China where few, if any, non-Chinese had visited. We were impressed by the tremendous efforts being made everywhere to improve the conditions and lives of this huge nation, and by the friendliness of everyone we met. Several women managed to borrow bicycles and went exploring early in the morning when the cities were waking up to a new day. They saw more of the real life of the country than those of us who stayed in bed – the day begins very early in China.

We shared a memorable night on the train between Xian and Chengdu with the mother-daughter team of Catherine Denholm and Ann Crosby. Our group had been assigned a whole car, with two wash-rooms – a Chinese toilet at one end and a western one at the other; both smelled, but the western one was reported to be so bad that I never went near it. Nancy and I shared one of the four-bunk compart-ments with Catherine and Ann. The bunks were two up, two down, and a long discussion ensued as to the up/down sleeping arrangements. I was recommended to the lower level, on account of my nocturnal expeditions to the washroom. Nancy too had been urged to sleep on the lower level, mostly from a sense of self-preservation with regard to the strength of the upper-berth supports. We watched the long legs of the mother-daughter duo get folded into the upper berths – being over seventy obviously didn't hamper Catherine's gymnastic ability.

The food was awful, but we drank much beer, always a good staple. After dinner, Catherine served us western-style instant coffee and we laced it with a tot from our reserve of whisky. Then Nancy went off to play cards with our next-door neighbours and we settled down for a nice talk, mostly about foreign affairs, with Madame Xu, our guide, and Xiang, the shy young interpreter. At the end, we all agreed that China could play an important role in trying to persuade the United States and the Soviet Union to begin peace negotiations. Then we made up our beds and searched for boiled water for drinking and tooth-cleaning. We arrived at Chengdu the following morning feeling rather scruffy and with slightly less enthusiasm for the imagined delights of the Trans-Siberian trip we'd so been looking forward to.

Travelling with Nancy is always an experience. This next story arises from a telephone conversation we had in the spring of 1989. 'I was wondering,' she said, 'whether I would ask you up to the cottage next weekend.' This may seem to be rather a strange way of issuing an invitation to a friend, but given the circumstances, it was not unreasonable. I had been to her island a few times when she first built the cottage on Go Home Bay, so I knew the terrain, but on earlier visits, I had been much better able to both see and walk on the rocky ground. This time, Nancy would have to act as my 'seeing-eye dog' as well as doing all the baggage-carrying and chores herself. We also discussed whether we would fight, arguments having been part of our relationship since we first met. We agreed that when Nancy faced a difficult situation it was useless for me to try to be helpful. It usually leads to a shouting match and bad feelings. I had learned that when Nancy gets into a 'snit,' the best action is get the hell out of the way.

The next day she phoned to say the trip was on, and we arranged food and times. We started off in mid-afternoon in her new (second-hand) Cadillac, towing the trailer that carried her Boston Whaler loaded with all kinds of hardware and supplies, and arrived, to Nancy's relief, before dark. The lake water was low, and she wanted to be able to see well when navigating the boat through the rocky approach. Anyone who has tried backing a car with a trailer attached knows that the steering is the opposite of what you think is logical. Nancy has become adept at this art, but it was one of those dicey occasions when I was ordered to make myself scarce. Then the boat slid into the water and Nancy started tinkering with the motor.

After a while she consulted with Ralph, the caretaker and resident expert on the landing. Several more false starts followed. They finally agreed that the motor was missing a part and, after much peering into the water, they saw something on the sandy bottom. The evening was quite chilly, and the water must still have been close to freezing. (The next morning, when we tried washing our faces, I decided instantly to remain unwashed.) Ralph, his wife, and I all looked at Nancy. 'OK, I guess someone has to get it,' said the boat-owner.

Nancy stripped off her heavy sweater, kicked off her shoes, and pulled off her corduroy pants, revealing to our gaze a voluptuous figure, a replica of those more-than-ample goddesses. Quite a vision. What no goddess had had was a very fancy black lace bra and a pair of very skimpy and very bright scarlet panties. Thus clad, and roaring and squeaking mightily, our heroine waded into the freezing water up to her shoulders. Then, feeling around with her toes, she miraculously found the part and brought it to the surface, enthusiastically applauded by her audience. After a brisk towelling, she donned her clothes and proceeded to help Ralph improvise a connection with a piece of wire. Luckily, the motor started and didn't stop.

The light was fading rapidly, so when we finally reached her dock, we hurried to unload before it got too dark to see. I couldn't see much anyway, especially with uneven boulders, loose rocks, low bushes, and scrub to confuse me. So, bless her, Nancy shouldered all the heavy baggage she could manage, and guided her half-blind, hobbling old friend over the hazards of the path, until we reached the comfortable haven of her cabin.

In August 1990, I was visiting Hornby again. We were just going swimming at Whaling Station beach one day when the alarm siren went and we saw a column of smoke rising at Helliwell Provincial Park about a mile away. A messenger came round telling us to evacuate the area.

It was one of the longest, hottest, and driest summers in memory. Hornby has only two little lakes and is often tinder-dry in the summer, with High Danger notices posted round the island. People are always very much aware of the danger of fire. One time, a very long time ago when I was still smoking, I put a cigarette butt out of the car onto the gravel road. And the butt was butted. But no matter. I got a ticking-off by everybody which I have obviously never forgotten.

This universal awareness among the Hornby islanders paid off that August. There was no need to call for volunteer firefighters. Hundreds were ready, some even clad in the requisite boots and long pants, and many were turned away. Radio communication with both individual firefighters and the authorities in Comox was extraordinarily good, and within about half an hour two water bombers were on the scene. After loading thirty tons of water in Whaling Station Bay, they roared over and dumped their loads. After half a dozen runs by the huge tankers, the fire was controlled and finally out.

The alarm had been given by hikers who noticed a tiny patch of smoke in the long dried-out grass near the cliffs and started stamping out the fire that was spreading with the wind. They saw a whole bush literally explode into flames. Dashing to the nearest house, some distance through the park, they gave the alarm. Every islander and most visitors knew what to do, or knew to keep out of the way, and thanks to organization and good fortune (the water bombers were nearby, the wind dropped), a disaster was miraculously avoided.

The community spirit on Hornby is truly remarkable. Besides cooperating in emergencies, islanders tend to generate their own entertainment. Dances in the Community Hall are very popular, particularly fancy-dress ones. I was on Hornby once for a Hallowe'en dance, and the ingenuity which went into those costumes was mind-boggling. There was an upside-down person, as well as animals, flowers, and houses. The night Sheila first met Dale, he was a cedar tree and she was a lemon (not too easy to manoeuvre in and out of the car). The dancing takes place in the main hall, and there's a special circular stone-built room with a huge log fire in it, which is reserved for beer-drinking and chit-chat. What I like most about these dances is that no one has to go with a partner. You can dance by yourself or with anyone, male or female, who takes a fancy to pairing up for a while.

A short way down the road is the island library, designed and built by the islanders, who raised all the money and cut all the lumber, including the shingles for the roof. The same process rebuilt and enlarged the Community Hall, where the Purcell Quartet came for a week-long event. On Saturday mornings, outside the Co-op, the local potters, weavers, and vegetable growers have a market. Every so often there is a 'Saturday evening salmon dinner,' which is crowded out in the summer. The Co-op is at a crossroads in the middle of the island, so that is where everyone puts up their For Sale and Lost and Found notices, announcement of ratepayers' meetings, and so on. If you aren't on the mail route or you haven't a phone, this is where you come to pick up your mail and make phone calls. I've met friends from all over Canada outside the Co-op, people I never dreamed I'd see on Hornby, but there they were.

One of the achievements of the community is the dump. The once smelly and unsightly dump is now one of Hornby's showplaces. This transformation began in the late seventies, and now garbage is carefully sorted and recycled. Hornby's original residents took care of their own waste, and some continue to compost, to feed their livestock, and burn or bury their own garbage. In 1970, the year-round population was 125, including 15 school-age children. Now it's over 850 adult residents and 320 children, not to mention the several thousand summer visitors. The official Class C Dump (a piece of Crown land, where, four times a year, volunteers burned and flattened the garbage, then covered it with gravel) had become inadequate, unsightly, and a hazard to health.

Many of Hornby's residents were already committed to conservation and pollution control, so needed little persuasion to introduce a do-it-yourself recycling program. Start-up expenses were provided by a grant from the provincial recycling program and the proceeds of the 1979 Hornby Quilt Raffle. Then the Regional Board was persuaded to hire a Waste Resources Coordinator, the only paid labour involved in the project until 1980.

The original ambitious multiple categories for recycling were reduced to three: burnables (paper, plastic); dry unburnables (cans, glass); and anything wet (kitchen waste, etc.). Rows of barrels containing cans and glass stand ready to be sent off for recycling. An incinerator, grandly labelled Hornby Island Sanitation Department, was constructed by a few scrap-metal wizards from an old boiler, among other things, and crowned by a curly corrugated stovepipe, which makes the whole thing look like an outsize top hat. A metal-crusher was constructed along similar lines. Commercially available models would have cost thousands of dollars to acquire; these cost a few hundred. Old cars are collected in batches of forty ('Rolls Royces on the left, pleez,' said a notice) and shipped off. In the Free Store, treasures such as ancient hats, paperback books, clothes, and functional bathtubs can be had for nothing. Clothing in excess of the islanders' needs is sent to Goodwill stores elsewhere.

Recycling continues. At the campsite, there's a notice that says, 'Leave crabs and fish cleanings below the tide line, please – the gulls do a better job than we can.'

With humour, common sense, and resourcefulness, the Hornby

Islanders have shown that a community can still work together for the common good. Like Yukoners and other pioneer types, they have shared and developed the building, engineering, and craft skills to make life worth living. I'm proud to add that my daughter Sheila is now the editor of the Hornby Island Press' newsletter, *The First Edition*, in which she deals with complainers with a firm hand, insisting they supply constructive suggestions.

In my time on Hornby, I have met peace workers, feminists, ecologists, artists, craft workers, and writers. What stays with me most is that sense of cooperation and community. It gives me the answer to the question so often asked, 'But what can one person do?' The answer is, 'Together, we can move mountains.' If ordinary men and women can combine their efforts, nothing is impossible. If we can save the environment on Hornby, we can save the planet. But only if each one of us contributes their share.

25

December 1990

One Sunday morning this December I finished peering at *The Globe and Mail* headlines and was wishing I had a built-in human reader. I'm too lazy to undertake sorting the newspaper sheets out for the reading machine that magnifies pages onto a screen, like a TV. Having to give up reading is my biggest complaint about becoming a handicapped person, though I could also mention bird-watching, tennis and ping-pong, dancing, and jigsaw puzzles as things I miss. The best remedy for all this is to remember there's always someone worse off.

And there's always the radio. On the CBC, the news reported George Bush dashing about South America, no doubt bringing everyone into line. Then it was J.S. Bach's cantata, 'Wachet Auf.' This was all I needed to start on a musical remembering trip. Brough and I had agreed that an organist was the one absolute essential for our wedding, and I walked up the aisle at Montreal's A and P (St Andrew and St Paul) to part of the 'Wachet Auf' cantata. We came back down the aisle to the 'Gigue Fugue,' which is wonderful skipping music.

I became as addicted to Bach and Mozart as Brough was. His devotion to Bach's *St Matthew Passion* was renowned. He must have attended most of the annual performances in Toronto, which began with Sir Ernest Macmillan in Convocation Hall. I remember when we discovered Haydn's *Lord Nelson Mass*, and when the U of T orchestra brought us a dazzling and thrilling *Carmina Burana* in the old Conservatory Concert Hall, where the Hydro Building now stands.

And I remember being doubly furious on December 7, 1941, when the performance of Brahms' *Second Piano Concerto* from Carnegie Hall was interrupted to announce the bombing of Pearl Harbour. But then again, the Beethoven's *Ninth* with Leonard Bernstein from the site of the Berlin Wall was an overwhelming experience for millions of people.

From this, I fell to thinking about how my enjoyment of Christmas, and Easter too, comes down to the music. The rest I can do without, although I don't have anything against parties and presents except that I am too lazy to prepare for them. In the meantime, I think of the Sunday and Christmas mornings when Brough and I carried our breakfast upstairs and sat munching and listening to cantatas and oratorios, reading the paper, and savouring each other's company. Today I'm doing what Brough would have hated, trying to listen to two cantatas at once and flipping the radio dial back and forth. With classical music offered by three Toronto FM radio stations, there's quite a choice.

My habit of phoning friends when there is music on radio or television which they might enjoy must have bugged many of them, but it generally pays off, for me anyway, in knowing that Mady is listening to the *B Minor Mass* or Moira to Joan Sutherland at the same time as I am.

We all know what an important role the telephone can play in our lives. Long before the term 'network' was common, women used telephone communication to keep in touch, to organize activity, and for a hundred other purposes. For anyone with limited sight, it is a life-support system and, sometimes literally, a life-saver. I am addicted to the phone, so it can disrupt an entire day. Recently, one call about the confrontations between Mohawks and the military in Quebec led to several mornings of planning What To Do. Or it can be a request for a recipe, a quotation, an opinion, a name, or a date. And off one goes searching for numbers, making notes, looking up references, urging others to act, and dashing about postponing all the actions previously lined up in one's mind for that particular time.

Besides, I have a host of wonderful and remarkable friends to talk to. And, since I am not one of those talented people who observe things like body language and atmosphere, or at least only minimally, I often rely on the perceptions of others to guide me. Actually, I almost find this easier to do by phone, where I can often tell by people's voices what they are feeling. I do have guidelines, worked out over the years, but often I forget them, and then I generally regret it. For instance: listening is better than telling. I am still learning this one. It needed my daughters and others to teach me that, when meeting a group of people, it is not a good idea to start in with what's on the tip of one's tongue, regardless of what others may be saying. They may be waiting for your news, but don't count on it. I've had instructions and reminders from friends about trying to *feel* how others feel and to ask them. On the subject of feelings, it's only comparatively recently that I got around to hugging, let alone kissing friends or family. As to telling anyone that I love them, that's the hardest of all.

I have to work hard to remember that, as people grow older, some become more radical and outspoken, some more reactionary and outspoken. Some remain open-minded, where others tend to be intolerant or reluctant to accept change. I tend to be of the latter group, which makes me cautious (if I remember) not to say, 'Oh we tried that, and it didn't work,' or 'Must we reinvent the wheel?' or that famous phrase learned from Sheila Macpherson, 'Heard it in grade 8.' I need my friends and family to remind me of all these things.

This week, several calls came from Muriel about flights to the CRIAW conference, then the Voice of Women office phoned about the planning of the annual meeting, and I had to make several more calls as a result. With Vi Thompson I discussed the delights of the Ontario NDP's first days in office as our new provincial government. Then we arranged to go to another women's conference with a few pieces of information to pass on to others. I commissioned more slippers to keep my feet warm, since knitting is also one of Vi's many skills, which she combines with the NDP meetings and everything else. I've had mitts, jackets, and socks and am very grateful for them. There followed discussions with four academic friends about questions to be answered (they hope) in my book.

In a normal week, when Ursula Franklin and I are both in Toronto, I get one or two telephone calls from her. Some of Ursula's most valued assessments have come by phone when she arrives at her office in the morning and hasn't yet started on her gruelling schedule. When I hear her drawling 'Hi,' I grab a pen (usually not within convenient reach, or working too well, for that matter) and prepare to hear something interesting. I may still be eating breakfast, or doing the washing, but I don't want to miss a word. Often I am caught with only a messy scrap of paper on which to note these pearls of wisdom, so I fear many of them come out in garbled and inadequate form. Subjects range from a new button that says, 'Military intelligence is a contradiction in terms,' to a concise analysis of American political choices or a piece of scurrilous gossip. It is foolish to raise questions with Ursula as to what meetings she is attending – the run-down of engagements, speeches, and articles to be dealt with is too daunting.

With the temperature getting lower, I've been bringing in the plants which shot up and proliferated during the hot, wet summer. So I finally called Montreal to ask my brother, the gardening expert, for instructions on taking cuttings from my hibiscus, which produced glorious flame-coloured flowers regularly all summer. He gave me detailed instructions, but at the moment I can't bear to cut any of it because it's still flowering.

One of my most precious delights, which has developed quite recently, is to get a phone call from Susan. Her calls range from intense fury, boredom, or despair, to enthusiasm, excitement, and delight. If the call begins with frustration or some other negative mood, gradually it works its way back up, ending with a cheerful, 'Well, if ever I get this done, then maybe I can get back to my studio and do some real work.'

Recently she's been serving on a dance jury in Ottawa. We talked sadly of the awful toll inflicted on the dance community by AIDS, and of the frustration and despair about the world's future expressed by David Suzuki, whom she ran into in the airport. He keeps on keeping on for the sake of his children. We've talked about Gananoque and our island, about teeth (when she was facing a root-canal job), about ceramics and her shows, and the two filtering machines she has had installed to keep the clay and glaze dust from their lethal effects on the lungs of workers in the studio.

Phone calls to the west coast are usually made late in the evening, and from west to east early in the morning. When I phone Sheila, I am often in bed, and she is finishing dinner or Darian is reading bedtime stories (he must be disgusted by the interruption). Conversations with Sheila are a wonderful mixture of news about Hornby, the events and celebrations of the island, household projects-in-progress, and family news. When we've finished gossiping along, I am filled with a nice comfortable feeling of affection and warmth.

I'm glad I've so often been to wherever my friends and family are. When you can picture how and where things are happening, it makes everything nearer and more familiar, something for which a conversation is better than a letter. Over the last fifteen to twenty years, my letter-writing has dwindled and almost dried up. Without a telephone, life wouldn't be the same.

Since Brough died, I have had several wonderful women living on my top floor. Back in the fall of 1987, Betty Fairbank came to keep me company for the winter. When Betty was preparing to go back, Shelley Mardiros' best friend, Mary McGeer, was looking for somewhere to live. She became an instant companion and friend, besides giving me insight into how a dedicated musician works. Students and visitors fill the top floor in the summertime, and sometimes it turns into what the inhabitants are pleased to call a Newfoundland ghetto.

But in spite of these invasions and other visitors dropping in and out, I still have quite a lot of time on my own. And the domestic routine still continues. Last Thursday, I set out to catch the Avenue Road bus to shop and have my hair cut. Walking in a light powdering of snow through the familiar part of Toronto around Yonge and Chaplin Crescent brought me to the stores I shopped at when we lived on Wilberton Road. Shopping there hasn't changed much. Although the hardware store has been run by a series of families since our children and theirs were at North Toronto Collegiate, I can still drop in for a chat. I began going to Karl and Gunther, the twin 'hairstylists' on Yonge Street at Davisville, when a haircut cost two dollars, and even now I can call them up for a haircut that is finished in half an hour flat, gossip and catching up included.

I used to enjoy getting up early on Saturday mornings to go to the farmer's market when it was still at the city limits on Yonge Street, and also later when it moved to the St Lawrence Market. After Mike and Mary Freeman's Healthbreads Bakery on College Street closed down, the Harbord Bakery became a regular shopping stop, as did the A & P stores which, to my great disgust, were closed down, one by one.

Walking with limited vision is rather like exploring new territory, and I felt a sense of achievement when I arrived on the east side of Yonge Street, having made it from Oriole Parkway over crossings and snow bumps and street lights. But I took a taxi home, and the driver told me he'd been parked exactly opposite the store I was in when he got the call. 'Never been so close to my fare before,' he said chattily.

At home 'my student,' Rachel, was efficiently sorting old files, and we found a speech of Helen Tucker's, given at the time of the Cuban Crisis. *Plus ça change.* Much of it was completely relevant today, including Voice of Women's condemnation of force and violence. Rachel was off soon to join her parents in London, so we wished each other happy holidays, and I caught up on my phoning. Mady was trying to find a Canadian to join Margaret Papandreou in going to Baghdad to appeal to Saddam Hussein. Here we are sitting politely waiting while George Bush plans to blow up the Middle East to save American oil. It's appalling.

Susan came in with some gorgeous new blue/black pottery and presents from Sheila: the garlic braids that I couldn't fit into my pack last August, Christmas cake, a lovely picture of Sheila and Darian collecting seaweed for garden fertilizer, and a note from Sheila's partner, Bill. Darian, he said, was making 'mosquito submarines' (what on earth?). I phoned them later. They all sounded fine, and I learned that mosquito submarines were small bottles containing mosquitoes, floating in the lake. It made perfect sense to children I spoke to later. A mosquito in a floating bottle, they explained, could keep an eye on its offspring, the eggs floating in the lake.

The next day, Ann Buttrick came for tea. We had an incredible and lengthy argument about who would buy, stuff, and cook a turkey. Talk about two evenly matched stubborn women! It was quite hilarious and eventually settled amicably. Nancy phoned to see if all was well, and dropped by for supper with Mary Ebert's three children, whom she was minding. It was a lovely party with extensive rides on the 'elevated railway' (the stairlift installed for Brough when he became weaker), decorating my pot of pine branches for a Christmas tree, and much carolsinging. Then Jean Woodsworth and I went to Tafelmusik's *Messiah*.

On Saturday, 'my editor' and I agreed we were partly working and mostly having fun at our 'editorial' meeting. Editing at the moment means Christine getting my writings into some sort of order, while I flounder among reminiscences and non-sequiturs. We have so many overlapping experiences and people: Janet Baker, Noel and Gertie, Flanders and Swann, and Joyce Grenfell. It's difficult not to be led astray.

Then I filled in until suppertime with some Christmas phoning and gossiping with Eric and Jo Adams and other friends, and there was just time to change before my old friend Anna Lou picked me up and we went off to meet Mady at the Royal Alex for *The Heidi Chronicles*. I hadn't been there for ages, and we enjoyed Mirvish's renovations right up to the top gallery. Mady even got me one of those theatre hearing aids, and the whole show was good old-fashioned American feminist fun. We found a restaurant afterwards for beer, tea, and pie, and Mady left me at Bedford Road subway for a nice, peaceful, damp walk home.

Now it's the Sunday before Christmas. First, I woke up and turned on the radio. *Le Tombeau de Couperin* played by Louis Lortie was enchanting. Telemann was to follow, but I switched just to try all the stations and found Bach's *Christmas Oratorio* on CJRT. That was it. Memories of Brough and me and the first time we heard Janet Baker at the Festival Hall. The absolutely right music for Christmas. Being alone in the house allows me to turn on the radio noisily, however early, which for Bach's trumpets is essential.

It's about 6:30 a.m. now, and here I am writing another piece about blessings, a diary of the last three days. Last night I was thinking that, despite all the horror and misery in the world today, I really am happy. However selfish and self-centred this may be, I felt I should catch the feeling of joy and thanksgiving to 'whatever powers there be' for being alive and able to feel – good feelings, happiness, love.

So let us end on a cheerful note: Jan Port is coming to breakfast and we are at Part V of the *Christmas Oratorio*.

Postscript

As this book comes to a close, we are facing the last decade of the twentieth century. What monumental changes have taken place during my life! I began by writing about a world which seemed smaller and simpler than that of today. Back then, one could hear a train rumbling through the city at night – no longer a frequent or familiar noise. The roar of transporter freight has been transferred to planes and superhighways. We seldom listen now to the wail of a train whistle on the prairies, or across the river at night at Hope or French River or Gananoque.

About thirty wars are being fought around the world, space is being conquered by man (sic), incredible microsurgery is now possible, and, far more sinister, man is changing the atmosphere, the oceans, and the earth itself. With all these tremendous developments, human beings have not been able to overcome their insatiable greed and struggle for power. We still don't seem able to care and provide for some of our fellow human beings without denying life and justice to others. Yet incredible acts of love and sacrifice take place daily as we struggle to make the world a better place – for some, if not for all.

Karen Ridd's stories of how the grass and trees can slowly and steadily grow up between cracks in the solid concrete of an old highway, or the story of the women in San Salvador offering hot coffee to violent men who have just bombed their offices – these can give one hope. Recently, Nobel Peace Prize winner Mairead McGuire answered the angry question 'How long are we going to go on feeding the poor?' by replying, 'I would ask, "How long are the poor going to go on feeding us?"'

Gloria Steinem urged women not to assume that the struggle for equality and justice was successful until each of us individually took upon ourselves the job of reaching every woman and man in the effort to change our political situation, by voting and by being an activist.

And so we 'keep on keeping on,' as they say. And those familiar sayings, new and old, still hold good for global strategy: love thy neighbour; do as you would be done by; until all of us have made it, none of us have made it. (Even: one who stands at the edge of a cliff is wise to define progress as one step backwards.) And let's talk to each other, to anyone we can. Some people are gifted in this way – I wish I were more so.

Although at present the future of the world looks uncertain, even bleak, we can also realize that tremendous strides have been made by the efforts of so many of the people I have written about in this book.

Chronology

1913	Kathleen Margaret Walker born in Uxbridge, England
1916	Richard Walker born
1917	Father dies
	Family moves to Branksome, outside Bournemouth
1920	Mother marries Maurice Sarson; family moves to Bedford
1932	Kay finishes school, begins physiotherapy training at St Thomas' Hospital, London
1933	Mother dies
1934	Kay completes physiotherapy training
1935	Works for five months in Selly Oak, near Birmingham
	Arrives in Montreal to work as physiotherapist
1935–41	In Hillside Tennis Club
1935–late 1950s	In CPA, Canadian Physiotherapy Association (1920–present)
1936–38	Spends summer holidays in England
1939	Kay makes first trip to west coast (Canada and US), by train
1939–41	Sings in Elgar Choir
1940–41	Makes summer camping trips to west coast by car
1941	Moves to Fredericton, New Brunswick
1942	Brough Macpherson arrives to teach at University of New Brunswick
1943	Kay visits Brough in Ottawa; gets engaged
	Marries Brough in Montreal; moves to Ottawa
1944	Kay and Brough move to Deer Park Crescent, Toronto
	Susan Macpherson born
1946	Stephen Macpherson born
1947	Kay and family move to Wilberton Road, Toronto
1948	Stillbirth of twins
1949	Sheila Macpherson born

1949–61	Kay in Home and School Associations
1949–69	Attends Ladies' Liquid Lunches
1950–64	Kay in Deer Park Residents' Association
1950–86	In AWE, Association of Women Electors (1937–86)
1952–53	Kay and family spend Brough's sabbatical in Oxford, England
1954–64	Kay first chair of Ontario Board of Directors of Physiotherapy, formerly Board of Regents of Physiotherapy (Regents 1925–53, Directors 1953–present)
1955–59	On Board of University Settlement (1910–present)
1957–59	President of AWE
1959–60	Kay and family spend Brough's sabbatical in London, England
1960–present	Kay in VOW, Voice of Women (1960–present)
1962	At VOW's first International Women's Peace Conference (Montreal)
1963–67	Kay president of VOW
1964	Kay and Thérèse Casgrain arrested in Paris after conference on NATO
	Kay and family move to Glengowan Road, Toronto
1964–75	Kay occasionally attends Lawrence Park Residents' Association
1966	Makes first visit to Hornby Island
	Attends meeting of national women's organizations which form the Committee on Equality and call for a royal commission on the status of women in Canada
	With VOW delegation to Soviet Union
1967–8	Kay and family spend sabbatical in Cambridge, England
1968	Kay visits Vietnam
1971–81	Kay in Ontario Committee on the Status of Women (1971–present)
1972	At Strategies for Change conference of NAC (now National Action Committee on the Status of Women)
	Helps found WPA, Women for Political Action (1972–82)
	Runs as independent candidate in federal election (St Paul's)
1972–76	In WPA
1972–present	In NAC (1972–present)
1973	To Mexico, then Australia
	To Women in Politics conference
	Joins NDP, attends federal NDP convention
1973–80	In CCLA, Canadian Civil Liberties Association (1964–present)

1974	Runs as NDP candidate in federal election (York East)
1975	Kay and Brough move to Boswell Avenue, Toronto
	Muriel Duckworth and Kay at Social Sciences Research Council consultation
	Kay to Cyprus for Famagusta 'Women Walk Home'
	Kay and Brough buy cabin on Hornby Island
1977–9	Kay president of NAC; starts publication of NAC's *MEMO*
Late 1970s–late 1980s	Works as school volunteer
1978	To Greece for Women's Union tour
1979	To Brussels for women's peace conference to coincide with meeting of NATO defence ministers
	Runs as NDP candidate in federal election (York East)
1980	Runs as NDP candidate in federal election (York East)
	Sheila has son, Darian
1981	Kay to Amsterdam for anti-nuclear conference
	Involved in Canadian constitutional conference
	Kay and Brough to Japan
1982	Kay and Brough to San Francisco and Mexico
	Kay helps found and chairs NAC's Survival Committee
	Speaks at UNSSOD rally in New York (after initially being turned back at US border)
	Receives Order of Canada
1983	Helps organize meeting for Margaret Papandreou to speak in Toronto
1983–6	Serves on Persons Award selection committee
1984	To Athens as one of the Canadians receiving thanks from Greek government to celebrate 10th anniversary of liberation from Colonels
	To China
1985	Helps organize International Women's Peace Conference in Halifax and prepare for Nairobi Congress ending the Decade of Women; serves on Secretary of State selection committee to fund travel to Nairobi
	To Greece for second tour by Women's Union
1986	At Department of National Defence consultation
1987	Receives honorary doctorate of law from York University
	Brough dies
	Kay receives Persons Award
1989	Stephen dies
1990	Kay in VOW's 30th anniversary film and celebrations

Heads of AWE, VOW, and NAC

Association of Women Electors of Metropolitan Toronto
(formerly Women Electors' Association)

1938–40	Mrs E.S. McCarty
1941–2	Mrs J.W. Falkner
1943–4	Mrs H.A. Luffman
1945–7	Mrs W.N. Robertson (later Mrs Norman Gunn)
1948–9	Mrs E.B. Dustan
1950	Mrs A.D. Stockwood
1951–2	Mrs P. Sandiford
1953–4	Mrs S.J. Allin
1955–6	Mrs S. Hermant
1957–8	Mrs C.B. Macpherson
1959	Mrs H.W. Rowlands
1959–60	Mrs W.D. Walker
1961–2	Mrs G.S. Vickers
1963–4	Mrs T.H. Murphy
1965–6	Mrs F. Burger
1967–8	Mrs D.M. Eisen
1969–70	Mrs H.W. Rowlands
1971–2	Mrs F.E. Burke
1973–4	Mrs W.O.C. Miller
1975–6	Mrs R. Wertheimer
1977–8	Mrs D. Price
1979–80	Mrs R. Wolfe
1981–2	Mrs T.H. Murphy
1983–6	Mrs R. Wolfe

Voice of Women

1960–2	Helen Tucker
1962–3	Thérèse Casgrain
1963–7	Kay Macpherson
1967–71	Muriel Duckworth
1971–4	National Coordinating Committee
1974–9	Donna Elliott (paid coordinator)
1980–6	Dorothy Smieciuch (volunteer coordinator)
1986–9	Board of Directors and Administrative Committee chaired by Martha Goodings
1989–present	Board of Directors and Administrative Committee chaired by Grace Hartman

National Action Committee on the Status of Women

1972–3	Laura Sabia
1974–5	Grace Hartman
1975–7	Lorna Marsden
1977–9	Kay Macpherson
1979–81	Lynn McDonald
1981	Jean Wood
1982–4	Doris Anderson
1984–6	Chaviva Hošek
1986–8	Louise Dulude
1988–90	Lynn Kaye
1990–3	Judy Rebick

Abbreviations

AGM	Annual general meeting
AWE	Association of Women Electors
Bs and Ps	Business and Professional Women's Clubs
CACSW	Canadian Advisory Council on the Status of Women
CARAL	Canadian Abortion Rights Action League
CBC	Canadian Broadcasting Corporation
CCF	Cooperative Commonwealth Federation, predecessor of the NDP
CCLA	Canadian Civil Liberties Association
CIDA	Canadian International Development Agency
CND	Campaign for Nuclear Disarmament
CNE	Canadian National Exhibition
CPA	Canadian Physiotherapy Association
CRIAW	Canadian Research Institute for the Advancement of Women
CTV	Canadian Television Network
CUPE	Canadian Union of Public Employees
FWTAO	Federation of Women Teachers' Associations of Ontario
ICY	International Cooperation Year
IODE	Imperial Order Daughters of the Empire
IWD	International Women's Day
LEAF	Women's Legal Education and Action Fund
LSE	London School of Economics
MLA	Member of Legislative Assembly
MLF	Multi-Lateral Force
NAC	National Action Committee on the Status of Women
NATO	North Atlantic Treaty Organization
NDP	New Democratic Party
NFB	National Film Board

NGO	Non-governmental organization
NORAD	North American Air Defense Command
OCSW	Ontario Committee on the Status of Women
OISE	Ontario Institute for Studies in Education
PASOK	Panhellenic Socialist Movement
PBS	Public Broadcasting Service (US)
RAF	Royal Air Force (UK)
RCAF	Royal Canadian Air Force
RCMP	Royal Canadian Mounted Police
RCSW	Royal Commission on the Status of Women
Ss, the	Susan, Stephen, and Sheila Macpherson
SALT	Strategic Arms Limitation Treaty
SRN	State Registered Nurse
St A and P	St Andrew and St Paul's Church in Montreal
TTC	Toronto Transit Corporation
U of T	University of Toronto
UN	United Nations
UNB	University of New Brunswick
UNESCO	United Nations Educational, Scientific, and Cultural Organization
UNSSOD	United Nations' Special Session on Disarmament
USSR	Union of Soviet Socialist Republics
VOW	Voice of Women
WFH	Wages for Housework
WILPF	Women's International League for Peace and Freedom
WMS	Women for Mutual Security, previously Women for a Meaningful Summit
WPA	Women for Political Action
WSP	Women Strike for Peace
YWCA	Young Women's Christian Association

Index

Photo Credits

Moira Armour: Kay with Thérèse Casgrain, 1965; NAC meeting with NDP caucus; NAC Executive, 1978; 'Persons Day' Dinner, 1980; 'Women and the Constitution' Conference, 1981

J. Goode/*Toronto Star*: anti–Vietnam war demonstration, 1968

Nanaimo Daily Free Press: discussing Amchitka explosion, 1971

Cyprus Mail: 'Women Walk Home,' 1975

Pamela Harris: Kay on telephone, 1980. The portrait of Kay Macpherson by Pamela Harris is from *Faces of Feminism* by Pamela Harris, published by Second Story Press.

John Evans Photography, Ottawa: Kay receiving Order of Canada, 1982

Andrew Oxenham: Susan Macpherson, 'Personal Collection,' 1985

All other photographs are reproduced by courtesy of Kay Macpherson and her family and friends.